Study Guide
with
Working Papers

Brian Zwicker

Grant MacEwan College

College Accounting
A Practical Approach

Canadian Ninth Edition

Jeffrey Slater

North Shore Community College

Brian Zwicker

Grant MacEwan College

PEARSON

Prentice
Hall

Toronto

ISBN 0-13-127818-5

Editor-in-Chief: Gary Bennett
Associate Editor: Kalpna Patel
Production Editor: Cheryl Jackson
Production Coordinator: Andrea Falkenberg

2 3 4 5   10 09 08 07 06

Printed and bound in Canada

PEARSON

Prentice
Hall

Contents

1

Accounting Concepts
and Procedures: An Introduction

SELF-REVIEW QUIZ 1-1

PETE O'BRIEN REAL ESTATE

	Assets		=	Liabilities	+	Owner's Equity
	Cash +	Computer Equipment =		Accounts Payable +		Pete O'Brien, Capital
TRANSACTION 1	+14,000	600		0		14,000
BALANCE	14,000		=			14,000
TRANSACTION 2	-600	+600		0		0
BALANCE	13,400	+600	=	0		14,000
TRANSACTION 3		-500	=	+500		
ENDING BALANCE	13,410 +	$1,100	=	$500	+	$14,000

14,500 = 14,500

SELF REVIEW QUIZ 1-2

Janning Company
Balance Sheet
November 30, 2007.

Assets				Liabilities and		
Cash	CASH-INVESTMENT	$8,000 00		Owners Equity		
Office Equipment		31,000 00				
		-600		Accounts Payable		30,000
				Owner's Equity		
				A. Janning, Capital		9,000
				Total Liabilities and		
Total Assets.		$39,000 00		Owners Equity.	$	39,000

SELF-REVIEW QUIZ 1-3

BING COMPANY

	Assets			= Liabilities +		Owner's Equity			
	Cash +	Accounts Receivable +	Cleaning Equipment =	Accounts Payable +	B. Bing, Capital -	B. Bing, Withdrawals +	Revenue -	Expenses	
BEGINNING BALANCE	$9,000 +	$2,500 +	$6,500 =	$1,000 +	$11,800 -	$ 800 +	$8,000 -	$2,000	
1.	4,000	2					4,000	1	
BALANCE	13,000	2,500	6,500 =	1,000	11,800	800	12,000	2,000	
2.		6,000					6,000		
BALANCE	13,000	8,500	6,500 =	1,000	11,800	800	18,000	2,000	
3.				+125				+125	
BALANCE	13,000	8,500	6,500 =	1,125	11,800	800	18,000	2,125	
4.	-500					+500			
BALANCE	12,500	8,500	6,500 =	1,125	11,800	1,300	18,000	2,125	
5.	+1,000	-1,000							
ENDING BALANCE	13,500 +	7,500 +	6,500 =	1,125 +	11,800 -	1,300 +	18,000 -	2,125	

27,500 = 87,500

SELF-REVIEW QUIZ 1-4

(1)

Rusty Realty
Income Statment
November 1, 30, 2008

		Dr.	Cr.
1. Revenue:			
Commisions Earned.			1500 00
Operating Expenses:			
Rent Expense		$200 00	
Advertising Expense		150 00	
Salaries Expense		90 00	
Total Operating Expenses			
			- 440 00
Net Income.			1060 00

(2)

Rusty Realty
Statement of Owner Equity.
FOR MONTH ENDED NOVEMBER 30, 2008

		Dr.	Cr.
R. Rusty, Capital, November 1, 2008.			5000 00
Net Income for November		1060 00	
Less: Withdraws for November		-100 00	
Increase in Capital			
R. Rusty, Capital, November 30, 2008			960 00
			5960 00

SELF-REVIEW QUIZ 1-4, Cont.

(3)

Rusty Realty
Balance Sheet
November 30, 2008

Assets					Liabilities and Owner's Equity				
Cash	4	000	00		Accounts Payable		$ 900	00	
Accounts Recivable	1	370	00						
Store furnature	1	490	00		Owner's Equity				
					R. Rusty, Capital				
					Total Liabilites and Owner's Equity		5 960	00	
Total Assets	6	860	00				6 860	00	

A Fresh Start
SUBWAY Case
Discussion Questions

1. Stan's company is not incorporated and he has no partners.
2. Stan and Subway are interdependent businesses because Subway earns its profits through Stan's business, and Stan relies on Subway for his products, recipes, advertising, location, service, training and managerial expertise.
3. a. Stan must satisfy Subway as to his financial ability to run a successful operation. Part of this process is sharing his personal financial situation.
   b. Yes, most do but the level of detail required sometimes varies a bit.
4. a. Whether the sales are increasing or decreasing and consequently whether the income is sufficient to pay the overheads.
   b. From the inventory reports Subway can tell if Stan is using too much or too little of the supplies.

FORMS FOR COMPREHENSIVE DEMONSTRATION PROBLEM

A.

MICHAEL BROWN, BARRISTER AND SOLICITOR

	Cash	+	Accounts Receivable	+	Office Equipment	=	Accounts Payable	+	M. Brown, Capital	−	M. Brown, Withdrawals	+	Revenue	−	Expenses
						Assets = Liabilities + Owner's Equity									
1.															
BALANCE						=									
2.															
BALANCE						=									
3.															
BALANCE						=									
4.															
BALANCE						=									
5.															
BALANCE						=									
6.															
BALANCE						=									
7.															
BALANCE						=									
8.															
BALANCE						=									
9.															
ENDING BALANCE						=									
						=									

B-1

MICHAEL BROWN, BARRISTER AND SOLICITOR

INCOME STATEMENT

FOR THE MONTH ENDED JUNE 30, 2006

FORMS FOR COMPREHENSIVE PROBLEM, Cont.

B-2

MICHAEL BROWN, BARRISTER AND SOLICITOR

STATEMENT OF OWNER'S EQUITY

FOR THE MONTH ENDED JUNE 30, 2006

B-3

MICHAEL BROWN, BARRISTER AND SOLICITOR

BALANCE SHEET

JUNE 30, 2006

ASSETS		LIABILITIES AND OWNER'S EQUITY	

NAME: _____ CLASS: _____ DATE: _____

FORMS FOR MINI EXERCISES

1.   a. _____
        b. _____
        c. _____
        d. _____
        e. _____
        f. _____

2.   a. _____
        b. _____
        c. _____

3.   a. _____
        b. _____

4.   _____
      _____
      _____

5.   _____
      _____
      _____
      _____

6.   _____
      _____
      _____

7.   a. _____
        b. _____
        c. _____
        d. _____

8.   a. _____
        b. _____
        c. _____
        d. _____
        e. _____
        f. _____
        g. _____
        h. _____

9.   a. _____
        b. _____
        c. _____
        d. _____

NAME: _____ CLASS: _____ DATE: _____

FORMS FOR EXERCISES

1-1.

a. _____

b. _____

c. _____

1-2.

	Assets	=	Liabilities	+	Owner's Equity
	Cash + Equipment				
a.					
b.					
c.					

1-3.

AVON'S CLEANERS

BALANCE SHEET

NOVEMBER 30, 2007

ASSETS		LIABILITIES AND OWNER'S EQUITY	

1-4.

WONG'S COMPUTER COMPANY

	Assets			= Liabilities +		Owner's Equity			
	Cash +	Accounts Receivable +	Computer Equipment =	Accounts Payable +	B. Wong, Capital -	B. Wong, Withdrawals +	Revenue -	Expenses
a.								
b.								
c.								
d.								
e.								
f.								
g.								
ENDING BALANCE								

FORMS FOR EXERCISES, Cont.

1-5.(a)

FRENCH REALTY

INCOME STATEMENT

FOR THE MONTH ENDED JUNE 30, 2007

1-5.(b)

FRENCH REALTY

STATEMENT OF OWNER'S EQUITY

FOR THE MONTH ENDED JUNE 30, 2007

1-5.(c)

FRENCH REALTY

BALANCE SHEET

JUNE 30, 2007

ASSETS   LIABILITIES AND OWNER'S EQUITY

END OF CHAPTER PROBLEMS

PROBLEM 1A-1 or 1B-1.

LEE'S NAIL CARE CENTRE

	Assets		=	Liabilities	+	Owner's Equity
				Accounts Payable		Lee Stone, Capital
	Cash +	Equipment	=		+	
Transaction a	18,000	0		0		18,000
BALANCE	18,000	0	=	0		18,000
Transaction b	-4,000	-44,000				
BALANCE	14,000	4000	=	0		18,000
Transaction c	0	+1000		-10.00		
BALANCE	14,000	5000	=	1000		18,000
Transaction d	-400	0		-400		
ENDING BALANCE	13,600 +	500	=	600	+	18,000

PROBLEM 1A-2 or 1B-2.

GREEN'S ADVERTISING SERVICE

BALANCE SHEET

SEPTEMBER 30, 2008

Assets		=	Liabilities and Owner's Equity	
1. CASH	10 000		Accounts Payable	30 000
2. Auto	35 000			
3. Equipment	14 000		R. Green, Capital	29 000
Total Assets	59 000		Total Liabilities + Equity	59 000

PROBLEM 1A-3 or 1B-3.

RICK FOX DESKTOP PUBLISHING SERVICE

	Assets			=	Liabilities	+	Owner's Equity				
	Cash +	Accounts Receivable +	Office Equipment	=	Accounts Payable	+	R. Fox, Capital	- R. Fox, Withdrawals	+ Revenue	- Expenses		
a.	12,000	0	0		0		12,000	0	0	0		
BALANCE	12,000	0	0	=	0		12,000	0	0	0		
b.	0	0	4,000		4,000		0	0	0	0		
BALANCE	12,000	0	4,000	=	4,000		12,000	0	0	0		
c.	500	0	0		0		0	0	500	0		
BALANCE	12,500	0	4,000	=	4,000		12,000	0	500	0		
d.	0	2,100	0		0		0	0	2,100	0		
BALANCE	12,500	2,100	4,000	=	4,000		12,000	0	2,600	0		
e.	-650	0	0		0		0	0	0	650		
BALANCE	11,850	2,100	4,000	=	4,000		12,000	0	2,600	650		
f.	-210	0	0		0		0	0	0	+210		
BALANCE	11,640	2,100	4,000	=	4,000		12,000	0	2,600	860		
g.	0	0	0	+	900		0	0	0	+900		
BALANCE	11,640	2,100	4,000	=	4,900		12,000	0	2,600	1760		
h.	-400	0	0		0		0	+400	0	0		
ENDING BALANCE	11,240 +	2,100 +	4,000	=	4,900 +		12,000 -	400 +	2,600 -	1760		

$$17,340 = 17,340$$

11,240
2,100
4,000

17,340

4,900
+12,000

16,900
- 400

16,500
+ 2,600

19,100
- 1,760

17,340

1-11

PROBLEM 1A-4 or 1B-4.

(a)

WEST'S STENCILLING SERVICE
INCOME STATEMENT
FOR MONTH ENDED JUNE 30, 2008

(b)

WEST'S STENCILLING SERVICE
STATEMENT OF OWNER'S EQUITY
FOR MONTH ENDED JUNE 30, 2008

PROBLEM 1A-4 or 1B-4.

(c)

WEST'S STENCILLING SERVICE

BALANCE SHEET

JUNE 30, 2008

Assets					Liabilities and Owner's Equity				

PROBLEM 1A-5 or 1B-5.

(1)

MARTIN'S CATERING SERVICE

	Assets			=	Liabilities	+	Owner's Equity			
	Cash +	Accounts Receivable +	Equipment	=	Accounts Payable	+	Jill Martin, Capital -	Jill Martin, Withdrawals +	Catering Revenue -	Expenses
10/26										
BALANCE				=						
10/29										
BALANCE				=						
10/30										
BALANCE				=						
10/31										
BALANCE				=						
11/1										
BALANCE				=						
11/5										
BALANCE				=						
11/8										
BALANCE				=						
11/12										
BALANCE				=						
11/15										
BALANCE				=						
11/16										
BALANCE				=						
11/17										
BALANCE				=						
11/26										
BALANCE				=						
11/28										
BALANCE				=						
11/30										
ENDING BALANCE	+	+		=		+	-	+	-	

PROBLEM 1A-5 or 1B-5, Cont.

(2)

MARTIN'S CATERING SERVICE

BALANCE SHEET

OCTOBER 31, 2007

Assets					Liabilities and Owner's Equity				

(3)

MARTIN'S CATERING SERVICE

INCOME STATEMENT

FOR MONTH ENDED NOVEMBER 30, 2007

PROBLEM 1A-5 or 1B-5, Cont.

(4)

MARTIN'S CATERING SERVICE

STATEMENT OF OWNER'S EQUITY

FOR MONTH ENDED NOVEMBER 30, 2007

(5)

MARTIN'S CATERING SERVICE

BALANCE SHEET

NOVEMBER 30, 2007

Assets		Liabilities and Owner's Equity	

PROBLEM 1C-1.

_____

	Cash	+	Computer Equipment	+	Office Equipment	=	Accounts Payable	+	Frances Baker, Capital
			Assets			=	Liabilities	+	Owner's Equity
TRANSACTION A									
BALANCE						=			
TRANSACTION B									
BALANCE						=			
TRANSACTION C									
BALANCE						=			
TRANSACTION D									
ENDING BALANCE		+		+		=		+	

PROBLEM 1C-2.

_____

_____

_____

PROBLEM 1C-3.

_____

	Cash	+	Accounts Receivable	+	Office Equipment	=	Accounts Payable	+	R. Owens, Capital	-	R. Owens, Withdrawals	+	Revenue	-	Expenses
A.																
BALANCE						=										
B.																
BALANCE						=										
C.																
BALANCE						=										
D.																
BALANCE						=										
E.																
BALANCE						=										
F.																
BALANCE						=										
G.																
BALANCE						=										
H.																
BALANCE						=										
I.																
ENDING BALANCE		+		+		=		+		-		+		-		

Assets = Liabilities + Owner's Equity

=

PROBLEM 1C-4.

(a)

_____

_____

_____

(b)

_____

_____

_____

PROBLEM 1C-4, Cont.

(c)

PROBLEM 1C-5.

(1)

	Assets			=	Liabilities	+		Owner's Equity		
	Cash +	Accounts Receivable +	Surveying Equipment	=	Accounts Payable	+	H. McGraw, Capital -	H. McGraw, Withdrawals +	Surveying Revenue -	Expenses
BALANCE				=						
BALANCE				=						
BALANCE				=						
BALANCE				=						
BALANCE				=						
BALANCE				=						
BALANCE				=						
BALANCE				=						
BALANCE				=						
BALANCE				=						
BALANCE				=						
BALANCE				=						
BALANCE				=						
ENDING BALANCE	+	+		=	+		-	+		-

PROBLEM 1C-5, Cont.

(2)

_____

_____

_____

(3)

_____

_____

_____

PROBLEM 1C-5, Cont.

(4)

_____

_____

_____

(5)

_____

_____

_____

REAL WORLD APPLICATION #1R-1.

Roger's Window Washing Company

Income Statement

For The Year Ended December 31, 2006

Insights

_____

_____

_____

_____

_____

REAL WORLD APPLICATION #1R-2.

(1)

LUNE CO.

BALANCE SHEET

DECEMBER 31, 2007

(2) _____
_____
_____
_____
_____

(3) _____

LUNE CO.

REVISED BALANCE SHEET

JANUARY 4, 2008

_____

Insight

Cash	Desks	Auto	J. Lune	Notes Payable

YOU MAKE THE CALL: CRITICAL THINKING/ETHICAL CASE (#1R-3.)

CONTINUING PROBLEM

1, 2.   _____

	Cash	+	Supplies	+	Computer Shop Equipment	+	Office Equipment	=	Accounts Payable	+	T. Freedman, Capital	−	T. Freedman, Withdrawals	+	Service Revenue	−	Expenses
					Assets			=	*Liabilities* +				*Owner's Equity*				
a																	
BALANCE									=								
b																	
BALANCE									=								
c																	
BALANCE									=								
d																	
BALANCE									=								
e																	
BALANCE									=								
f																	
BALANCE									=								
g																	
BALANCE									=								
h																	
BALANCE									=								
i																	
BALANCE									=								
j																	
ENDING BALANCE		+		+		+		=		+		−		+		−	

CONTINUING PROBLEM, Cont.

3.

_____

_____

_____

_____

_____

_____

CONTINUING PROBLEM, Cont.

3.

_____

_____

_____

CHAPTER 1

CHAPTER SUMMARY TEST

Part A

Fill in the blank to complete the statement.

1. Assets = _____ + _____ .
2. The recording function of the accounting process is called _____ .
3. A summary of assets, liabilities, and owner's equity as of a particular date is reported on a statement called the _____ _____ .
4. The owner's current net investment or equity in the assets of a business is called _____ .
5. Revenue earned from a sale on account creates an asset called _____ _____ .
6. An outward or potential outward flow of assets usually causes _____ .
7. A report which shows how well a business has performed over a period of time is called the _____ _____ .
8. Personal expenses unrelated to the business are _____ .
9. The ending figure from the income statement is placed on the _____ _____ _____ _____ .
10. The report that shows changes in capital over a period of time is called the _____ _____ _____ _____ .

Part B

Answer true or false to the following statements.

1. Assets plus liabilities equal owner's equity.
2. Business transactions are recorded in cash equivalent terms.
3. Capital equals cash.
4. Revenue is a liability.
5. The balance sheet lists assets, owner's equity, and liabilities.
6. Bookkeeping is a major component of accounting.
7. Revenue is a subdivision of owner's equity.
8. Expenses create an outward flow of assets.
9. The balance sheet shows financial details of a business at a point in time.
10. "Withdrawals" is one subdivision of liabilities.
11. Expenses are listed on the balance sheet.
12. Withdrawals and expenses are both listed on the income statement.
13. Revenue is shown on the income statement.
14. "Withdrawals" is listed on the statement of owner's equity.
15. The income statement updates the statement of owner's equity, and indirectly helps update the balance sheet.

Part C

In column 2, record the appropriate codes that properly identify the recording of the transactions in column 1.

1. Increase in assets
2. Decrease in assets
3. Increase in liabilities
4. Decrease in liabilities

5. Increase in capital
6. Increase in revenues
7. Increase in expenses
8. Increase in withdrawals

Column 1	Column 2
1. EXAMPLE: Joan Beck invested $4,000 in her business.	*1,5*
2. Bought supplies on account for $60.	_____
3. Bought equipment for $500 cash.	_____
4. Paid salaries of $350.	_____
5. Received $3,000 in cash from revenue earned.	_____
6. Paid rent expense of $80 cash.	_____
7. Paid half the amount owed on supplies previouly purchased on account.	_____
8. Paid utilities expense of $85.	_____
9. Earned revenue of $900 to be received later.	_____
10. Bought additional equipment of $2,000, half paid in cash and half charged.	_____
11. Customer paid $100 of amount previously owed.	_____
12. Paid for cleaning expense $40.	_____
13. Joan paid home phone bill from the company's cash $25.	_____
14. Charged customer $100 for service performed.	_____
15. Advertising expense bill received. Due next month. $125.	_____

SOLUTIONS TO CHAPTER 1 SUMMARY TEST

Part A

1. Liabilities, Owner's Equity
2. Bookkeeping
3. Balance Sheet
4. Capital

5. Accounts Receivable
6. Expenses
7. Income Statement

8. Withdrawals
9. Statement of Owner's Equity
10. Statement of Owner's Equity

Part B

1. False
2. True
3. False
4. False
5. True

6. False
7. True
8. True
9. True
10. False

11. False
12. False
13. True
14. True
15. True

Part C

1. 1,5
2. 1,3
3. 1,2
4. 2,7
5. 1,6

6. 2,7
7. 2,4
8. 2,7
9. 1,6
10. 1,2,3

11. 1,2
12. 2,7
13. 2,8
14. 1,6
15. 3,7

2

Debits and Credits: Analyzing and Recording Business Transactions

SELF-REVIEW QUIZ 2-1

1. _____	4. _____	
2. _____	5. _____	
3. _____		

SELF-REVIEW QUIZ 2-2

A.

1. Accounts Affected	2. Category	3. ↑ ↓	4. Rules	5. T-Account Update

B.

1. Accounts Affected	2. Category	3. ↑ ↓	4. Rules	5. T-Account Update

C.	1.	2.	3.	4.	5.
	Accounts Affected	Category	↑↓	Rules	T-Account Update

D.	1.	2.	3.	4.	5.
	Accounts Affected	Category	↑↓	Rules	T-Account Update

E.	1.	2.	3.	4.	5.
	Accounts Affected	Category	↑↓	Rules	T-Account Update

SELF-REVIEW QUIZ 2-3

Cash   111

	300
4,500	100
2,000	1,200
1,000	1,300
300	2,600

Accounts Payable   211

	700
300	

Salon Fees   411

	3,500
	1,000

Accounts Receivable   121

1,000	300

Pam Jay, Capital   311

	4,000

Rent Expense   511

1,200	

Salon Equipment   131

700	

Pam Jay, Withdrawals   321

100	

Salon Supplies Exp.   521

1,300	

Salaries Expense   531

2,600	

SELF-REVIEW QUIZ 2-3, Cont.

(1)

_____

_____

_____

(2)

_____

_____

_____

SELF-REVIEW QUIZ 2-3, Cont.

(3)

_____

_____

_____

(4)

_____

_____

Debits on the Left...
SUBWAY Case
Discussion Questions

1. The cash account reflects a net result of cash inflows and outflows. It also helps to determine the liquidity of the business (its ability to meet its financial obligations) -- an important consideration when considering ongoing viability.
2. Many small business owners start by doing their own bookkeeping and accounting work in order to save money. However, for the most part, business ownership skills are different from bookkeeping/accounting skills and, as a business grows, owners tend to hire others to handle the tasks they no longer have time to do.
3. Not really. These terms are fairly technical and of interest mostly to people who are attempting to understand the basics of bookkeeping. Since Stan is managing his own bookkeeping and accounting at the moment, they are important now, but will cease to be important to Stan in due course. It will still be of interest to the person in charge of the bookkeeping, of course.

FORMS FOR COMPREHENSIVE DEMONSTRATION PROBLEM

1, 2, 3.

D=22,100   C   D   C=7,700   D = 700   O   S.

Cash	111		Accounts Payable	211		Advertising Expense	511
210,000	1,200		B7,000			c700	
	D1,200		c700				
E15,000	F3,000 5900						
J 3,000	91,250						
28,000	I 300		C=10,000			D.1,250	
	K 150		Mel Free, Capital	311		Gas Expense	512
Accounts Receivable 112							
H. 4,000	J. 3,000		10,000	a 10,000		G.1,250	
D= 1,000							

D=1200   D=150   D = 3,000

Office Equipment	121		Mel Free, Withdrawals	312		Salaries Expense	513
D.1,200			K. 150			F 3,000	

D=7000   C=19,000   D= 300

Delivery Trucks	122		Delivery Fees Earned	411		Telephone Expense	514
B7,000			E. 15,000			I 300	
			H. 4,000				

FORMS FOR COMPREHENSIVE DEMONSTRATION PROBLEM, Cont.

4.

MEL'S DELIVERY SERVICE

TRIAL BALANCE

JULY 31, 2007

	D	C
CASH	22100	
ACCOUNTS REICIVABLE	1000	
OFFICE EQUIPMENT	12000	
DELIVERY TRUCKS	7000	
ACCOUNTS PAYABLE		17700
MEL FREE CAPITAL		10000
MEL FREE WITHDRAWS	150	
DELIVERY FEES EARNED		19000
ADVERTISING EXPENSE	700	
GAS EXPENSE	1250	
SALARIES EXPENSE	3000	
TELEPHONE EXPENSE	300	
TOTALS.	46700	46700

5.(a)

MEL'S DELIVERY SERVICE

INCOME STATEMENT

FOR THE MONTH ENDED JULY 31, 2007

	D	C
REVENUE:		
DELIVERY FEES Earned		19000
Operating Expenses:		
Advertising Expenses	700	
Gas Expenses	1250	
Salaries Expense	3000	
Telephone Expense.	300	
Total Operating Expenses.		5250
Net Income		13750

2-6 © 2006 Pearson Canada All Rights Reserved

FORMS FOR COMPREHENSIVE DEMONSTRATION PROBLEM, *Cont.*

5.(b)

MEL'S DELIVERY SERVICE
STATEMENT OF OWNER'S EQUITY
FOR MONTH ENDED JULY 31, 2007   C   D.

	C	D
MEL - CAPITAL 09/2007		10 000
NET INCOME 09/2007	13 750	
-WITH DRAWS 09/2007	150	
Increase in Capital		13 600
MEL FREE CAPITAL, JULY 31, 2007.		23 600

5.(c)

MEL'S DELIVERY SERVICE
BALANCE SHEET
JULY 31, 2007

Assets		Liabilities and Owner's Equity	
Cash	22 100	Liabilites.	1
Accounts Recivable	1 000	Accounts Payable	17 700
OFFIC EQUIPMENT	1 200		
Delivery Trucs.	17 000		
		Owner's Equity.	
		Mel Free Capital	23 600
Total Assets	41 300		41 300

FORMS FOR MINI EXERCISES

1.

Cash			110
6/9 4,000		4/8	500
7/14 8,000			

C. Clark, Capital		311
	7,000	3/7
	3,000	3/9
	6,000	4/12

2. A. _____ _____ _____ _____

B. _____ _____ _____ _____

C. _____ _____ _____ _____

D. _____ _____ _____ _____

E. _____ _____ _____ _____

F. _____ _____ _____ _____

G. _____ _____ _____ _____

3.

1. Accounts Affected	2. Category	3. ↑↓	4. Rules	T-Account Update

4. _____

_____

_____

_____

_____

_____

_____

_____

_____

_____

5. A. _____

B. _____

C. _____

D. _____

E. _____

F. _____

G. _____

H. _____

I. _____

J. _____

K. _____

EXERCISES

EXERCISE 2-1.

_____
_____
_____
_____
_____
_____
_____
_____
_____
_____
_____
_____
_____
_____
_____
_____
_____
_____
_____

EXERCISE 2-4.

	Dr.	Cr.
A.	8	1
B.		
C.		
D.		
E.		
F.		
G.		
H.		
I.		

EXERCISE 2-2.

1. Accounts Affected	2. Category	3. ↑↓	4. Rules	5. T-Account Update

EXERCISE 2-3.

ACCOUNT   CATEGORY   ↑   ↓   FINANCIAL REPORT

_____
_____
_____
_____
_____
_____
_____

EXERCISES, Cont.

2-5. (1)

HALL'S CLEANERS

INCOME STATEMENT

FOR THE MONTH ENDED JULY 31, 2009

2-5. (2)

HALL'S CLEANERS

STATEMENT OF OWNER'S EQUITY

FOR THE MONTH ENDED JULY 31, 2009

2-5. (3)

HALL'S CLEANERS

BALANCE SHEET

JULY 31, 2009

ASSETS			LIABILITIES AND OWNER'S EQUITY		

END OF CHAPTER PROBLEMS

PROBLEM 2A-1 or 2B-1.

Accounts Affected	Category	Inc. ↑	Dec. ↓	Rules	T-Account Update
a.					
b.					
c.					
d.					
e.					
f.					

PROBLEM 2A-2 or 2B-2.

Cash   111

Office Equipment   121

Accounts Payable   211

M. Slater, Capital   311

M. Slater, Withdrawals   312

Travel Fees Earned   411

Advertising Expense   511

Rent Expense   512

PROBLEM 2A-3 or 2B-3.

(a)

Cash 111	Accounts Payable 211	Fees Earned 411

Accounts Receivable 112	Mike Frank, Capital 311	Rent Expense 511

Office Equipment 121	Mike Frank, Withdrawals 312	Utilities Expense 512

(b)

MIKE'S WINDOW WASHING SERVICE

TRIAL BALANCE

MAY 31, 2007

PROBLEM 2A-4 or 2B-4.

(a)

| GRACE LANTZ |
| BARRISTER AND SOLICITOR |
| INCOME STATEMENT |
| FOR THE MONTH ENDED MAY 31, 2008 |

(b)

| GRACE LANTZ |
| BARRISTER AND SOLICITOR |
| STATEMENT OF OWNER'S EQUITY |
| FOR THE MONTH ENDED MAY 31, 2008 |

PROBLEM 2A-4 or 2B-4, Cont.

(c)

| GRACE LANTZ |
| BARRISTER AND SOLICITOR |
| BALANCE SHEET |
| MAY 31, 2008 |

Assets					Liabilities and Owner's Equity								

PROBLEM 2A-5 or 2B-5.

1., 2., 3.

| Cash | 111 | Accounts Payable | 211 | Advertising Expense | 511 |

| | | Alice Angel, Capital | 311 | Gas Expense | 512 |

| Accounts Receivable | | | | | |

| | | Alice Angel, Withdrawals | 312 | Salaries Expense | 513 |

| Office Equipment | 121 | | | | |

| | | Delivery Fees Earned | 411 | Telephone Expense | 514 |

| Delivery Trucks | 122 | | | | |

4.

ANGEL'S DELIVERY SERVICE
TRIAL BALANCE
MARCH 31, 2007

PROBLEM 2A-5 or 2B-5.

5.(a)

ANGEL'S DELIVERY SERVICE

INCOME STATEMENT

FOR MONTH ENDED MARCH 31, 2007

5.(b)

ANGEL'S DELIVERY SERVICE

STATEMENT OF OWNERS'S EQUITY

FOR MONTH ENDED MARCH 31, 2007

5.(c)

ANGEL'S DELIVERY SERVICE

BALANCE SHEET

MARCH 31, 2007

Assets					*Liabilities and Owner's Equity*			

PROBLEM 2C-1.

Accounts Affected	Category	Inc. ↑	Dec. ↓	Rules	T-Account Update
A.					
B.					
C.					
D.					
E.					
F.					

PROBLEM 2C-2.

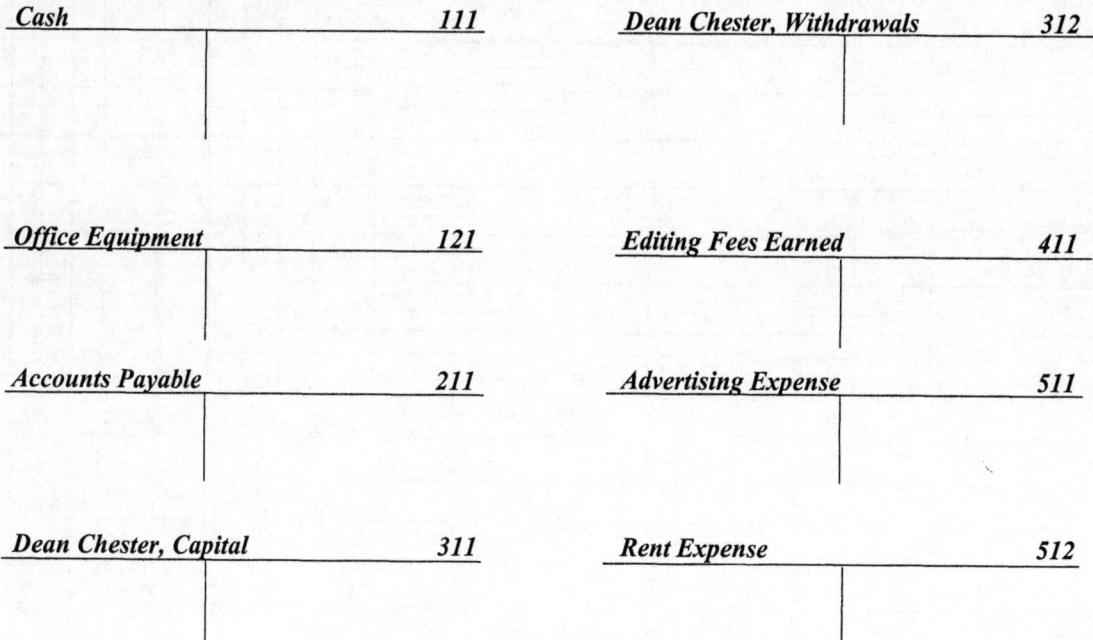

Cash	111	Dean Chester, Withdrawals	312
Office Equipment	121	**Editing Fees Earned**	411
Accounts Payable	211	**Advertising Expense**	511
Dean Chester, Capital	311	**Rent Expense**	512

PROBLEM 2C-3.

(a)

Cash	111		Accounts Receivable	112		Equipment	121

Accounts Payable	211		Ricky Cheung, Capital	311		Ricky Cheung, Withdrawals	312

Fees Earned	411		Rent Expense	511		Utilities Expense	512

(b)

PROBLEM 2C-4. (a)

_____

_____

_____

2C-4. (b)

_____

_____

_____

2C-4. (c)

_____

_____

_____

PROBLEM 2C-5.

1, 2, 3.

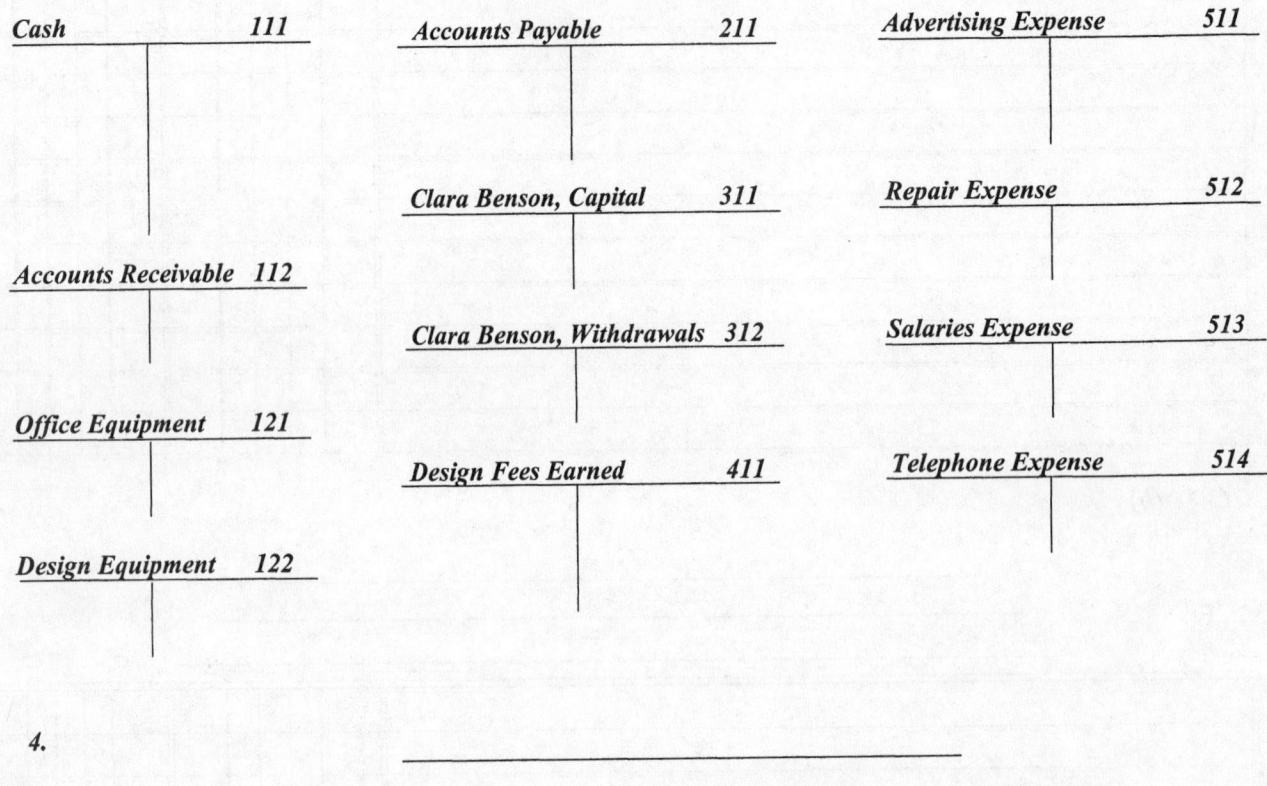

Cash	111
Accounts Receivable	112
Office Equipment	121
Design Equipment	122

Accounts Payable	211
Clara Benson, Capital	311
Clara Benson, Withdrawals	312
Design Fees Earned	411

Advertising Expense	511
Repair Expense	512
Salaries Expense	513
Telephone Expense	514

4.

PROBLEM 2C-5. 5(a)

5(b)

5(c)

REAL WORLD APPLICATION #2R-1.

_____

_____

_____

REAL WORLD APPLICATION #2R-2.

Situation	Total of Trial Balance	Effects on Accounts
1		
2		
3		
4		
5		
6		

REAL WORLD APPLICATION #2R-1 and 2R-2. (Continued)

_____
_____
_____
_____
_____
_____
_____
_____
_____
_____
_____
_____
_____
_____
_____
_____
_____
_____
_____
_____
_____
_____
_____

YOU MAKE THE CALL: CRITICAL THINKING/ETHICAL CASE -- #2R-3.

_____
_____
_____
_____
_____
_____
_____
_____
_____
_____
_____
_____
_____

CONTINUING PROBLEM

1, 2, 3.

Cash	1000
3,850	

Accounts Receivable 1020

Prepaid Rent	1025

Supplies	1030
250	

Computer Shop Equipment	1080
1,200	

Office Equipment	1090
600	

Accounts Payable	2000
	335

T. Freedman, Capital	3000
	4,500

T. Freedman, Withdrawals	3010
100	

Service Revenue	4000
	1,650

Advertising Expense	5010

Rent Expense	5020
400	

Utilities Expense	5030
85	

Phone Expense	5040

Supplies Expense	5050

Insurance Expense	5060

Postage Expense	5070

4.

_____

_____

_____

CONTINUING PROBLEM, Continued

5.

2-25

CHAPTER 2
CHAPTER SUMMARY TEST

PART A:

Fill in the blank(s) to complete the statement.

1. The right side of a T account is called the _____ _____ .
2. _____ accumulate information in a book called the ledger.
3. Balancing an account involves _____ .
4. _____ decrease an asset account.
5. The names and numbering system of general ledger accounts is summarized in the _____ _____ _____ .
6. Transaction analysis charts assist with recording _____ _____ .
7. Withdrawals are increased by a _____ .
8. An informal report that lists account names and balances is called a _____ _____ .
9. A group of accounts is called a _____ .
10. The income statement, statement of owner's equity, and balance sheet are prepared from a _____ _____ .
11. Increasing revenue ultimately causes owner's equity to_____ .
12. Cash, Accounts Receivable, and Equipment are examples of_____ .
13. A debit to one asset and a credit to another asset for the same transaction reflects a _____ in assets.
14. The accounts payable account is an example of a _____ account.
15. An increase in utilities expense is a _____ by rules of debits and credits.

PART B:

Ellen Leung started a courier company. From the following chart of accounts, indicate in column 2 (by account number) which account(s) will be debited or credited because of the transaction in column 1.

Chart of Accounts

ASSETS	LIABILITIES	EXPENSES
100 Cash	210 Accounts Payable	500 Advertising
120 Accounts Receivable		510 Gas
170 Equipment-Office	OWNER'S EQUITY	550 Salaries
180 Van		560 Telephone
	300 E. Leung, Capital	
	310 E. Leung, Withdrawals	
	REVENUE	
	400 Fees Earned	

COLUMN 1			COLUMN 2	
			Debit(s)	Credit(s)
1. EXAMPLE: Ellen Leung invested $25,000 in the courier company.			100	300
2. Bought equipment on account for $6,000.				
3. Purchased a van on account for $40,000.				
4. Ellen paid home utility bill from company chequebook, $20.				
5. Telephone bill received, not due until next month.				
6. Customer charged a courier pick-up of $20.				
7. Received partial payment for transaction #6 of $10.				
8. Collected $100 in cash from courier fees earned.				
9. Paid driver salaries of $450.				
10. Paid advertising bill, $32.				
11. Purchased additional office equipment for cash, $900.				
12. Bought graphic design for van on account for $360.				

PART C:

Are the following statements true or false?

1. A trial balance could be in balance, but incorrect.
2. Debit and credit columns are found on the three financial reports.
3. In double-entry bookkeeping, the sum of all debits is equal to the sum of all credits.
4. Each ledger page is numbered as in a text book.
5. Withdrawals are listed in the debit column of the trial balance.
6. The rules of debit and credit have not changed in 500 years.
7. Withdrawals are increased by a debit.
8. An expense always creates a liability.
9. Transaction analysis charts are commonly used in business.
10. A shift in assets means the total of assets does not change.
11. A debit means an account is decreasing.
12. The chart of accounts helps in locating and identifying accounts quickly.
13. The right side of an account is the credit side.
14. The statement of owner's equity is typically prepared after the balance sheet.
15. A trial balance is the final step before statements are prepared.
16. Credits increase revenue accounts.
17. Credit means something good.
18. Withdrawals are listed on the balance sheet.

SOLUTION TO CHAPTER 2 TEST

PART A

1. Credit side
2. Accounts
3. Footings
4. Credits
5. Chart of Accounts

6. Business Transactions
7. Debit
8. Trial Balance
9. Ledger
10. Trial Balance

11. Increase
12. Assets
13. Shift
14. Liability
15. Debit

PART B

	DEBIT	CREDIT		DEBIT	CREDIT		DEBIT	CREDIT
1.	100	300	5.	560	210	9.	550	100
2.	170	210	6.	120	400	10.	500	100
3.	180	210	7.	100	120	11.	170	100
4.	310	100	8.	100	400	12.	500	210

PART C

1. True
2. False
3. True
4. False
5. True

6. True
7. True
8. False
9. False
10. True

11. False
12. True
13. True
14. False
15. True -- but see Chapter Four

16. True
17. False
18. False

3

Beginning the Accounting Cycle: Journalizing, Posting, and the Trial Balance

SELF-REVIEW QUIZ 3-1

LOWE'S REPAIR SERVICE
GENERAL JOURNAL

Page 1

Date		Account Title and Description	Post Ref.	Dr.	Cr.

SELF-REVIEW QUIZ 3-1, Cont.

LOWE'S REPAIR SERVICE
GENERAL JOURNAL

Page 1   (Cont.)

Date	Account Title and Description	Post Ref.	Dr.	Cr.

SELF-REVIEW QUIZ 3-2

CLARK'S DESKTOP PUBLISHING SERVICES
GENERAL JOURNAL

Page 1

Date 2007		Account Titles and Description	Post. Ref.	Dr.	Cr.
May	1	Cash		10 0 0 0 0 0	
		Brenda Clark, Capital			10 0 0 0 0 0
		Initial investment of cash by owner			
	1	Desktop Publishing Equipment		6 0 0 0 0 0	
		Cash			1 0 0 0 0 0
		Accounts Payable			5 0 0 0 0 0
		Purchase of equipment from Ben Co.			
	1	Prepaid Rent		1 2 0 0 0 0	
		Cash			1 2 0 0 0 0
		Rent Paid in advance (3 months)			
	3	Office Supplies		6 0 0 0 0	
		Accounts Payable			6 0 0 0 0
		Purchase of supplies on account from Norris Co.			
	7	Cash		3 0 0 0 0 0	
		Desktop Publishing Fees			3 0 0 0 0 0
		Cash received for services rendered			
	11	Office Salaries Expense		6 5 0 0 0	
		Cash			6 5 0 0 0
		Payment of office salaries			
	18	Advertising Expense		2 5 0 0 0	
		Accounts Payable			2 5 0 0 0
		Bill received from Al's News Co., but not paid			
	20	Brenda Clark, Withdrawals		6 2 5 0 0	
		Cash			6 2 5 0 0
		Personal withdrawal of cash			
	22	Accounts Receivable		5 0 0 0 0 0	
		Desktop Publishing Fees			5 0 0 0 0 0
		Billed Morris Co. for fees earned			

SELF-REVIEW QUIZ 3-2, Cont.

CLARK'S DESKTOP PUBLISHING SERVICES
GENERAL JOURNAL

Page 2

Date 2007		Account Title and Description	Post. Ref.	Dr.	Cr.
May	25	Office Salaries Expense		6 5 0 00	
		Cash			6 5 0 00
		Payment of office salaries			
	28	Accounts Payable		2 5 0 0 00	
		Cash			2 5 0 0 00
		Paid half the amount owed Ben Co.			
	29	Telephone Expense		2 2 0 00	
		Cash			2 2 0 00
		Paid telephone bill			

PARTIAL LEDGER OF CLARK'S DESKTOP PUBLISHING SERVICES

NAME: __CASH__ ACCOUNT NO. ___111___

Date	Explanation	Post. Ref.	Debit	Credit	D R C R	Balance

NAME: __ACCOUNTS RECEIVABLE__ ACCOUNT NO. ___112___

Date	Explanation	Post. Ref.	Debit	Credit	D R C R	Balance

SELF-REVIEW QUIZ 3-2, Cont.

NAME: __OFFICE SUPPLIES_____ ACCOUNT NO. ____114

Date		Explanation	Post Ref.	Debit	Credit	D R C R	Balance

NAME: __PREPAID RENT_____ ACCOUNT NO. ____115

Date		Explanation	Post Ref.	Debit	Credit	D R C R	Balance

NAME: __DESKTOP PUBLISHING EQUIPMENT_____ ACCOUNT NO. ____121

Date		Explanation	Post Ref.	Debit	Credit	D R C R	Balance

NAME: __ACCOUNTS PAYABLE_____ ACCOUNT NO. ____211

Date		Explanation	Post Ref.	Debit	Credit	D R C R	Balance

NAME: __BRENDA CLARK, CAPITAL_____ ACCOUNT NO. ____311

Date		Explanation	Post Ref.	Debit	Credit	D R C R	Balance

SELF-REVIEW QUIZ 3-2, Cont.

NAME: __BRENDA CLARK, WITHDRAWALS__   ACCOUNT NO. ____312__

Date	Explanation	Post Ref.	Debit	Credit	DR CR	Balance

NAME: __DESKTOP PUBLISHING FEES__   ACCOUNT NO. ____411__

Date	Explanation	Post Ref.	Debit	Credit	DR CR	Balance

NAME: __OFFICE SALARIES EXPENSE__   ACCOUNT NO. ____511__

Date	Explanation	Post Ref.	Debit	Credit	DR CR	Balance

NAME: __ADVERTISING EXPENSE__   ACCOUNT NO. ____512__

Date	Explanation	Post Ref.	Debit	Credit	DR CR	Balance

NAME: __TELEPHONE EXPENSE__   ACCOUNT NO. ____513__

Date	Explanation	Post Ref.	Debit	Credit	DR CR	Balance

SELF-REVIEW QUIZ 3-3

1.

_____

_____

_____

2.

GENERAL JOURNAL

Page 4

Date		Account Title and Description	Post Ref.	Dr.	Cr.

FORMS FOR COMPREHENSIVE DEMONSTRATION PROBLEM

a.

ABBY'S EMPLOYMENT AGENCY - GENERAL JOURNAL

Page 1

Date		Account Title and Description	Post Ref.	Dr.	Cr.

FORMS FOR COMPREHENSIVE DEMONSTRATION PROBLEM, Cont.

b.

| ABBY'S EMPLOYMENT AGENCY - GENERAL LEDGER |

NAME: _CASH_____ ACCOUNT NO. ____111____

Date		Explanation	Post Ref.	Debit	Credit	D R C R	Balance

NAME: _ACCOUNTS RECEIVABLE_____ ACCOUNT NO. ____112____

Date		Explanation	Post Ref.	Debit	Credit	D R C R	Balance

NAME: _SUPPLIES_____ ACCOUNT NO. ____131____

Date		Explanation	Post Ref.	Debit	Credit	D R C R	Balance

NAME: _EQUIPMENT_____ ACCOUNT NO. ____141____

Date		Explanation	Post Ref.	Debit	Credit	D R C R	Balance

NAME: _ACCOUNTS PAYABLE_____ ACCOUNT NO. ____211____

Date		Explanation	Post Ref.	Debit	Credit	D R C R	Balance

NAME: _A. TODD, CAPITAL_____ ACCOUNT NO. ____311____

Date		Explanation	Post Ref.	Debit	Credit	D R C R	Balance

NAME: _A. TODD, WITHDRAWALS_____ ACCOUNT NO. ____321____

Date		Explanation	Post Ref.	Debit	Credit	D R C R	Balance

FORMS FOR COMPREHENSIVE DEMONSTRATION PROBLEM, Cont.

b.

NAME: __EMPLOYMENT FEES EARNED_____ ACCOUNT NO. __411__

Date		Explanation	Post Ref.	Debit	Credit	D R C R	Balance

NAME: __WAGES EXPENSE_____ ACCOUNT NO. __511__

Date		Explanation	Post Ref.	Debit	Credit	D R C R	Balance

NAME: __TELEPHONE EXPENSE_____ ACCOUNT NO. __521__

Date		Explanation	Post Ref.	Debit	Credit	D R C R	Balance

NAME: __ADVERTISING EXPENSE_____ ACCOUNT NO. __531__

Date		Explanation	Post Ref.	Debit	Credit	D R C R	Balance

c.

ABBY'S EMPLOYMENT AGENCY
TRIAL BALANCE
MARCH 31, 2007

FORMS FOR MINI EXERCISES

1.

a. _____   e. _____

b. _____   f. _____

c. _____   g. _____

d. _____   h. _____

i. _____

2.

(A) _____

(B) _____

(C) _____

3.

NAME: ___CASH_____   ACCOUNT NO. ___111___

Date 2006		Explanation	Post Ref.	Debit	Credit	D R C R	Balance
June	2		GJ1	1 5 0 0			
	5		GJ1	6 0 0			
	9		GJ2		4 0 0		
	10		GJ3	1 0 0			

4.

LARKIN COMPANY
TRIAL BALANCE
OCTOBER 31, 2008

5.

Date		Account Title and Description	Post Ref.	Dr.	Cr.

NAME: _____   CLASS: _____   DATE: May 25

FORMS FOR EXERCISES

3-1.

2008 Date Oct.	Account Title and Description	Post Ref.	Dr.	Cr.
Oct. 1.	Cash		40000	
	Equipment		2000	
	W. Lantz, Capital			42000
Oct 3	Building		60000	
	Accounts Payable			60000
Oct 13	Truck		18000	
	Cash			18000
Oct 17	Supplies		700	
	Accounts Payable			700
			120,700	120,700

3-2.

2007 Date	Account Title and Description	Post Ref.	Dr.	Cr.
Jan 2	Cash		16000	
	R. Long, capital			16000
Jan 5	Equipment		7000	
	Cash			7000
Jan 8	Equipment		6000	
	Accounts Payable			6000
Jan 15	Cash		900	
	Revenue			900
Jan 18	Account Reicievable		900	
	Revene			900
Jan 22	Withdrawl R. Long		300	
	Cash			300
			31,100	31,100

EXERCISES, Cont.

3-3.

2006 Date	Account Title and Description	Post Ref.	Dr.	Cr.
April 6	Cash		15 000	
	A. King, Capital			15 000
	Cash investment.			
April 14	Equipment		9000	
	Cash			4000
	Accounts Payable			5000

NAME: CASH   ACCOUNT NO. _____ 111

2006 Date	Explanation	Post Ref.	Debit	Credit	DR CR	Balance
April 6	Cash	111	15 000		DR	15 000
	R. Long Cash Investment					

NAME: EQUIPMENT   ACCOUNT NO. _____ 121

2006 Date	Explanation	Post Ref.	Debit	Credit	DR CR	Balance
April 14	Equipment	121	900		DR	900
	Auto Repair Equipment					

NAME: ACCOUNTS PAYABLE   ACCOUNT NO. _____ 211

2006 Date	Explanation	Post Ref.	Debit	Credit	DR CR	Balance
April 14	Accounts Payable.	211		5000	CR	5000
	Equipment bought on					
	account					

NAME: A. KING, CAPITAL   ACCOUNT NO. _____ 311

Date	Explanation	Post Ref.	Debit	Credit	DR CR	Balance
April 6	A. King Capital	311		15 000	CR	15 000
	Cash Investmen.					

EXERCISES, Cont.

3-4 (a)

2008 Date	Account Title and Description	Post Ref.	Dr.	Cr.
July 2	Cash		6000	
	J. Lowe, Capital			6000
	Cash Investment			
July 4	Equipment		800	
	Accounts Payable.			800
	Purchase of Equipment.			
July 15	Cash		4000	
	Accounts Reicievable			4000
	Billed Friend Co.			
July 18	Cash		5000	
	Revenue			5000
	Services Rendered.			

(b)

NAME: _CASH_ ACCOUNT NO. ___111___

Date	Explanation	Post Ref.	Debit	Credit	D R C R	Balance

NAME: _ACCOUNTS RECEIVABLE_ ACCOUNT NO. ___112___

Date	Explanation	Post Ref.	Debit	Credit	D R C R	Balance

EXERCISE 3-4, Cont.

NAME: __EQUIPMENT__   ACCOUNT NO. ___121___

Date	Explanation	Post Ref.	Debit	Credit	DR CR	Balance

NAME: __ACCOUNTS PAYABLE__   ACCOUNT NO. ___211___

Date	Explanation	Post Ref.	Debit	Credit	DR CR	Balance

NAME: __J. LOWE, CAPITAL__   ACCOUNT NO. ___311___

Date	Explanation	Post Ref.	Debit	Credit	DR CR	Balance

NAME: __J. LOWE, WITHDRAWALS__   ACCOUNT NO. ___312___

Date	Explanation	Post Ref.	Debit	Credit	DR CR	Balance

NAME: __FEES EARNED__   ACCOUNT NO. ___411___

Date	Explanation	Post Ref.	Debit	Credit	DR CR	Balance

NAME: __SALARIES EXPENSE__   ACCOUNT NO. ___511___

Date	Explanation	Post Ref.	Debit	Credit	DR CR	Balance

EXERCISE 3-4, Cont.

(c)

LOWE COMPANY

TRIAL BALANCE

JULY 31, 2008

EXERCISE 3-5.

SUN CO.

TRIAL BALANCE

MARCH 31, 2006

EXERCISE 3-6.

GENERAL JOURNAL

Date	Account Title and Description	Post Ref.	Dr.	Cr.

END OF CHAPTER PROBLEMS

PROBLEM 3A-1 or 3B-1.

AL'S FITNESS CENTRE
GENERAL JOURNAL

Page 1

Date		Account Title and Description	Post Ref.	Dr.	Cr.

PROBLEM 3A-1 or PROBLEM 3B-1, Cont.

AL'S FITNESS CENTRE
GENERAL JOURNAL

Page 2

Date	Account Title and Description	Post Ref.	Dr.	Cr.

PROBLEM 3A-2 or 3B-2.

a.

TAYLOR'S DANCE STUDIO - GENERAL JOURNAL

Page 1

Date	Account Title and Description	Post Ref.	Dr.	Cr.

PROBLEM 3A-2 or 3B-2, Cont.

b.

GENERAL LEDGER OF TAYLOR'S DANCE STUDIO

NAME: CASH 2008   ACCOUNT NO. _____ 111

Date	Explanation	Post. Ref.	Debit	Credit	DR CR	Balance
June 2	Initial Investment	111	9000 —		D	9000 —
June 2	Rent Expense	111		1000 —	C	1000 —
5	Workshop Revenue	111	900		D	9900 —
9	Supplies purchased	111		300	C	1300 —
11	wage expense.	111		400	C	1700 —
16	cash withdrawals	111		150	C	1850 —
27	Electrical expense	111		125	C	1975 —
36	telephone expense	111		190	C	2165 —

NAME: ACCOUNTS RECEIVABLE June 2008   ACCOUNT NO. _____ 112

Date	Explanation	Post. Ref.	Debit	Credit	DR CR	Balance
Jue 10	Dance Lessons	112	2100 —		D	2100 —

NAME: PREPAID RENT   ACCOUNT NO. _____ 114

Date	Explanation	Post. Ref.	Debit	Credit	DR CR	Balance
June 2	Rent expense	114	1000		D	1000 —

NAME: SUPPLIES   ACCOUNT NO. _____ 121

Date	Explanation	Post. Ref.	Debit	Credit	DR CR	Balance
June 9	Supplies	121	300		D	300 —

NAME: EQUIPMENT   ACCOUNT NO. _____ 131

Date	Explanation	Post. Ref.	Debit	Credit	DR CR	Balance
June 3	Equipement Purchase	131	700 —		D	700 —

NAME: ACCOUNTS PAYABLE   ACCOUNT NO. _____ 211

Date	Explanation	Post. Ref.	Debit	Credit	DR CR	Balance
June 3	Equipement Purchase	211		700 —	C	700 —

NAME: Christina Sharlow   CLASS: _____   DATE: _____

PROBLEM 3A-2 or 3B-2, Cont.

b.

NAME: MOLLY TAYLOR, CAPITAL   ACCOUNT NO. _____ 311

Date	Explanation	Post Ref.	Debit	Credit	DR CR	Balance
June 2008 2	Initial Investment	311		9000 —	C	9000 —

NAME: MOLLY TAYLOR, WITHDRAWALS   ACCOUNT NO. _____ 312

Date	Explanation	Post Ref.	Debit	Credit	DR CR	Balance
June 2008 16	Withdrawals	312	150 —		D	150 —

NAME: FEES EARNED   ACCOUNT NO. _____ 411

Date	Explanation	Post Ref.	Debit	Credit	DR CR	Balance
June 2008 5	Revenue	411		900 —	C	900 —
June 2008 10	Revenue	411		2100 —	C	3000 —

NAME: ELECTRICAL EXPENSE   ACCOUNT NO. _____ 511

Date	Explanation	Post Ref.	Debit	Credit	DR CR	Balance
June 2008 27	Electrical Expense	511	125 —		D	125 —

NAME: SALARIES EXPENSE   ACCOUNT NO. _____ 512

Date	Explanation	Post Ref.	Debit	Credit	DR CR	Balance
June 2008 11	Wage Expense	512	400 —		D	400 —

NAME: TELEPHONE EXPENSE   ACCOUNT NO. _____ 531

Date	Explanation	Post Ref.	Debit	Credit	DR CR	Balance
June 2009 30	Telephone Expense	531	190 —		D	190 —

NAME: Christina Sharla CLASS: _____ DATE: _____

PROBLEM 3A-2 or 3B-2, Cont.

c.

TAYLOR'S DANCE STUDIO

TRIAL BALANCE

JUNE 30, 2008

Cash	7735 —	
Accounts Recievable	2100	
Prepaid Rent	1000	
Supplies	300	
Equipment	700	
Accounts Payable		700
Molly Taylor, capital		900
Molly Taylor, withdrawals.	450	
Fees Earned		3000
Electrical Expense	125	
Salaries Expense	400	
Telephone Expense	190	
	12700	12700

PROBLEM 3A-3 or 3B-3.

a.

A. FRENCH PLACEMENT AGENCY -- GENERAL JOURNAL

Date		Account Title and Description	Post. Ref.		Dr.					Cr.			

PROBLEM 3A-3 or 3B-3, Cont.

b.

| GENERAL LEDGER OF A. FRENCH PLACEMENT AGENCY |

NAME: _CASH_ ACCOUNT NO. ___111___

Date		Explanation	Post Ref.	Debit	Credit	D R C R	Balance

NAME: _ACCOUNTS RECEIVABLE_ ACCOUNT NO. ___112___

Date		Explanation	Post Ref.	Debit	Credit	D R C R	Balance

NAME: _SUPPLIES ON HAND_ ACCOUNT NO. ___131___

Date		Explanation	Post Ref.	Debit	Credit	D R C R	Balance

NAME: _EQUIPMENT_ ACCOUNT NO. ___141___

Date		Explanation	Post Ref.	Debit	Credit	D R C R	Balance

NAME: _ACCOUNTS PAYABLE_ ACCOUNT NO. ___211___

Date		Explanation	Post Ref.	Debit	Credit	D R C R	Balance

PROBLEM 3A-3 or 3B-3, Cont.

b.

NAME: A. FRENCH, CAPITAL   ACCOUNT NO. 311

Date	Explanation	Post Ref.	Debit	Credit	D R C R	Balance

NAME: A. FRENCH, WITHDRAWALS   ACCOUNT NO. 321

Date	Explanation	Post Ref.	Debit	Credit	D R C R	Balance

NAME: PLACEMENT FEES EARNED   ACCOUNT NO. 411

Date	Explanation	Post Ref.	Debit	Credit	D R C R	Balance

NAME: WAGES EXPENSE   ACCOUNT NO. 511

Date	Explanation	Post Ref.	Debit	Credit	D R C R	Balance

NAME: TELEPHONE EXPENSE   ACCOUNT NO. 521

Date	Explanation	Post Ref.	Debit	Credit	D R C R	Balance

NAME: ADVERTISING EXPENSE   ACCOUNT NO. 531

Date	Explanation	Post Ref.	Debit	Credit	D R C R	Balance

PROBLEM 3A-3 or 3B-3, Cont.

c.

A. FRENCH PLACEMENT AGENCY

TRIAL BALANCE

JUNE 30, 2006

PROBLEM 3C-1.

_____

_____   *Page 1*

Date		Account Title and Description	Post Ref.		Dr.				Cr.			

PROBLEM 3C-1, Cont.

_____

_____   *Page 2*

Date		Account Title and Description	Post Ref.	Dr.					Cr.				

PROBLEM 3C-2. _____

_____   Page 1

Date		Account Titles and Description	Post Ref.	Dr.	Cr.

PROBLEM 3C-2, Cont.

NAME: CASH _____ ACCOUNT NO. ____111____

Date		Explanation	Post Ref.	Debit	Credit	D R C R	Balance

NAME: ACCOUNTS RECEIVABLE _____ ACCOUNT NO. ____112____

Date		Explanation	Post Ref.	Debit	Credit	D R C R	Balance

NAME: PREPAID RENT _____ ACCOUNT NO. ____114____

Date		Explanation	Post Ref.	Debit	Credit	D R C R	Balance

NAME: SUPPLIES _____ ACCOUNT NO. ____121____

Date		Explanation	Post Ref.	Debit	Credit	D R C R	Balance

NAME: EQUIPMENT _____ ACCOUNT NO. ____131____

Date		Explanation	Post Ref.	Debit	Credit	D R C R	Balance

NAME: ACCOUNTS PAYABLE _____ ACCOUNT NO. ____211____

Date		Explanation	Post Ref.	Debit	Credit	D R C R	Balance

PROBLEM 3C-2, Cont.

NAME: DOUG ST. JAMES, CAPITAL   ACCOUNT NO. 311

Date	Explanation	Post Ref.	Debit	Credit	DR CR	Balance

NAME: DOUG ST. JAMES, WITHDRAWALS   ACCOUNT NO. 321

Date	Explanation	Post Ref.	Debit	Credit	DR CR	Balance

NAME: FEES EARNED   ACCOUNT NO. 411

Date	Explanation	Post Ref.	Debit	Credit	DR CR	Balance

NAME: ADVERTISING EXPENSE   ACCOUNT NO. 511

Date	Explanation	Post Ref.	Debit	Credit	DR CR	Balance

NAME: ELECTRICAL EXPENSE   ACCOUNT NO. 515

Date	Explanation	Post Ref.	Debit	Credit	DR CR	Balance

NAME: SALARIES EXPENSE   ACCOUNT NO. 521

Date	Explanation	Post Ref.	Debit	Credit	DR CR	Balance

NAME: TELEPHONE EXPENSE   ACCOUNT NO. 531

Date	Explanation	Post Ref.	Debit	Credit	DR CR	Balance

PROBLEM 3C-2, Cont.

PROBLEM 3C-3.

_____

_____   Page 1

Date		Account Titles and Description	Post Ref.	Dr.	Cr.

PROBLEM 3C-3, Cont.

NAME: CASH _____ ACCOUNT NO. _____ 111

Date		Explanation	Post Ref.	Debit	Credit	D R C R	Balance

NAME: ACCOUNTS RECEIVABLE _____ ACCOUNT NO. _____ 112

Date		Explanation	Post Ref.	Debit	Credit	D R C R	Balance

NAME: SUPPLIES _____ ACCOUNT NO. _____ 131

Date		Explanation	Post Ref.	Debit	Credit	D R C R	Balance

NAME: EQUIPMENT _____ ACCOUNT NO. _____ 141

Date		Explanation	Post Ref.	Debit	Credit	D R C R	Balance

NAME: ACCOUNTS PAYABLE _____ ACCOUNT NO. _____ 211

Date		Explanation	Post Ref.	Debit	Credit	D R C R	Balance

PROBLEM 3C-3, Cont.

NAME: __M. NEPOOSE, CAPITAL_____ ACCOUNT NO. ____311____

Date	Explanation	Post Ref.	Debit	Credit	D R C R	Balance

NAME: __M. NEPOOSE, WITHDRAWALS_____ ACCOUNT NO. ____321____

Date	Explanation	Post Ref.	Debit	Credit	D R C R	Balance

NAME: __INVESTIGATIVE FEES EARNED_____ ACCOUNT NO. ____411____

Date	Explanation	Post Ref.	Debit	Credit	D R C R	Balance

NAME: __WAGE EXPENSE_____ ACCOUNT NO. ____511____

Date	Explanation	Post Ref.	Debit	Credit	D R C R	Balance

NAME: __TELEPHONE EXPENSE_____ ACCOUNT NO. ____521____

Date	Explanation	Post Ref.	Debit	Credit	D R C R	Balance

NAME: __ADVERTISING EXPENSE_____ ACCOUNT NO. ____531____

Date	Explanation	Post Ref.	Debit	Credit	D R C R	Balance

PROBLEM 3C-3, Cont.

REAL WORLD APPLICATION #3R-1.

HAMPTON CO.

TRIAL BALANCE

JUNE 30, 2007

REAL WORLD APPLICATIONS #3R-2.

_____
_____
_____
_____
_____
_____
_____
_____
_____
_____
_____
_____
_____
_____
_____
_____
_____
_____
_____
_____
_____
_____
_____
_____
_____
_____

YOU MAKE THE CALL: CRITICAL THINKING/ETHICAL CASE #3R-3.

_____
_____
_____
_____
_____
_____
_____
_____
_____

CONTINUING PROBLEM

1.   **ELDORADO COMPUTER CENTRE - GENERAL JOURNAL**   *Page 1*

Date	Account Titles and Description	Post Ref.	Dr.	Cr.

CONTINUING PROBLEM, Cont.

2.   GENERAL LEDGER OF ELDORADO COMPUTER CENTRE

NAME: CASH   ACCOUNT NO. ____1000____

Date 2007		Explanation	Post. Ref.	Debit	Credit	DR CR	Balance
Sept.	1	Balance Forward	✔			Dr	2 8 6 5 0 0

NAME: ACCOUNTS RECEIVABLE   ACCOUNT NO. ____1020____

Date 2007		Explanation	Post. Ref.	Debit	Credit	DR CR	Balance
Sept.	1	Balance forward	✔			Dr	8 5 0 0 0

NAME: PREPAID RENT   ACCOUNT NO. ____1025____

Date 2007		Explanation	Post. Ref.	Debit	Credit	DR CR	Balance

NAME: SUPPLIES   ACCOUNT NO. ____1030____

Date 2007		Explanation	Post. Ref.	Debit	Credit	DR CR	Balance
Sept.	1	Balance forward	✔			Dr.	4 5 0 0 0

NAME: COMPUTER SHOP EQUIPMENT   ACCOUNT NO. ____1080____

Date 2007		Explanation	Post. Ref.	Debit	Credit	DR CR	Balance
Sept.	1	Balance forward	✔			Dr	1 2 0 0 0 0

NAME: OFFICE EQUIPMENT   ACCOUNT NO. ____1090____

Date 2007		Explanation	Post. Ref.	Debit	Credit	DR CR	Balance
Sept.	1	Balance forward	✔			Dr.	6 0 0 0 0

2.   **GENERAL LEDGER OF ELDORADO COMPUTER CENTRE, Cont.**

NAME: ACCOUNTS PAYABLE   ACCOUNT NO.   2000

Date 2007		Explanation	Post. Ref.	Debit	Credit	D R C R	Balance
Sept.	1	Balance forward	✔			Cr	4 0 5 0 0

NAME: T. FREEDMAN, CAPITAL   3000

Date 2007		Explanation	Post. Ref.	Debit	Credit	D R C R	Balance
Sept.	1	Balance forward	✔			Cr.	4 5 0 0 0 0

NAME: T. FREEDMAN, WITHDRAWALS   ACCOUNT NO.   3010

Date 2007		Explanation	Post. Ref.	Debit	Credit	D R C R	Balance
Sept.	1	Balance forward	✔			Dr.	1 0 0 0 0

NAME: SERVICE REVENUE   ACCOUNT NO.   4000

Date 2007		Explanation	Post. Ref.	Debit	Credit	D R C R	Balance
Sept.	1	Balance forward	✔			Cr	3 4 0 0 0 0

NAME: ADVERTISING EXPENSE   5010

Date 2007		Explanation	Post. Ref.	Debit	Credit	D R C R	Balance
Sept.	1	Balance forward	✔			Dr.	1 4 0 0 0 0

NAME: RENT EXPENSE   ACCOUNT NO.   5020

Date 2007		Explanation	Post. Ref.	Debit	Credit	D R C R	Balance
Sept.	1	Balance forward	✔			Dr.	4 0 0 0 0

CONTINUING PROBLEM, Cont.

2.   **GENERAL LEDGER OF ELDORADO COMPUTER CENTRE, Cont.**

NAME: _UTILITIES EXPENSE_ _____   ACCOUNT NO.   ___5030___

Date 2007		Explanation	Post. Ref.	Debit	Credit	D R C R	Balance
Sept.	1	Balance forward	✔			Dr	8 5 0 0

NAME: _PHONE EXPENSE_ _____   ACCOUNT NO.   ___5040___

Date 2007		Explanation	Post. Ref.	Debit	Credit	D R C R	Balance
Sept.	1	Balance forward	✔			Dr	1 5 5 0 0

NAME: _SUPPLIES EXPENSE_ _____   ACCOUNT NO.   ___5050___

Date 2007		Explanation	Post. Ref.	Debit	Credit	D R C R	Balance

NAME: _INSURANCE EXPENSE_ _____   ACCOUNT NO.   ___5060___

Date 2007		Explanation	Post. Ref.	Debit	Credit	D R C R	Balance
Sept.	1	Balance forward	✔			Dr.	1 5 0 0 0

NAME: _POSTAGE EXPENSE_ _____   ACCOUNT NO.   ___5070___

Date 2007		Explanation	Post. Ref.	Debit	Credit	D R C R	Balance
Sept.	1	Balance forward	✔			Dr.	5 0 0 0

CONTINUING PROBLEM, Cont.

3.

ELDORADO COMPUTER CENTRE

TRIAL BALANCE

SEPTEMBER 30, 2007

4.

ELDORADO COMPUTER CENTRE

INCOME STATEMENT

FOR THE THREE MONTHS ENDING SEPTEMBER 30, 2007

CONTINUING PROBLEM, Cont.

4.

ELDORADO COMPUTER CENTRE

STATEMENT OF OWNER'S EQUITY

FOR THE THREE MONTHS ENDING SEPTEMBER 30, 2007

4.

ELDORADO COMPUTER CENTRE

BALANCE SHEET

SEPTEMBER 30, 2007

CHAPTER 3
CHAPTER SUMMARY TEST

PART A:

1. Reports prepared for parts of a fiscal year (monthly, quarterly, etc.) are called _____ _____.

2. An accounting period that runs for any 12 consecutive months is called a _____ _____.

3. The _____ _____ _____ eliminates the need for footings.

4. Recording transactions in a journal is referred to as _____.

5. The usual balance of each account is referred to as its _____ _____.

6. The portion of a journal entry which is indented and placed below the debits and credits is called the _____.

7. Entries are journalized in _____ order.

8. A ledger is often referred to as a book of _____ _____.

9. Supplies on hand is a(n) _____ on the balance sheet.

10. When supplies are used up or consumed they become a(n) _____.

11. A journal entry requiring more than a single debit and credit is called a _____ _____.

12. Transferring information from a journal to a ledger is called _____.

13. The book of original entry corresponds to a(n) _____.

14. Recording $885.00 as $858.00 is an example of a _____.

15. The process of updating the PR of the journal from the account number of the ledger to indicate which account in the ledger information has been posted to is referred to as _____ .

PART B:

Match the terms in column 1 to the definition, example or phrase in column 2. Be careful to use a letter only once.

COLUMN 1	COLUMN 2
___g___ 1. EXAMPLE: Withdrawals	a. Accounting period
_____ 2. Posting	b. Interim reports
_____ 3. Book of original entry	c. 2740--27400
_____ 4. Slide	d. Transferring information from a journal to a ledger
_____ 5. Transposition	e. Chronological order
_____ 6. Journalizing	f. Decreased by a debit
_____ 7. Cross-reference	g. Expenditure unrelated to business
_____ 8. General journal	h. Compound journal entry
_____ 9. A fiscal year	i. General journal
_____ 10. Balance sheet prepared monthly	j. 1980--1890
_____ 11. Revenue	k. Updating PR column of journal from ledger account
_____ 12. List of all GL accounts with amounts	l. Trial balance
	m. Record transactions here

PART C:

Are the following statements True or False?

1. *The normal balance of withdrawals account is a credit.*
2. *The running balance of an account can be kept in a three-column account.*
3. *The totals of a trial balance may possibly not balance due to transpositions.*
4. *3259 written by mistake as 3529 is an example of a transposition.*
5. *The ledger is a book of original entry.*
6. *An accounting cycle may be from May 1 to April 30.*
7. *The post reference column of a ledger records the page number of the journal.*
8. *Information from the journal is posted to the journal.*
9. *The journal keeps accounts in alphabetical order.*
10. *If the totals of a trial balance balance, the individual accounts must be correct.*
11. *A fiscal year could be a calendar year.*
12. *750 written by mistake as 570 is an example of a slide.*
13. *Interim reports cover an entire fiscal year.*
14. *The income statement is prepared for a stated accounting period.*
15. *Journals and ledgers are usually in the same book.*
16. *Ruling is eliminated in the three-column account.*
17. *The normal balance of an account is on the opposite side from that which increases it.*
18. *Cross-referencing means only updating the post reference column of the journal.*
19. *The trial balance is prepared from the ledger.*
20. *Equal debits and credits on a trial balance does not guarantee that transactions have been properly recorded.*

SOLUTIONS TO SUMMARY CHAPTER 3 TEST

PART A

1. *Interim reports*
2. *Fiscal year*
3. *Three column account*
4. *Journalizing*
5. *Normal balance*
6. *Explanation*
7. *Chronological*
8. *Final entry*
9. *Asset*
10. *Expense*
11. *Compound journal entry*
12. *Posting*
13. *Journal*
14. *Transposition*
15. *Cross-referencing*

PART B

1. *g*
2. *d*
3. *i*
4. *c*
5. *j*
6. *e*
7. *k*
8. *m*
9. *a*
10. *b*
11. *f*
12. *l*

PART C

1. *false*
2. *true*
3. *true*
4. *true*
5. *false*
6. *true*
7. *true*
8. *false*
9. *false*
10. *false*
11. *true*
12. *false*
13. *false*
14. *true*
15. *false*
16. *true*
17. *false*
18. *false*
19. *true*
20. *true*

4

The Accounting Cycle Continued: Preparing Worksheets and Financial Reports

SELF-REVIEW QUIZ 4-1

Use a blank fold-out worksheet located at the end of this study guide.

SELF-REVIEW QUIZ 4-2

(1)

_____

_____

(2)

_____

_____

SELF-REVIEW QUIZ 4-2, Cont.

(3):

SUBWAY: Where the Dough Goes
Discussion Questions

1. Amortization for each year = $200 ($3,000 - $1,000 = $2,000 / 10 years);
   Amortization for each month =$16.67 ($200 / 12 months).

2. Lila would have checked with the Subway field consultant for an estimate of the bake oven's residual value and useful life. Subway headquarters would have historic information from its Subway franchises as to how long bake ovens like Stan's last and approximately how much they can get for an old bake oven.

3. A clean worksheet is helpful even after that month's statements have been prepared because it is often necessary to consult it months later to resolve a question or problem -- especially at tax time. An indecipherable worksheet can cause big problems later.

FORMS FOR COMPREHENSIVE DEMONSTRATION PROBLEM

(1) Use a blank fold-out worksheet located at the end of this study guide.

(2)

FROST COMPANY
INCOME STATEMENT
FOR THE MONTH ENDED DECEMBER 31, 2008

(2)

FROST COMPANY
STATEMENT OF OWNER'S EQUITY
FOR THE MONTH ENDED DECEMBER 31, 2008

(2)

FROST COMPANY

BALANCE SHEET

DECEMBER 31, 2008

ASSETS

LIABILITIES AND OWNER'S EQUITY

CHAPTER 4
FORMS FOR MINI EXERCISES

1. a. _____
   _____
   _____

   b.

1. Accounts Affected	2. Category	3. ↑↓	4. Rules	5. T-Account Update

   c. _____
   _____
   _____

2. a. _____
   _____
   _____

   b.

1. Accounts Affected	2. Category	3. ↑↓	4. Rules	5. T-Account Update

   c. _____

3. a. _____
   b. _____

   c.

1. Accounts Affected	2. Category	3. ↑↓	4. Rules	5. T-Account Update

   d. _____
   _____

FORMS FOR MINI EXERCISES, Cont.

4. a.

1. Accounts Affected	2. Category	3. ↑↓	4. Rules	5. T-Account Update

b. _____
_____

5. a. _____   h. _____

    b. _____   i. _____

    c. _____   j. _____

    d. _____   k. _____

    e. _____   l. _____

    f. _____   m. _____

    g. _____   n. _____

6. _____
_____
_____
_____
_____
_____
_____
_____
_____

FORMS FOR EXERCISES

4-1.

Account	Category	Normal Balance	Found on which Financial Report(s)

4-2.

Accounts Affected	Category	↑ ↓	Rules
a.			
b.			

4-3.

a.	
b.	

4-4.

Use a blank fold-out worksheet located at the end of this study guide.

FORMS FOR EXERCISES, Cont.

4-5. a.

J. TRENT

INCOME STATEMENT

FOR THE MONTH ENDED DECEMBER 31, 2008

b.

J. TRENT

STATEMENT OF OWNER'S EQUITY

FOR THE MONTH ENDED DECEMBER 31, 2008

c.

J. TRENT

BALANCE SHEET

DECEMBER 31, 2008

ASSETS			LIABILITIES & OWNER'S EQUITY		

END OF CHAPTER PROBLEMS

NOTE: For Problems 4A-1, 4A-2, 4A-3(1), 4B-1, 4B-2 and 4B-3(1), please use a blank, fold-out worksheet which is found at the end of this study guide.

PROBLEM 4A-3 or 4B-3.

2.

KEVIN'S MOVING CO.
INCOME STATEMENT
FOR THE MONTH ENDED OCTOBER 31, 2008

KEVIN'S MOVING CO.
STATEMENT OF OWNER'S EQUITY
FOR THE MONTH ENDED OCTOBER 31, 2008

KEVIN'S MOVING CO.
BALANCE SHEET
OCTOBER 31, 2008

ASSETS				LIABILITIES & OWNER'S EQUITY			

REAL WORLD APPLICATIONS #4R-2 and
YOU MAKE THE CALL: Critical Thinking/Ethical Cases #4R-3.

CONTINUING PROBLEM

ELDORADO COMPUTER CENTRE
WORK SHEET
FOR THREE MONTHS ENDED SEPTEMBER 30, 2007

Account Titles	Trial Balance		Adjustments	
	Dr.	Cr.	Dr.	Cr.

CONTINUING PROBLEM, Cont.

ELDORADO COMPUTER CENTRE
WORK SHEET - CONTINUED
FOR THREE MONTHS ENDED SEPTEMBER 30, 2007

Adjusted Trial Balance		Income Statement		Balance Sheet	
D r.	C r.	D r.	C r.	D r.	C r.

CONTINUING PROBLEM, Cont.

ELDORADO COMPUTER CENTRE

INCOME STATEMENT

FOR THE THREE MONTHS ENDING SEPTEMBER 30, 2007

ELDORADO COMPUTER CENTRE

STATEMENT OF OWNER'S EQUITY

FOR THE THREE MONTHS ENDING SEPTEMBER 30, 2007

CONTINUING PROBLEM, Cont.

ELDORADO COMPUTER CENTRE

BALANCE SHEET

SEPTEMBER 30, 2007

ASSETS

LIABILITIES & OWNER'S EQUITY

CHAPTER 4

CHAPTER SUMMARY TEST

PART A

1. _____ affect both the balance sheet and income statement.
2. The adjustment for supplies usually reflects the amount of supplies_____ _____ .
3. Adjustments are due to _____ transactions.
4. Accumulated Amortization, a contra-asset account, is shown on the_____ _____ .
5. Supplies Expense is found on the income statement. Supplies are found on the _____
   _____ .
6. _____ _____ reflects the transaction amount of equipment at time of purchase.
7. Amortization Expense is shown on the _____ _____ .
8. _____ is a contra-asset account that has a credit balance.
9. The figure for net loss on the worksheet would be carried over to the _____ column of the balance sheet section.
10. After the completion of the worksheet, _____ _____ are prepared.
11. _____ cost of an auto less _____ _____ reflects the net book value of an auto on the balance sheet.
12. Withdrawals are listed in the _____ column of the adjusted trial balance of the worksheet.
13. Salaries Payable is a liability that will appear in the _____ column of the _____ _____ section of the worksheet.
14. A worksheet is a(n) _____ report.

PART B

Choose the best answer to the following statements by circling the letter corresponding to your choice.

1. The historical or original cost of an asset
   a. sometimes changes
   b. never changes
   c. continually changes
   d. is carried over to the balance sheet columns (credit column)

2. A worksheet is usually completed
   a. one column at a time
   b. two columns at a time
   c. three columns at a time
   d. all columns at once

3. Adjustments affect
   a. the income statement accounts
   b. the balance sheet accounts
   c. both a and b
   d. neither a nor b

4. Net income on the worksheet is
    a. carried over to the adjusted trial balance (credit column)
    b. carried over to the balance sheet columns (debit column)
    c. carried over to the trial balance (credit column)
    d. carried over to the balance sheet columns (credit column)
5. Accumulated Amortization is found on
    a. a worksheet
    b. an income statement
    c. both a worksheet and an income statement
    d. both a worksheet and a balance sheet
6. Accumulated Amortization, a contra-asset, is increased by a
    a. debit
    b. credit
    c. neither a nor b
    d. both a and b
7. The adjustment for supplies requires one to know
    a. supplies on hand for beginning and end of period
    b. supplies purchased
    c. supplies used up
    d. any two of a, b, or c
8. The _____ is an informal report.
    a. balance sheet
    b. income statement
    c. worksheet
    d. statement of owner's equity
9. Withdrawals on the worksheet are found in the
    a. debit column of the income statement
    b. debit column of the balance sheet
    c. credit column of the income statement
    d. credit column of the balance sheet
10. The worksheet specifically shows
    a. the beginning figure for owner's capital, including any additional contributions
    b. the ending figure for owner's capital
    c. the average figure for owner's capital
    d. no exact figure for owner's capital
11. The adjustment for amortization affects
    a. the income statement
    b. the balance sheet
    c. both a and b
    d. neither a nor b
12. The total of the assets on a formal balance sheet will _____ equal the total of the debit column
    of the balance sheet on the worksheet.
    a. always
    b. sometimes
    c. never
    d. neither a nor b
13. The purpose of adjustments is to
    a. bring ledger accounts up to proper balances in the journal
    b. bring ledger accounts to proper balance
    c. bring the general journal up to date
    d. correct for errors encountered
14. Book value equals cost less
    a. amortization expense
    b. accumulated amortization
    c. neither a nor b
    d. a plus b

PART C

Answer true or false to the following statements.

1. Supplies on hand is an expense with a debit balance.
2. Debits and credits are used on formal reports.
3. Historical cost relates only to buildings.
4. The totals of the adjustments columns may agree but be incorrect.
5. Prepaid rent is found on the balance sheet.
6. Rent expense is found on the statement of owner's equity.
7. An expense is recorded only when it is paid.
8. The adjustment for amortization increases cash on hand.
9. As Accumulated Amortization increases, the historical cost decreases.
10. Accumulated Amortization is found on the balance sheet.
11. The net income on the worksheet is the same amount as shown on the income statement.
12. Prepaid rent is an expense of a future period.
13. The ending figure for owner's capital is found on the worksheet.
14. Withdrawals have the same type of balance as does Accumulated Amortization.
15. Salaries Payable is shown on the balance sheet.
16. Net loss is never shown on a worksheet.
17. Cost less amortization expense equals book value.
18. Canadian worksheets always use dollar signs.
19. The worksheet helps in preparing financial reports.

SOLUTIONS TO CHAPTER SUMMARY TEST

PART A

1. adjustments
2. used up (on hand)
3. internal
4. balance sheet
5. balance sheet
6. historical (original) cost
7. income statement
8. Accumulated Amortization
9. debit
10. financial statements
11. Historical, accumulated amortization
12. debit
13. credit, balance sheet
14. informal

PART B

1. b	6. b	11. c
2. b	7. either a and b; or c	12. b
3. c	8. c	13. b
4. d	9. b	14. b
5. d	10. a	

PART C

1. false	5. true	10. true	15. true
2. false	6. false	11. true	16. false
3. false	7. false	12. true	17. false
4. true	8. false	13. false	18. false
	9. false	14. false	19. true

5

The Accounting Cycle Completed: Adjusting, Closing, and the Post-Closing Trial Balance

SELF-REVIEW QUIZ 5-1

(1)

Date	Account Title and Description	Post Ref.	Dr.	Cr.

5-1

(2) Partial Ledger*

Amortization Expense, Store Equipment	511		Accumulated Amortization, Store Equipment	122
			4	

Prepaid Insurance	116		Insurance Expense	516
3				

Store Supplies	114		Supplies Expense	514
5				

Salaries Expense	512		Salaries Payable	212
8				

* Some accounts are not listed in order in attempt to highlight relationship of adjustments.

SELF-REVIEW QUIZ 5-2

(1) _____

P. Logan, Capital	310	Revenue from Clients	410	Supplies Expense	514
	14		25	4	

P. Logan, Withdrawals	311	Amortization Expense, Store Equipment	510	Insurance Expense	516
3		1		2	

Income Summary	312	Salaries Expense	512	Rent Expense	518
		11		2	

(2) _____

_____

_____

SELF-REVIEW QUIZ 5-3

_____

_____

Please see page 5-48 for suggested solutions for the Subway Case Discussion Questions.

FORMS FOR COMPREHENSIVE DEMONSTRATION PROBLEM

Use a blank fold-out worksheet which is located at the end of this study guide.

ROLO COMPANY
GENERAL JOURNAL

Page 1

Date	Account Title and Description	Post. Ref.	Dr.	Cr.

FORMS FOR COMPREHENSIVE DEMONSTRATION PROBLEM, Cont.

ROLO COMPANY
GENERAL JOURNAL

Page 2

Date	Account Title and Description	Post. Ref.	Dr.	Cr.

FORMS FOR COMPREHENSIVE DEMONSTRATION PROBLEM, Cont.

NAME: CASH   ACCOUNT NO. _____ 111

Date		Explanation	Post Ref.	Debit	Credit	D R C R	Balance

NAME: ACCOUNTS RECEIVABLE   ACCOUNT NO. _____ 112

Date		Explanation	Post Ref.	Debit	Credit	D R C R	Balance

NAME: PREPAID RENT   ACCOUNT NO. _____ 114

Date		Explanation	Post Ref.	Debit	Credit	D R C R	Balance

NAME: OFFICE SUPPLIES   ACCOUNT NO. _____ 115

Date		Explanation	Post Ref.	Debit	Credit	D R C R	Balance

NAME: OFFICE EQUIPMENT   ACCOUNT NO. _____ 121

Date		Explanation	Post Ref.	Debit	Credit	D R C R	Balance

NAME: ACCUMULATED AMORTIZATION, OFFICE EQUIPMENT   ACCOUNT NO. _____ 122

Date		Explanation	Post Ref.	Debit	Credit	D R C R	Balance

FORMS FOR COMPREHENSIVE DEMONSTRATION PROBLEM, Cont.

NAME: ACCOUNTS PAYABLE   ACCOUNT NO. 211

Date	Explanation	Post Ref.	Debit	Credit	D R C R	Balance

NAME: SALARIES PAYABLE   ACCOUNT NO. 212

Date	Explanation	Post Ref.	Debit	Credit	D R C R	Balance

NAME: ROLO KERN, CAPITAL   ACCOUNT NO. 311

Date	Explanation	Post Ref.	Debit	Credit	D R C R	Balance

NAME: ROLO KERN, WITHDRAWALS   ACCOUNT NO. 312

Date	Explanation	Post Ref.	Debit	Credit	D R C R	Balance

NAME: INCOME SUMMARY   ACCOUNT NO. 313

Date	Explanation	Post Ref.	Debit	Credit	D R C R	Balance

NAME: FEES EARNED   ACCOUNT NO. 411

Date	Explanation	Post Ref.	Debit	Credit	D R C R	Balance

NAME: SALARIES EXPENSE   ACCOUNT NO. 511

Date	Explanation	Post Ref.	Debit	Credit	D R C R	Balance

FORMS FOR COMPREHENSIVE DEMONSTRATION PROBLEM, Cont.

NAME: ADVERTISING EXPENSE _____ ACCOUNT NO. ___512___

Date	Explanation	Post. Ref.	Debit	Credit	D R C R	Balance

NAME: RENT EXPENSE _____ ACCOUNT NO. ___513___

Date	Explanation	Post. Ref.	Debit	Credit	D R C R	Balance

NAME: OFFICE SUPPLIES EXPENSE _____ ACCOUNT NO. ___514___

Date	Explanation	Post. Ref.	Debit	Credit	D R C R	Balance

NAME: AMORTIZATION EXPENSE, OFFICE EQUIPMENT _____ ACCOUNT NO. ___515___

Date	Explanation	Post. Ref.	Debit	Credit	D R C R	Balance

ROLO COMPANY

INCOME STATEMENT

FOR THE MONTH ENDED JANUARY 31, 2007

FORMS FOR COMPREHENSIVE DEMONSTRATION PROBLEM, Cont.

ROLO COMPANY

STATEMENT OF OWNER'S EQUITY

FOR MONTH ENDED JANUARY 31, 2007

ROLO COMPANY

BALANCE SHEET

JANUARY 31, 2007

ASSETS					LIABILITIES & OWNER'S EQUITY				

FORMS FOR COMPREHENSIVE DEMONSTRATION PROBLEM, *Concluded*

ROLO COMPANY

POST-CLOSING TRIAL BALANCE

JANUARY 31, 2007

CHAPTER 5

FORMS FOR MINI EXERCISES

1.

GENERAL JOURNAL

Page 3

Date		Account Title and Description	Post Ref.	Dr.	Cr.

Prepaid Insurance	115		Insurance Expense	510
10				

Store Supplies	116		Amort. Exp., Store Equipment	512
15				

Acc. Amort., Store Equipment	119		Supplies Expense	514
	12			

Salaries Payable	210		Salaries Expense	516
			7	

2. _____

_____

_____

_____

_____

FORMS FOR MINI EXERCISES

3.

GENERAL JOURNAL

Date	Account Title and Description	Post Ref.	Dr.	Cr.

4.

Income Summary   314

Temporary or Permanent: _____

5.

Mel Blanc, Capital   310

Balance: _____

5-1.

FORMS FOR EXERCISES

Date		Account Title and Description	Post Ref.	Dr.	Cr.

5-2.   TEMPORARY   PERMANENT   WILL BE CLOSED

1. *Income Summary*
2. *Melissa Bryant, Capital*
3. *Salary Expense*
4. *Melissa Bryant, Withdrawals*
5. *Fees Earned*
6. *Accounts Payable*
7. *Cash*

5-3.

Date		Account Title and Description	Post Ref.	Dr.	Cr.

EXERCISES, Cont.

5-4.

Date		Account Title and Description	Post Ref.	Dr.				Cr.			

5-5.

WEY CO.
POST-CLOSING TRIAL BALANCE
DECEMBER 31, 2009

	Dr.				Cr.			

PROBLEM 5A-1 or 5B-1.

1. Use a blank fold-out worksheet which is located at the end of this study guide.

2.

LOU'S CONSULTING SERVICE
GENERAL JOURNAL

Page 3

Date	Account Title and Description	Post Ref.	Dr.	Cr.

PROBLEM 5A-2 or 5B-2.

(1)

POTTER CLEANING SERVICE
GENERAL JOURNAL

Page 2

Date		Account Title and Description	Post Ref.	Dr.	Cr.

PROBLEM 5A-2 or 5B-2, Cont.

(2) GENERAL LEDGER OF POTTER CLEANING SERVICE

NAME: __CASH__   ACCOUNT NO. ___112___

Date	Explanation	Post Ref.	Debit	Credit	DR CR	Balance

NAME: __PREPAID INSURANCE__   ACCOUNT NO. ___114___

Date	Explanation	Post Ref.	Debit	Credit	DR CR	Balance

NAME: __CLEANING SUPPLIES__   ACCOUNT NO. ___115___

Date	Explanation	Post Ref.	Debit	Credit	DR CR	Balance

NAME: __AUTO__   ACCOUNT NO. ___121___

Date	Explanation	Post Ref.	Debit	Credit	DR CR	Balance

NAME: __ACCUMULATED AMORTIZATION, AUTO__   ACCOUNT NO. ___122___

Date	Explanation	Post Ref.	Debit	Credit	DR CR	Balance

NAME: __ACCOUNTS PAYABLE__   ACCOUNT NO. ___212___

Date	Explanation	Post Ref.	Debit	Credit	DR CR	Balance

PROBLEM 5A-2 or 5B-2, Cont.

(2)

NAME: ____SALARIES PAYABLE_____ ACCOUNT NO. ____213____

Date		Explanation	Post Ref.	Debit	Credit	D R C R	Balance

NAME: ____B. POTTER, CAPITAL_____ ACCOUNT NO. ____312____

Date		Explanation	Post Ref.	Debit	Credit	D R C R	Balance

NAME: ____B. POTTER, WITHDRAWALS_____ ACCOUNT NO. ____313____

Date		Explanation	Post Ref	Debit	Credit	D R C R	Balance

NAME: ____INCOME SUMMARY_____ ACCOUNT NO. ____314____

Date		Explanation	Post Ref.	Debit	Credit	D R C R	Balance

NAME: ____CLEANING FEES_____ ACCOUNT NO. ____412____

Date		Explanation	Post Ref.	Debit	Credit	D R C R	Balance

NAME: ____SALARIES EXPENSE_____ ACCOUNT NO. ____513____

Date		Explanation	Post Ref.	Debit	Credit	D R C R	Balance

PROBLEM 5A-2 or 5B-2, Cont.

(2)

NAME: __TELEPHONE EXPENSE_____ ACCOUNT NO. ____514__

Date		Explanation	Post Ref.	Debit	Credit	DR CR	Balance

NAME: __ADVERTISING EXPENSE_____ ACCOUNT NO. ____515__

Date		Explanation	Post Ref.	Debit	Credit	DR CR	Balance

NAME: __GAS EXPENSE_____ ACCOUNT NO. ____516__

Date		Explanation	Post Ref.	Debit	Credit	DR CR	Balance

NAME: __INSURANCE EXPENSE_____ ACCOUNT NO. ____517__

Date		Explanation	Post Ref.	Debit	Credit	DR CR	Balance

NAME: __CLEANING SUPPLIES EXPENSE_____ ACCOUNT NO. ____518__

Date		Explanation	Post Ref.	Debit	Credit	DR CR	Balance

NAME: __AMORTIZATION EXPENSE, AUTO_____ ACCOUNT NO. ____519__

Date		Explanation	Post Ref.	Debit	Credit	DR CR	Balance

PROBLEM 5A-2 or PROBLEM 5B-2, Concluded

(2)

POTTER CLEANING SERVICE
POST-CLOSING TRIAL BALANCE
MARCH 31, 2007

	Dr.	Cr.

PROBLEM 5A-3 OR 5B-3.

Use a blank fold-out worksheet which is located at the end of this study guide.

PROBLEM 5C-1.

(1) Use a blank fold-out worksheet which is located at the end of this study guide.

(2)

Date	Account Titles and Description	Post Ref.	Dr.	Cr.

PROBLEM 5C-2.

_____

(1) _____ Page 1

Date		Account Title and Description	Post Ref.	Dr.					Cr.				

PROBLEM 5C-2, Cont.

Date	Account Title and Description	Post Ref.	Dr.	Cr.

(2)

NAME: _CASH_ ACCOUNT NO. ___1100

Date 2006		Explanation	Post Ref.	Debit	Credit	D R C R	Balance
Nov	30	Bal. Fwd.				Dr	2 3 6 6 4 8

NAME: _PREPAID INSURANCE_ ACCOUNT NO. ___1120

Date 2006		Explanation	Post Ref.	Debit	Credit	D R C R	Balance
Nov	30	Bal. Fwd.				Dr	7 1 4 5 6

NAME: _ACCOUNTS RECEIVABLE_ ACCOUNT NO. ___1140

Date 2006		Explanation	Post Ref.	Debit	Credit	D R C R	Balance
Nov	30	Bal Fwd.				Dr	5 2 7 7 4 2

NAME: _REPAIR PARTS AND SUPPLIES_ ACCOUNT NO. ___1160

Date 2006		Explanation	Post Ref.	Debit	Credit	D R C R	Balance
Nov	30	Bal. Fwd.				Dr	1 5 9 7 4 7

PROBLEM 5C-2, Cont.

(2)

NAME: _VAN_   ACCOUNT NO. _1200_

Date 2006		Explanation	Post Ref.	Debit	Credit	DR CR	Balance
Nov	30	Bal. Fwd.				Dr	2 1 6 7 5 0 0

NAME: _ACCUMULATED AMORTIZATION, VAN_   ACCOUNT NO. _1250_

Date 2006		Explanation	Post Ref.	Debit	Credit	DR CR	Balance
Nov	30	Bal. Fwd.				Cr	8 1 0 3 6 5

NAME: _ACCOUNTS PAYABLE_   ACCOUNT NO. _2100_

Date 2006		Explanation	Post Ref.	Debit	Credit	DR CR	Balance
Nov	30	Bal. Fwd.				Cr	3 7 7 2 6 0

NAME: _SALARIES PAYABLE_   ACCOUNT NO. _2150_

Date		Explanation	Post Ref.	Debit	Credit	DR CR	Balance

NAME: _MEGAN TRAN, CAPITAL_   ACCOUNT NO. _3100_

Date 2006		Explanation	Post Ref.	Debit	Credit	DR CR	Balance
Nov	30	Bal. Fwd.				Cr	1 3 6 6 3 5 8

NAME: _MEGAN TRAN, WITHDRAWALS_   ACCOUNT NO. _3150_

Date 2006		Explanation	Post Ref.	Debit	Credit	DR CR	Balance
Nov	30	Bal. Fwd.				Dr	2 6 0 0 0 0

PROBLEM 5C-2, Cont.

(2)

NAME: __INCOME SUMMARY__ ACCOUNT NO. __3199__

Date 2006	Explanation	Post Ref.	Debit	Credit	DR CR	Balance

NAME: __REPAIR REVENUE__ ACCOUNT NO. __4100__

Date 2006		Explanation	Post Ref.	Debit	Credit	DR CR	Balance
Nov	30	Bal. Fwd.				Cr	1 6 4 5 8 70

NAME: __ADVERTISING EXPENSE__ ACCOUNT NO. __5100__

Date 2006		Explanation	Post Ref.	Debit	Credit	DR CR	Balance
Nov	30	Bal. Fwd.				Dr	7 1 4 38

NAME: __AUTOMOTIVE EXPENSE__ ACCOUNT NO. __5112__

Date 2006		Explanation	Post Ref.	Debit	Credit	DR CR	Balance
Nov	30	Bal. Fwd.				Dr	2 3 4 5 51

NAME: __BANK CHARGES EXPENSE__ ACCOUNT NO. __5114__

Date	Explanation	Post Ref.	Debit	Credit	DR CR	Balance

NAME: __CLEANING EXPENSE__ ACCOUNT NO. __5120__

Date 2006		Explanation	Post Ref.	Debit	Credit	DR CR	Balance
Nov	30	Bal. Fwd.				Dr	3 7 5 00

PROBLEM 5C-2, Cont.

(2)

NAME: AMORTIZATION EXPENSE, VAN ACCOUNT NO. 5125

Date	Explanation	Post Ref.	Debit	Credit	D R C R	Balance

NAME: INSURANCE EXPENSE ACCOUNT NO. 5140

Date	Explanation	Post Ref.	Debit	Credit	D R C R	Balance

NAME: MISCELLANEOUS EXPENSE ACCOUNT NO. 5145

Date 2006		Explanation	Post Ref.	Debit	Credit	D R C R	Balance
Nov	30	Bal. Fwd.				Dr	1 7 8 1 4

NAME: POSTAGE AND OFFICE EXPENSE ACCOUNT NO. 5160

Date 2006		Explanation	Post Ref.	Debit	Credit	D R C R	Balance
Nov	30	Bal. Fwd.				Dr	2 8 4 1 7

NAME: SALARIES EXPENSE ACCOUNT NO. 5180

Date 2006		Explanation	Post Ref.	Debit	Credit	D R C R	Balance
Nov	30	Bal. Fwd.				Dr	3 8 7 0 4 0

NAME: SUPPLIES EXPENSE ACCOUNT NO. 5185

Date	Explanation	Post Ref.	Debit	Credit	D R C R	Balance

PROBLEM 5C-2, Cont.

(2)

_____

_____

_____

PROBLEM 5C-3.

Use a blank fold-out worksheet which is located at the end of this study guide.

_____

_____   Page 1

Date		Account Title and Description	Post Ref.	Dr.	Cr.

PROBLEM 5C-3, Cont.

_____

_____

Date	Account Title and Description	Post Ref.	Dr.	Cr.

PROBLEM 5C-3, Cont.

_____

_____   *Page 3*

Date		Account Title and Description	Post Ref.	Dr.	Cr.

PROBLEM 5C-3, Cont.

NAME: _____ ACCOUNT NO. _____

Date		Explanation	Post Ref.	Debit				Credit				DR CR	Balance			

NAME: _____ ACCOUNT NO. _____

Date		Explanation	Post Ref.	Debit			Credit			DR CR	Balance		

NAME: _____ ACCOUNT NO. _____

Date		Explanation	Post Ref.	Debit			Credit			DR CR	Balance		

NAME: _____ ACCOUNT NO. _____

Date		Explanation	Post Ref.	Debit			Credit			DR CR	Balance		

NAME: _____ ACCOUNT NO. _____

Date		Explanation	Post Ref.	Debit			Credit			DR CR	Balance		

PROBLEM 5C-3, Cont.

NAME: _____ ACCOUNT NO. _____

Date		Explanation	Post Ref.	Debit	Credit	D R C R	Balance

NAME: _____ ACCOUNT NO. _____

Date		Explanation	Post Ref.	Debit	Credit	D R C R	Balance

NAME: _____ ACCOUNT NO. _____

Date		Explanation	Post Ref.	Debit	Credit	D R C R	Balance

NAME: _____ ACCOUNT NO. _____

Date		Explanation	Post Ref.	Debit	Credit	D R C R	Balance

NAME: _____ ACCOUNT NO. _____

Date		Explanation	Post Ref.	Debit	Credit	D R C R	Balance

NAME: _____ ACCOUNT NO. _____

Date		Explanation	Post Ref.	Debit	Credit	D R C R	Balance

PROBLEM 5C-3, Cont.

NAME: _____ ACCOUNT NO. _____

Date		Explanation	Post Ref.	Debit	Credit	D R C R	Balance

NAME: _____ ACCOUNT NO. _____

Date		Explanation	Post Ref.	Debit	Credit	D R C R	Balance

NAME: _____ ACCOUNT NO. _____

Date		Explanation	Post Ref.	Debit	Credit	D R C R	Balance

NAME: _____ ACCOUNT NO. _____

Date		Explanation	Post Ref.	Debit	Credit	D R C R	Balance

NAME: _____ ACCOUNT NO. _____

Date		Explanation	Post Ref.	Debit	Credit	D R C R	Balance

NAME: _____ ACCOUNT NO. _____

Date		Explanation	Post Ref.	Debit	Credit	D R C R	Balance

PROBLEM 5C-3, Cont.

NAME: _____ ACCOUNT NO. _____

Date		Explanation	Post Ref.	Debit				Credit			D R C R	Balance			

NAME: _____ ACCOUNT NO. _____

Date		Explanation	Post Ref.	Debit				Credit			D R C R	Balance			

NAME: _____ ACCOUNT NO. _____

Date		Explanation	Post Ref.	Debit				Credit			D R C R	Balance			

NAME: _____ ACCOUNT NO. _____

Date		Explanation	Post Ref.	Debit				Credit			D R C R	Balance			

NAME: _____ ACCOUNT NO. _____

Date		Explanation	Post Ref.	Debit				Credit			D R C R	Balance			

PROBLEM 5C-3, Cont.

_____

_____

_____

_____

PROBLEM 5C-3, Cont.

PROBLEM 5C-3, Concluded

_____

_____

_____

REAL WORLD APPLICATIONS #5R-1, 5R-2, and

You Make the Call: Critical Thinking/Ethical Case #5R-3.

_____

_____

_____

_____

_____

_____

_____

_____

_____

_____

_____

_____

_____

_____

_____

_____

_____

_____

_____

_____

_____

_____

_____

_____

_____

_____

_____

_____

_____

_____

_____

Closing Time
SUBWAY Case
Discussion Questions

1. The salaries expense would be increased by $175. Her accrued wages would be placed in the Salaries Payable account.

2. The closing balance will be off by $20 x 3 x 2 = $120. The closing balances in the accounts "Uniforms" and "Accounts Payable" will be understated.

3. Doing a monthly closing allows Stan to compare performance over time and identify net profit or losses for each time period. It also helps with budgetting and when comparing his business to other Subways.

5-48   © 2006 Pearson Canada All Rights Reserved

CONTINUING PROBLEM

1.　　　　　　**ELDORADO COMPUTER CENTRE - GENERAL JOURNAL**　　　*Page 2*

Date	Account Titles and Description	Post Ref.	Dr.	Cr.

5-49

CONTINUING PROBLEM, Cont.

GENERAL LEDGER OF ELDORADO COMPUTER CENTRE

NAME: CASH   1000

Date 2007		Explanation	Post Ref.	Debit	Credit	D R C R	Balance
Sept.	30	Balance forward	✔			Dr	1 6 4 5 0 0

NAME: ACCOUNTS RECEIVABLE   1020

Date 2007		Explanation	Post Ref.	Debit	Credit	D R C R	Balance
Sept.	30	Balance forward	✔			Dr	2 6 0 0 0 0

NAME: PREPAID RENT   ACCOUNT NO. 1025

Date 2007		Explanation	Post Ref.	Debit	Credit	D R C R	Balance
Sept.	30	Balance forward	✔			Dr	1 2 0 0 0 0

NAME: SUPPLIES   ACCOUNT NO. 1030

Date 2007		Explanation	Post Ref.	Debit	Credit	D R C R	Balance
Sept.	30	Balance forward	✔			Dr	4 5 0 0 0

NAME: COMPUTER SHOP EQUIPMENT   ACCOUNT NO. 1080

Date 2007		Explanation	Post Ref.	Debit	Credit	D R C R	Balance
Sept.	30	Balance forward	✔			Dr	2 4 0 0 0 0

NAME: ACCUM. AMORTIZATION. COMPUTER SHOP EQUIPMENT   ACCOUNT NO. 1081

Date 2007		Explanation	Post Ref.	Debit	Credit	D R C R	Balance

NAME: OFFICE EQUIPMENT   ACCOUNT NO. 1090

Date 2007		Explanation	Post Ref.	Debit	Credit	D R C R	Balance
Sept.	30	Balance forward	✔			Dr	6 0 0 0 0

CONTINUING PROBLEM, Cont.

GENERAL LEDGER OF ELDORADO COMPUTER CENTRE

NAME: _ACCUMULATED AMORTIZATION, OFFICE EQUIPMENT_ _____ _1091_

Date 2007		Explanation	Post Ref.	Debit	Credit	D R C R	Balance

NAME: _ACCOUNTS PAYABLE_ _____ _2000_

Date 2007		Explanation	Post Ref.	Debit	Credit	D R C R	Balance
Sept.	30	Balance forward	✔			Cr	2 1 0 0 0

NAME: _T. FREEDMAN, CAPITAL_ _____ ACCOUNT NO. _3000_

Date 2007		Explanation	Post Ref.	Debit	Credit	D R C R	Balance
Sept.	30	Balance forward	✔			Cr	4 5 0 0 0 0

NAME: _T. FREEDMAN, WITHDRAWALS_ _____ ACCOUNT NO. _3010_

Date 2007		Explanation	Post Ref.	Debit	Credit	D R C R	Balance
Sept.	30	Balance forward	✔			Dr	1 0 0 0 0

NAME: _INCOME SUMMARY_ _____ ACCOUNT NO. _3020_

Date 2007		Explanation	Post Ref.	Debit	Credit	D R C R	Balance

NAME: _SERVICE REVENUE_ _____ ACCOUNT NO. _4000_

Date 2007		Explanation	Post Ref.	Debit	Credit	D R C R	Balance
Sept.	30	Balance forward	✔			Cr	6 6 8 5 0 0

CONTINUING PROBLEM, Cont.

GENERAL LEDGER OF ELDORADO COMPUTER CENTRE

NAME: __ADVERTISING EXPENSE_____ ACCOUNT NO. ____5010____

Date 2007		Explanation	Post Ref.	Debit	Credit	DR CR	Balance
Sept.	30	Balance forward	✔			Dr	1 4 0 0 0

NAME: __RENT EXPENSE_____ ACCOUNT NO. ____5020____

Date 2007		Explanation	Post Ref.	Debit	Credit	DR CR	Balance
Sept.	30	Balance forward	✔			Dr	4 0 0 0 0

NAME: __UTILITIES EXPENSE_____ ACCOUNT NO. ____5030____

Date 2007		Explanation	Post Ref.	Debit	Credit	DR CR	Balance
Sept.	30	Balance forward	✔			Dr	1 8 0 0 0

NAME: __PHONE EXPENSE_____ ACCOUNT NO. ____5040____

Date 2007		Explanation	Post Ref.	Debit	Credit	DR CR	Balance
Sept.	30	Balance forward	✔			Dr	2 2 0 0 0

NAME: __SUPPLIES EXPENSE_____ ACCOUNT NO. ____5050____

Date 2007		Explanation	Post Ref.	Debit	Credit	DR CR	Balance

NAME: __INSURANCE EXPENSE_____ ACCOUNT NO. ____5060____

Date 2007		Explanation	Post Ref.	Debit	Credit	DR CR	Balance
Sept.	30	Balance forward	✔			Dr	1 5 0 0 0

CONTINUING PROBLEM, Cont.

GENERAL LEDGER OF ELDORADO COMPUTER CENTRE

NAME: __POSTAGE EXPENSE_____ ACCOUNT NO. ___5070___

Date 2007		Explanation	Post Ref.	Debit	Credit	D R C R	Balance
Sept.	30	Balance forward	✔			Dr	5 0 0 0

NAME: __AMORTIZATION EXPENSE, COMPUTER SHOP EQUIPMENT__ ACCOUNT NO. ___5080___

Date 2007		Explanation	Post Ref.	Debit	Credit	D R C R	Balance

NAME: __AMORTIZATION EXPENSE, OFFICE EQUIPMENT_____ ACCOUNT NO. ___5090___

Date 2007		Explanation	Post Ref.	Debit	Credit	D R C R	Balance

CONTINUING PROBLEM, Cont.

ELDORADO COMPUTER CENTRE

POST-CLOSING TRIAL BALANCE

SEPTEMBER 30, 2007

CHAPTER 5

CHAPTER SUMMARY TEST

PART A

Fill in the blank(s) to complete each statement

1. Examples of temporary accounts are _____ _____ and _____ .
2. After all closing entries are posted, owner's Capital account will contain the_____

   _____ .
3. At the end of each fiscal year, Income Summary is _____ .
4. Temporary account _____ will not be carried over to the next accounting period.
5. To close expense to Income Summary a _____ to each individual expense and a _____
   to Income Summary is required.
6. A list of permanent accounts after the adjusting and closing entries have been posted to the ledger from the
   journal is called _____ _____ _____ .
7. To close revenue to Income Summary, a_____ to each revenue account and a _____
   to Income Summary is required.
8. After closing, each temporary account in the ledger will have a_____ balance.
9. To close withdrawals a _____ is required and the offsetting amount transferred to owner's
   Capital by a _____ .
10. When all closing entries have been posted, Income Summary has a _____ balance.
11. To close the balance of Income Summary, a _____ to Income Summary and a _____
    to owner's Capital is required if the company made a profit.
12. Journalizing adjustments are usually prepared from the _____ .
13. Income Summary is a _____ account.
14. Closing entries can be prepared from the_____ .
15. Cash, Equipment,and Supplies are called _____accounts.

PART B

The following is a chart of accounts for Jane's Computer Repair Co. From the chart, indicate in column 2
(by account number) which accounts will be debited or credited due to the transactions in column 1.

CHART OF ACCOUNTS

ASSETS
110 Cash
112 Accounts Receivable
116 Prepaid Rent
118 Prepaid Insurance
119 Computer Supplies
150 Delivery Van
151 Accumulated Amortization, Van

LIABILITIES
210 Accounts Payable
216 Salaries Payable

OWNER'S EQUITY
300 J. Ramey, Capital
310 J. Ramey, Withdrawals
330 Income Summary

REVENUE
400 Repair Fees Earned

EXPENSES
510 Advertising
520 Amortization Expense, Van
530 Insurance
560 Rent
570 Salaries
575 Computer Supplies

COLUMN 1

COLUMN 2

	DEBIT(S)	CREDIT(S)
1. Closed balance in revenue account to Income Summary.	_____	_____
2. Closed balance in individual expenses to Income Summary.	_____	_____
3. Closed balance in Income Summary to owner's Capital. (Assume that it is a net income.)	_____	_____
4. Closed withdrawals to owner's Capital.	_____	_____
5. Recorded computer supplies used up.	_____	_____
6. Recorded amortization on van.	_____	_____
7. Brought Salaries Expense up to date (an adjustment).	_____	_____

PART C

Answer true or false to the following statements.

1. All companies journalize and post closing entries before the end of their calendar year.
2. Adjustments are journalized before preparing the worksheet.
3. Closing entries can only clear permanent accounts.
4. Income Summary is a temporary account.
5. Interim reports can be prepared from worksheets.
6. To clear expenses in the closing process, a compound entry is appropriate.
7. Withdrawals is a temporary account.
8. Income Summary helps update withdrawals.
9. Accumulated Amortization is a temporary account.
10. Cash, Repairs Expense, and Accounts Payable need to be closed at the end of the period.
11. Closing entries do not relate to the worksheet.
12. Revenue is closed by a credit.
13. Expenses are placed on the debit side of the Income Summary account.

6

Banking Procedures and Control of Cash

SELF-REVIEW QUIZ 6-1

SITUATION	ADD TO BANK BALANCE	DEDUCT FROM BANK BALANCE	ADD TO CHEQUEBOOK BALANCE	DEDUCT FROM CHEQUEBOOK BALANCE
1				
2				
3				
4				
5				
6				
7				

SELF-REVIEW QUIZ 6-2

GENERAL JOURNAL

Page 6

SELF REVIEW QUIZ 6-2

AUXILIARY PETTY CASH RECORD

Date	Voucher No.	Description	Receipts	Payment	Category of Payment					
					Delivery Expense	General Expense	Sundry		
							Account		Amount	

Counting Down the Cash
SUBWAY Case

1. An advisory council interprets policies and is a place to bring common concerns. Franchisees need an advisory council so that they can voice concerns that they have with regard to policies sent from the head office. They can get clarity on issues or policies that they don't understand. At the advisory council, franchisees can be brought up to date on new technologies that everyone is to use.

2. Some small business owners don't use the computer much and fear they won't understand what to do. They might be so busy that learning a new tool seems a waste of time.

3. Stan would catch a discrepancy in the Cash account by knowing the beginning change fund and adding the cash register total. That should equal the cash on hand. If it does not, the amount will have to be recorded in the Cash Short and Over account. The journal entry would be

Cash	XXX	
Cash Short and Over	XX	
Sales		XXX
To record cash shortage.		

4. Subway invests in cash handling systems because it recognizes that the easier cash handling is for shop employees and owners, the greater its profits will be in the long run.

FORMS FOR MINI EXERCISES

1. a. _____
    b. _____
    c. _____
    d. _____
    e. _____
    f. _____

2. _____
    _____
    _____

3.
Woody Co.
Bank Reconciliation
May 31, 2007

Chequebook	*Bank Statement*

4. a. _____   d. _____
    b. _____   e. _____
    c. _____   f. _____

MINI EXERCISES, Cont.

5.   **GENERAL JOURNAL**

Date	Account Title and Description	Post. Ref.	Dr.	Cr.

6.   **GENERAL JOURNAL**

Date	Account Title and Description	Post. Ref.	Dr.	Cr.

FORMS FOR EXERCISES

6-1.

FAITH CO.
BANK RECONCILIATION AS OF JULY 31, 2007

CHEQUEBOOK BALANCE   BALANCE PER BANK

Ending Chequebook Balance   _____   Ending Bank Statement Balance   _____
                                            Add: _____
Deduct: _____
                                                   _____   _____
_____
_____   Deduct: _____
_____   _____
                                                   _____   _____

Reconciled Balance   _____   Reconciled Balance   _____

EXERCISES, Cont.

6-2.

6-3.

6-4.

6-5.

PROBLEM 6A-1 or 6B-1.

		Chequebook Balance														
		Balance per Bank Statement														

GENERAL JOURNAL

Date		Account Title and Description	Post Ref.	Dr.	Cr.

PROBLEM 6A-2 or 6B-2.

BANK OF SASKATCHEWAN
MAIN BRANCH
REGINA, SASKATCHEWAN

This form is provided to help you balance your bank statement. If no errors are reported to the bank within 30 days , the account will be considered correct.

Please notify us of any change in address.

Cheques outstanding
(not charged to account)

Cheque No.	Amount
Total	

Sort the cheques numerically or by date issued. Check off the stubs of your chequebook with each cheque paid by bank. List the numbers and amounts of cheques still outstanding in the space provided at the left.

Verify the deposits in your chequebook with deposits credited on this statement.

Bank balance shown on this statement $ _____

Plus: deposits not credited on this
statement $ _____
Subtotal $ _____
Less: Cheques outstanding $ _____
Balance $ _____

If your chequebook does not agree, enter any necessary adjustment:

_____
_____
_____

Correct chequebook balance $ _____

GENERAL JOURNAL

Date	Account Title and Description	Post Ref.	Dr.	Cr.

PROBLEM 6A-3 or 6B-3.

MERRY CO.
GENERAL JOURNAL   *Page 2*

Date		Account Title and Description	Post Ref.	Dr.				Cr.			

PROBLEM 6A-3 or 6B-3, Cont.

MERRY CO.
AUXILIARY PETTY CASH RECORD

Date	Voucher No.	Description	Receipts	Payments	Category of Payment				
					Postage Expense	Office Supplies Expense	Sundry		
							Account	Amount	

PROBLEM 6A-4 or 6B-4, Concluded

LOGAN CO.

AUXILIARY PETTY CASH RECORD

Date	Voucher No.	Description	Receipts	Payments	Category of Payment				
					Postage Expense	Delivery Expense	Account	Sundry	Amount

PROBLEM 6A-4 or 6B-4.

LOGAN CO.
GENERAL JOURNAL   *Page 33*

Date		Account Title and Description	Post Ref.	Dr.	Cr.

PROBLEM 6A-5 or 6B-5.

CASING SUPPLIERS LTD.
BANK RECONCILIATION AS OF MARCH 31, 2009

CHEQUEBOOK BALANCE   BALANCE PER BANK

Ending Chequebook Balance _____   Ending Bank Statement Balance _____
  Add: _____ _____   Add: _____ _____
Subtotal   Subtotal
  Deduct: _____   Deduct: _____

  _____ _____   _____ _____
  _____ _____   _____ _____
  _____ _____   _____ _____
  _____ _____   _____ _____

Reconciled Balance   _____   Reconciled Balance   _____

PROBLEM 6C-1.

		Chequebook Balance										
		Balance per Bank Statement										

GENERAL JOURNAL

Date		Account Title and Description	Post Ref.	Dr.			Cr.		

PROBLEM 6C-2.

BANK OF INDUSTRY AND COMMERCE
MAIN BRANCH
HALIFAX, NS

This form is provided to help you balance your bank statement. If no errors are reported to the bank within 30 days, the account will be considered correct.

Please notify us of any change in address.

Cheques outstanding
(not charged to account)

Cheque No.	Amount
Total	

Sort the cheques numerically or by date issued. Check off on the stubs of your chequebook each cheque paid by bank. List the numbers and amounts of cheques still outstanding in the space provided at the left.
Verify the deposits in your chequebook with deposits credited on this statement.
Bank balance shown on this statement $ _____
Plus:
Deposits not credited on this statement $ _____
   $ _____
Subtotal $ _____
Less: Cheques outstanding $ _____
Balance $ _____
If your chequebook does not agree, enter any necessary adjustment:

_____
_____
_____

Correct chequebook balance $ _____

THE FRESH FLOWER SHOP
GENERAL JOURNAL

Date	Account Title and Description	Post Ref.	Dr.	Cr.

PROBLEM 6C-3.

SAMUEL & CO.
GENERAL JOURNAL   *Page 2*

Date		Account Title and Description	Post Ref.	Dr.					Cr.				

PROBLEM 6C-3, Cont.

SAMUEL & CO.
AUXILIARY PETTY CASH RECORD

Date	Voucher No.	Description	Receipts	Payments	Category of Payment				
					Postage Expense	Office Supplies Expense	Sundry		
							Account	Amount	

PROBLEM 6C-4.

CARON CO.
GENERAL JOURNAL

Page 22

Date		Account Title and Description	Post Ref.	Dr.	Cr.

PROBLEM 6C-4, Concluded

CARON CO.

AUXILIARY PETTY CASH RECORD

Date	Voucher No.	Description	Receipts	Payments	Category of Payment				
					Postage Expense	Delivery Expense	Account	Sundry	Amount

PROBLEM 6C-5.

BANK RECONCILIATION

Balance per Bank Statement _____   *Balance per G/L - Unadjusted* _____
Add: *Add:*

_____ _____   _____ _____
                       _____   _____

Less: *Less:*
  Outstanding Cheques

  _____ _____   _____ _____
  _____ _____   _____ _____
  _____ _____   _____ _____

                       _____   _____

Reconciled Balance   _____   *Reconciled Balance*   _____

REAL WORLD APPLICATIONS

6R-1.

HOOP CO.
GENERAL JOURNAL

Page 13

Date		Account Title and Description	Post Ref.	Dr.	Cr.

_____
_____
_____

6R-2.

GINGER COMPANY
BANK RECONCILIATION
NOVEMBER 30, 2007

Bank Statement	_Chequebook_

_____
_____
_____

REAL WORLD APPLICATIONS

6R-3.

_____

_____

_____

_____

_____

_____

_____

_____

_____

_____

_____

_____

_____

_____

_____

_____

_____

_____

_____

_____

_____

_____

_____

_____

YOU MAKE THE CALL: CRITICAL THINKING/ETHICAL CASE

6R-4.

_____

_____

_____

_____

_____

_____

_____

_____

_____

_____

CONTINUING PROBLEM

1.

ELDORADO COMPUTER CENTRE - GENERAL JOURNAL

Page 3

Date	Account Title and Description	Post Ref.	Dr.	Cr.

CONTINUING PROBLEM, Cont.

ELDORADO COMPUTER CENTRE
AUXILIARY PETTY CASH RECORD

Date	Voucher No.	Description	Receipts	Payments	Category of Payment				
					Postage Expense	Supplies Expense	Sundry Account	Amount	

NAME: _____ CLASS: _____ DATE: _____

CONTINUING PROBLEM, Cont.
GENERAL LEDGER OF ELDORADO COMPUTER CENTRE

NAME: _CASH_   ACCOUNT NO. ___1000___

Date 2007		Explanation	Post Ref.	Debit	Credit	DR CR	Balance
Sept.	30	Balance Forward	✔			Dr	1 6 4 5 0 0

NAME: _PETTY CASH_   ACCOUNT NO. ___1010___

Date 2007		Explanation	Post Ref.	Debit	Credit	DR CR	Balance

NAME: _ACCOUNTS RECEIVABLE_   ACCOUNT NO. ___1020___

Date 2007		Explanation	Post Ref.	Debit	Credit	DR CR	Balance
Sept.	30	Balance forward	✔			Dr	2 6 0 0 0 0

NAME: _PREPAID RENT_   ACCOUNT NO. ___1025___

Date 2007		Explanation	Post Ref.	Debit	Credit	DR CR	Balance
Sept.	30	Balance forward	✔			Dr	4 0 0 0 0

NAME: _SUPPLIES_   ACCOUNT NO. ___1030___

Date 2007		Explanation	Post Ref.	Debit	Credit	DR CR	Balance
Sept.	30	Balance forward	✔			Dr	9 0 0 0

CONTINUING PROBLEM, Cont.

GENERAL LEDGER OF ELDORADO COMPUTER CENTRE, Cont.

NAME: ___COMPUTER SHOP EQUIPMENT___   ACCOUNT NO. ___1080___

Date 2007		Explanation	Post Ref.	Debit	Credit	DR CR	Balance
Sept.	30	Balance forward	✔			Dr	2 4 0 0 00

NAME: ___ACCUMULATED AMORTIZATION, COMPUTER SHOP___   ACCOUNT NO. ___1081___

Date 2007		Explanation	Post Ref.	Debit	Credit	DR CR	Balance
Sept.	30		✔			Cr	9 9 00

NAME: ___OFFICE EQUIPMENT___   ACCOUNT NO. ___1090___

Date 2007		Explanation	Post Ref.	Debit	Credit	DR CR	Balance
Sept.	30	Balance forward	✔			Dr	6 0 0 00

NAME: ___ACCUMULATED AMORTIZATION, OFFICE EQUIPMENT___   ACCOUNT NO. ___1091___

Date 2007		Explanation	Post Ref.	Debit	Credit	DR CR	Balance
Sept.	30	Balance forward	✔			Cr	2 0 00

NAME: ___ACCOUNTS PAYABLE___   ACCOUNT NO. ___2000___

Date 2007		Explanation	Post Ref.	Debit	Credit	DR CR	Balance
Sept.	30	Balance forward	✔			Cr	2 1 0 00

NAME: ___T. FREEDMAN, CAPITAL___   ACCOUNT NO. ___3000___

Date 2007		Explanation	Post Ref.	Debit	Credit	DR CR	Balance
Sept.	30	Balance forward	✔			Cr	7 4 0 6 00

CONTINUING PROBLEM, Cont.

GENERAL LEDGER OF ELDORADO COMPUTER CENTRE, Cont'd

NAME: T. FREEDMAN, WITHDRAWALS   ACCOUNT NO. _____3010_____

Date 2007	Explanation	Post Ref.	Debit	Credit	D R C R	Balance

NAME: INCOME SUMMARY   ACCOUNT NO. _____3020_____

Date 2007	Explanation	Post Ref.	Debit	Credit	D R C R	Balance

NAME: SERVICE REVENUE   ACCOUNT NO. _____4000_____

Date 2007	Explanation	Post Ref.	Debit	Credit	D R C R	Balance

NAME: ADVERTISING EXPENSE   ACCOUNT NO. _____5010_____

Date 2007	Explanation	Post Ref.	Debit	Credit	D R C R	Balance

NAME: RENT EXPENSE   ACCOUNT NO. _____5020_____

Date 2007	Explanation	Post Ref.	Debit	Credit	D R C R	Balance

NAME: UTILITIES EXPENSE   ACCOUNT NO. _____5030_____

Date 2007	Explanation	Post Ref.	Debit	Credit	D R C R	Balance

CONTINUING PROBLEM, Cont.

GENERAL LEDGER OF ELDORADO COMPUTER CENTRE, Cont'd

NAME: _PHONE EXPENSE_   ACCOUNT NO. _____5040_____

Date 2007	Explanation	Post Ref.	Debit	Credit	DR CR	Balance

NAME: _SUPPLIES EXPENSE_   ACCOUNT NO. _____5050_____

Date 2007	Explanation	Post Ref.	Debit	Credit	DR CR	Balance

NAME: _INSURANCE EXPENSE_   ACCOUNT NO. _____5060_____

Date 2007	Explanation	Post Ref.	Debit	Credit	DR CR	Balance

NAME: _POSTAGE EXPENSE_   ACCOUNT NO. _____5070_____

Date 2007	Explanation	Post Ref.	Debit	Credit	DR CR	Balance

NAME: _AMORTIZATION EXPENSE, COMPUTER SHOP EQUIPMENT_   ACCOUNT NO. _____5080_____

Date 2007	Explanation	Post Ref.	Debit	Credit	DR CR	Balance

NAME: _AMORTIZATION EXPENSE, OFFICE EQUIPMENT_   _____5090_____

Date 2007	Explanation	Post Ref.	Debit	Credit	DR CR	Balance

NAME: _MISCELLANEOUS EXPENSE_   ACCOUNT NO. _____5100_____

Date 2007	Explanation	Post Ref.	Debit	Credit	DR CR	Balance

CONTINUING PROBLEM, Cont.

ELDORADO COMPUTER CENTRE

TRIAL BALANCE

OCTOBER 31, 2007

CONTINUING PROBLEM, Cont.

ELDORADO COMPUTER CENTRE
BANK RECONCILIATION AS OF SEPTEMBER 30, 2007

BALANCE PER BANK		CHEQUEBOOK BALANCE	
Bank Statement Balance	_____	Chequebook Balance	_____
Add:		Add:	
_____		_____	
Subtotal	_____	Subtotal	_____
Deduct:		Deduct:	
_____	_____	_____	_____
Subtotal	_____	Subtotal	_____
Reconciled Balance	_____	Reconciled Balance	_____

CHAPTER 6
CHAPTER SUMMARY TEST

Part A

Fill in the blank(s) to complete the statement.

1. Adjustments to the chequebook balance in the reconciliation process will be followed by _____ _____ .

2. Cheques not yet processed by the bank at the time the bank statement is prepared are referred to as _____ _____ .

3. Deposits in transit are _____ _____ the bank balance.

4. Further negotiations of a cheque are prohibited by a _____ _____ .

5. The auxiliary petty cash record is a _____ _____ .

6. Petty cash is a(n) _____ with a _____ balance.

7. An asset used to make change for customer is called the _____ _____ .

8. When a bank debits your account, your balance will _____ .

9. The procedure whereby the bank does not return the actual cheque is called _____ .

10. A cash overage will be shown on the _____ _____ .

Part B

Prepare a bank reconciliation based on the following facts. The chequebook balance of Terry Company is $3,615.57. The bank statement shows a bank balance of $5,244.26. The bank statement shows interest earned of $26.00 and a service charge of $31.15. There is a deposit in transit of $1,206.96. Outstanding cheques are No. 1407 for $415.20 plus No. 1411 for $1,725.60. The bank collected a note for Terry for $3,100.00. Terry Company forgot to deduct a cheque for $2,400.00 during the month.

Part C

Answer true or false to the following statements.

1. A petty cash voucher records the expense into the ledger.
2. The petty cash account has a debit balance.
3. The balance in the company cash account will usually equal the bank balance before the bank statement is received.
4. Replenishment of petty cash requires a new cheque.
5. Deposit slips are needed for writing cheques.
6. The expenses paid from petty cash are journalized at the time of replenishment.
7. The signature card must always be consulted when a cheque is cashed.
8. Internal control only affects large companies.
9. The auxiliary petty cash record is posted daily.
10. The petty cash fund must be replenished monthly.
11. The establishment of petty cash may require some judgment as to the amount of petty cash needed.
12. Cheques outstanding have reached the bank but have not been recorded in the chequebook.
13. The drawer is the person who receives the cheque.
14. Petty cash is a liability found on the balance sheet.
15. A debit memo will increase the depositor's balance.
16. Cheques returned from the bank are placed in numerical order.
17. A change fund uses only coins.
18. The cash payments journal has a record of all cheques written.
19. The payee is the person or company to whom the cheque is payable.
20. Bank service charges represent miscellaneous income to a business.

SOLUTIONS TO CHAPTER SUMMARY TEST

Part A

1. journal entries
2. outstanding cheques
3. added to
4. restrictive endorsement
5. memorandum record

6. asset, debit
7. change fund
8. decrease
9. safekeeping
10. income statement

Part B

TERRY COMPANY
BANK RECONCILIATION

Chequebook Balance			Bank Balance		
Ending Balance		$3,615.57	Ending Balance		$5,244.26
Add:			Add:		
Interest	$26.00		Deposit in		
Collection			transit		1,206.96
of note	3,100.00	3,126.00			6,451.22
		6,741.57	Deduct:		
Deduct:			Cheques outstanding		
Service Chg.	31.15		Chq. 1407	$ 415.20	
Error	2,400.00	2,431.15	Chq. 1411	1,725.60	2,140.80
Reconciled Balance		$4,310.42	Reconciled Balance		$4,310.42

Part C

1. false	6. true	11. true	16. true
2. true	7. false	12. false	17. false
3. false	8. false	13. false	18. true
4. true	9. false	14. false	19. true
5. false	10. false	15. false	20. false

7

Payroll Concepts and Procedures: Employee Taxes

SELF-REVIEW QUIZ 7-1

Gross Pay:

_____   _____

_____   _____

_____   _____

Total Gross Pay   _____   _____

Deductions:

_____   _____

_____   _____

Total Deductions   _____   _____

Net Pay   _____   _____

Net Pay   ═════════════════════

SELF-REVIEW QUIZ 7-2

Gross Pay:

_____   _____

Deductions:

_____   _____

_____   _____

_____   _____

_____   _____

Total Deductions   _____   _____

Net Pay   _____   _____

Net Pay   ═════════════════════

SELF-REVIEW QUIZ 7-3

1. _____   3. _____   5. _____   7. _____

2. _____   4. _____   6. _____

SUBWAY Case
Payroll Records: A Full-Time Job
Discussion Questions

1.   *The payroll records Stan needs to keep are employee name, address, phone number, Social Insurance Number, TD1 forms, rate of pay, hours worked per pay period, gross pay and deductions per pay period.*

2.   *Stan might also want alternative phone numbers for each employee, as well as a schedule of the hours that each is available for work, so that he can reach them in an emergency. Name, address, and phone numbers of next of kin are usually also requested for use in emergencies.*

3.   *The payroll register helps Stan prepare the payroll by providing the data for journalizing the payroll entry in the general journal. He then journalizes entries to pay a payroll. Finally, he updates each individual employee earnings record.*

FORMS FOR CHAPTER 7 MINI EXERCISES

1.   A. _____
_____
_____
      B. _____
_____
_____
_____

2.   _____
_____
_____
_____

3.   _____
_____
_____
_____

4.   A. _____   D. _____
      B. _____   E. _____
      C. _____   F. _____

5.   A. _____
      B. _____
      C. _____
      D. _____
      E. _____

NAME: _____ CLASS: _____ DATE: _____

FORMS FOR EXERCISES

7-1.

	Regular Hours	Overtime Hours	Total Pay
Jean Knott	_____	_____	_____
Abe Janzen	_____	_____	_____
Mike Toth	_____	_____	_____

7-2.

	Abe Smith	May Cheung
Gross Pay	_____	_____
Deductions:		
_____	_____	_____
_____	_____	_____
_____	_____	_____
		_____
Total Deductions	_____	_____
Net Pay	_____	_____

7-3.

	Account Category	Dr/Cr	Appears on which Financial Report?
CPP Payable	_____	_____	_____
Income Tax Payable	_____	_____	_____
Medical Insurance Payable	_____	_____	_____
Wages and Salaries Payable	_____	_____	_____
Office Salaries Expense	_____	_____	_____
Marketing Wages Expense	_____	_____	_____

7-4.

_____

_____

_____

_____

_____

_____

7-5.

GENERAL JOURNAL

Page 20

Date	Account Title and Description	Post Ref.	Dr.	Cr.

END OF CHAPTER PROBLEMS

PROBLEM 7A-1 or 7B-1.

	EMPLOYEE	HOURLY RATE	REG. HOURS	O/T HOURS	GROSS EARNINGS
a.	Stephen Post	_____	_____	_____	_____
b.	Jean Nicola	_____	_____	_____	_____
c.	Maria Cardinal	_____	_____	_____	_____
d.	Tony Lee	_____	_____	_____	_____

Calculation space:

a.

b.

c.

d.

PROBLEM 7A-2 or 7B-2.

MONTANA COMPANY -- PAYROLL REGISTER

Employee	Net Claim Code	Weekly Salary							
Jenny Quan									
Frank Sloan									
Alberta Nobel									
Jeremy Gold									
Nancy James									

PROBLEM 7A-2 or 7B-2, Cont.

MONTANA COMPANY - PAYROLL REGISTER

Deductions				Net Pay	Chq. No.	Expense Accounts	
I T*	C P P	E I	Union Dues			Office	Sales

Income Tax:	Federal Income Tax +	Provincial Income Tax =	*Total Income Tax
Jenny Quan	_____	_____	_____
Frank Sloan	_____	_____	_____
Alberta Nobel	_____	_____	_____
Jeremy Gold	_____	_____	_____
Nancy James	_____	_____	_____
Total Income Tax			_____

PROBLEM 7A-3 or 7B-3.

PINTO CO. - PAYROLL REGISTER

Employee	Net Claim Code	Daily Time						Total Hrs.		Rate of Pay	Earnings		Gross Earnings
		M	T	W	Th	F	S	Reg.	O/T		Regular	Overtime	
Mary Cardinal													
Bill Smith													
Joe Kingle													
Anita Tsui													

PINTO CO.
GENERAL JOURNAL

Page 13

Date	Account Title and Description	Post Ref.	Dr.	Cr.

PROBLEM 7A-3 or 7B-3, Cont.

PINTO CO. - PAYROLL REGISTER

Deductions				Net Pay	Chq. No.	Expense Accounts	
I T*	C P P	E I	Health			Office	Sales

Income Tax: Federal Income Tax +   Provincial Income Tax =   *Total Income Tax

Mary Cardinal   _____   _____   _____
Bill Smith   _____   _____   _____
Joe Kingle   _____   _____   _____
Anita Tsui   _____   _____   _____

Total Income Tax   _____

PROBLEM 7A-4 or 7B-4.

BYSCANE CO. -- PAYROLL REGISTER

Employee	Net Claim Code	Weekly Salary	Cumulative C P P	I T*
Jim Ryan				
Emma LaPierre				
Jean Arnold				
Bob Sylvan				

BYSCANE CO.
GENERAL JOURNAL
Page 9

Date	Account Title and Description	Post. Ref.	Dr.	Cr.

Income Tax: Federal Income Tax +   Provincial Income Tax =   *Total Income Tax

Income Tax:	Federal Income Tax	Provincial Income Tax	*Total Income Tax
Jim Ryan	_____	_____	_____
Emma LaPierre	_____	_____	_____
Jean Arnold	_____	_____	_____
Bob Sylvan	_____	_____	_____
Total Income Tax			_____

PROBLEM 7A-4 or 7B-4, Cont.

BYSCANE CO. -- PAYROLL REGISTER

Deductions				Net Pay	Chq. No.	Expense Accounts	
C P P	E I	Union Dues	Health			Factory	Office

BYSCANE CO.
CASH DISBURSEMENTS JOURNAL   Page 20

Date	Chq. No.	Account Payment to	Post. Ref.	Sundry Dr.	Accounts Payable Dr.	Salaries Payable Dr.	Purchases Discounts Cr.	Cash Cr.
		Jim Ryan						
		Emma LaPierre						
		Jean Arnold						
		Bob Sylvan						

Alternative Solution

BYSCANE CO.
GENERAL JOURNAL   Page 10

Date	Account Title and Description	Post. Ref.	Dr.	Cr.

NAME: _____ CLASS: _____ DATE: _____

PROBLEM 7A-4 or 7B-4, Cont.

NAME: __INCOME TAX PAYABLE_____ ACCOUNT NO. ___210___

Date	Explanation	Post Ref.	Debit	Credit	D R C R	Balance

NAME: __CPP PAYABLE_____ ACCOUNT NO. ___212___

Date	Explanation	Post Ref.	Debit	Credit	D R C R	Balance

NAME: __EI PAYABLE_____ ACCOUNT NO. ___214___

Date	Explanation	Post Ref.	Debit	Credit	D R C R	Balance

NAME: __UNION DUES PAYABLE_____ ACCOUNT NO. ___216___

Date	Explanation	Post Ref.	Debit	Credit	D R C R	Balance

NAME: __HEALTH INSURANCE PAYABLE_____ ACCOUNT NO. ___218___

Date	Explanation	Post Ref.	Debit	Credit	D R C R	Balance

NAME: __SALARIES PAYABLE_____ ACCOUNT NO. ___220___

Date	Explanation	Post Ref.	Debit	Credit	D R C R	Balance

NAME: __FACTORY SALARIES EXPENSE_____ ACCOUNT NO. ___610___

Date	Explanation	Post Ref.	Debit	Credit	D R C R	Balance

NAME: __OFFICE SALARIES EXPENSE_____ ACCOUNT NO. ___612___

Date	Explanation	Post Ref.	Debit	Credit	D R C R	Balance

PROBLEM 7C-1.

EMPLOYEE	HOURLY RATE	REG. HOURS	O/T HOURS	GROSS EARNINGS
A .	_____	_____	_____	_____
B .	_____	_____	_____	_____
C .	_____	_____	_____	_____
D .	_____	_____	_____	_____
E .	_____	_____	_____	_____

Calculation space:

A.

B.

C.

D.

E.

PROBLEM 7C-2.

Employee	Net Claim Code	Weekly Salary	Deductions... IT*

Income Tax:

Employee Name	Federal Income Tax +	Provincial Income Tax =	*Total Income Tax

Total Income Tax

PROBLEM 7C-3.

Employee	Net Claim Code	Weekly Salary	Deductions... IT**

Income Tax:

Employee Name	Federal Income Tax +	Provincial Income Tax =	**Total Income Tax

Total Income Tax

PROBLEM 7C-2, Cont.

	Deductions, Cont.				Net Pay	Chq. No.
CPP	EI	Medical Plan	Union Dues			

PROBLEM 7C-3, Cont.

	Deductions, Cont.				Net Pay	Chq. No.
CPP	EI	Medical Plan	Union Dues			

PROBLEM 7C-4.

Date		Account Title and Description	Post Ref.	Dr.					Cr.				

PROBLEM 7C-5.

Date		Account Title and Description	Post Ref.	Dr.	Cr.

PROBLEM 7C-6.

Employee	Net Claim Code	Rate	Hours			Weekly Earnings
			Regular	Overtime	Total	

Working Space for Calculations regarding Earnings:

PROBLEM 7C-6, Cont.

_____

			Deductions			Net Pay	Chq. No.	Expense Accounts		
I T*	C P P	E I	Union Dues	Medical				Sales	Admin.	Manager

Income Tax:

Employee Name	Federal Income Tax +	Provincial Income Tax =	*Total Income Tax
_____	_____	_____	_____
_____	_____	_____	_____
_____	_____	_____	_____
_____	_____	_____	_____
	_____	_____	_____

Total Income Tax

Date	Account Title and Description	Post. Ref.	Dr.	Cr.

PROBLEM 7C-7.

Employee	Net Claim Code	Gross Earnings					Cumulative CPP					IT*				

Working Space for Calculations Regarding Earnings

Income Tax:

Employee Name	Federal Income Tax +	Provincial Income Tax =	*Total Income Tax
_____	_____	_____	_____
_____	_____	_____	_____
_____	_____	_____	_____
_____	_____	_____	_____
_____	_____	_____	_____

Total Income Tax _____   _____

PROBLEM 7C-7, Cont.

Deductions																			Net Pay					Chq. No.
CPP				EI				Life Ins.				Disability				Medical				Charitable						

PROBLEM 7C-7, Cont.

_____

_____

Page 21

Date		Account Title and Description	Post Ref.		Dr.			Cr.		

PROBLEM 7C-7, Cont.

_____

_____

Page 8

Date		Chq. No.	Account Payment to	Post Ref.	Sundry Account Dr.			Accounts Payable Dr.			Wages & Salaries Payable Dr.			Cash Cr.		

REAL WORLD APPLICATION #7R-1.

_____
_____
_____
_____
_____
_____
_____
_____
_____
_____
_____
_____
_____
_____
_____
_____
_____

REAL WORLD APPLICATION #7R-2.

_____
_____
_____
_____
_____
_____
_____
_____
_____
_____
_____
_____
_____
_____
_____
_____

YOU MAKE THE CALL: CRITICAL THINKING/ETHICAL CASE, #7R-3.

_____
_____
_____
_____
_____

CONTINUING PROBLEM

1. **ELDORADO COMPUTER CENTRE - GENERAL JOURNAL** *Page 4*

Date		Account Title and Description	Post Ref.	Dr.	Cr.

CONTINUING PROBLEM, Cont.

1.　　　　　**ELDORADO COMPUTER CENTRE - GENERAL JOURNAL**　　　*Page 5*

Date	Account Title and Description	Post Ref.	Dr.	Cr.

NAME: _____ CLASS: _____ DATE: _____

CONTINUING PROBLEM, Cont.
GENERAL LEDGER OF ELDORADO COMPUTER CENTRE

NAME: CASH   ACCOUNT NO. _1000_

Date 2007		Explanation	Post Ref.	Debit	Credit	D R C R	Balance
Nov.	1	Balance Forward	✔			Dr	4 2 9 3 0 0

NAME: PETTY CASH   ACCOUNT NO. _1010_

Date 2007		Explanation	Post Ref.	Debit	Credit	D R C R	Balance
Nov.	1	Balance Forward	✔			Dr	1 0 0 0 0

NAME: ACCOUNTS RECEIVABLE   ACCOUNT NO. _1020_

Date 2007		Explanation	Post Ref.	Debit	Credit	D R C R	Balance
Nov.	1	Balance Forward	✔			Dr	4 2 0 0 0 0

NAME: PREPAID RENT   ACCOUNT NO. _1025_

Date 2007		Explanation	Post Ref.	Debit	Credit	D R C R	Balance
Nov.	1	Balance Forward	✔			Dr	1 6 0 0 0 0

CONTINUING PROBLEM, Cont.

GENERAL LEDGER OF ELDORADO COMPUTER CENTRE, Cont'd

NAME: SUPPLIES   ACCOUNT NO. ____1030____

Date 2007		Explanation	Post Ref.	Debit	Credit	D R C R	Balance
Nov.	1	Balance Forward	✔			Dr	1 3 2 0 0

NAME: COMPUTER SHOP EQUIPMENT   ACCOUNT NO. ____1080____

Date 2007		Explanation	Post Ref.	Debit	Credit	D R C R	Balance
Nov.	1	Balance Forward	✔			Dr	2 4 0 0 0 0

NAME: ACCUMULATED AMORTIZATION, COMPUTER SHOP EQUIPMENT   ACCOUNT NO. ____1081____

Date 2007		Explanation	Post Ref.	Debit	Credit	D R C R	Balance
Nov.	1	Balance Forward	✔			Cr	9 9 0 0

NAME: OFFICE EQUIPMENT   ACCOUNT NO. ____1090____

Date 2007		Explanation	Post Ref.	Debit	Credit	D R C R	Balance
Nov.	1	Balance Forwatd	✔			Dr	6 0 0 0 0

NAME: ACCUMULATED AMORTIZATION, OFFICE EQUIPMENT   ACCOUNT NO. ____1091____

Date 2007		Explanation	Post Ref.	Debit	Credit	D R C R	Balance
Nov.	1	Balance Forward	✔			Cr	2 0 0 0

NAME: ACCOUNTS PAYABLE   ACCOUNT NO. ____2000____

Date 2007		Explanation	Post Ref.	Debit	Credit	D R C R	Balance
Nov.	1	Balance Forward	✔			Cr	5 0 0 0

CONTINUING PROBLEM, Cont.
GENERAL LEDGER OF ELDORADO COMPUTER CENTRE, Cont.

NAME: WAGES PAYABLE _____ ACCOUNT NO. ____2010____

Date 2007	Explanation	Post Ref.	Debit	Credit	D R C R	Balance

NAME: INCOME TAXES PAYABLE _____ ACCOUNT NO. ____2020____

Date 2007	Explanation	Post Ref.	Debit	Credit	D R C R	Balance

NAME: CPP PAYABLE _____ ACCOUNT NO. ____2030____

Date 2007	Explanation	Post Ref.	Debit	Credit	D R C R	Balance

NAME: EI PAYABLE _____ ACCOUNT NO. ____2040____

Date 2007	Explanation	Post Ref.	Debit	Credit	D R C R	Balance

NAME: T. FREEDMAN, CAPITAL _____ ACCOUNT NO. ____3000____

Date 2007	Explanation	Post Ref.	Debit	Credit	D R C R	Balance
	Balance Forward	✔			Cr	7 4 0 6 0 0

CONTINUING PROBLEM, Cont.

GENERAL LEDGER OF ELDORADO COMPUTER CENTRE, Cont'd

NAME: _T. FREEDMAN, WITHDRAWALS_____ ACCOUNT NO. ___3010___

Date 2007		Explanation	Post Ref.	Debit	Credit	D R C R	Balance
Nov.	1	Balance Forward	✔			Dr	2 0 1 5 00

NAME: __SERVICE REVENUE_____ ACCOUNT NO. ___4000___

Date 2007		Explanation	Post Ref.	Debit	Credit	D R C R	Balance
Nov.	1	Balance Forward	✔			Cr	7 8 0 0 00

NAME: _ADVERTISING EXPENSE_____ ACCOUNT NO. ___5010___

Date 2007	Explanation	Post Ref.	Debit	Credit	D R C R	Balance

NAME: _RENT EXPENSE_____ ACCOUNT NO. ___5020___

Date 2007	Explanation	Post Ref.	Debit	Credit	D R C R	Balance

NAME: _UTILITIES EXPENSE_____ ACCOUNT NO. ___5030___

Date 2007	Explanation	Post Ref.	Debit	Credit	D R C R	Balance

NAME: _PHONE EXPENSE_____ ___5040___

Date 2007	Explanation	Post Ref.	Debit	Credit	D R C R	Balance

NAME: _SUPPLIES EXPENSE_____ ACCOUNT NO. ___5050___

Date 2007	Explanation	Post Ref.	Debit	Credit	D R C R	Balance

CONTINUING PROBLEM, Cont.

GENERAL LEDGER OF ELDORADO COMPUTER CENTRE, Cont'd

NAME: INSURANCE EXPENSE   ACCOUNT NO. ____5060____

Date 2007		Explanation	Post Ref.	Debit	Credit	D R C R	Balance

NAME: POSTAGE EXPENSE   ACCOUNT NO. ____5070____

Date 2007		Explanation	Post Ref.	Debit	Credit	D R C R	Balance
Nov.	1	Balance Forward	✔			Dr	2 5 0 0

NAME: AMORTIZATION, COMPUTER SHOP EQUIPMENT   ACCOUNT NO. ____5080____

Date 2007		Explanation	Post Ref.	Debit	Credit	D R C R	Balance

NAME: AMORTIZATION, OFFICE EQUIPMENT   ACCOUNT NO. ____5090____

Date 2007		Explanation	Post Ref.	Debit	Credit	D R C R	Balance

NAME: MISCELLANEOUS EXPENSE   ____5100____

Date 2007		Explanation	Post Ref.	Debit	Credit	D R C R	Balance
Nov.	1	Balance Forward	✔			Dr	1 0 0 0

NAME: WAGES EXPENSE   ACCOUNT NO. ____5110____

Date 2007		Explanation	Post Ref.	Debit	Credit	D R C R	Balance

CONTINUING PROBLEM, Cont.

CONTINUING PROBLEM, Cont.

ELDORADO COMPUTER CENTRE - PAYROLL REGISTER

Date 2007	Employee	Chq #	Net Claim Code	Total Hrs. Reg.	Total Hrs. O/T	Rate of Pay	Earnings Regular	Earnings Overtime	Gross Earnings	I T*	Deductions CPP	Deductions E I	Net Pay
Nov 7	Lance Kumm												
7	Aurelle Hall												
Nov 14	Lance Kumm												
14	Aurelle Hall												

Income Tax: Employee Name
Nov. 7 Lance Kumm
Nov. 7 Aurelle Hall

Nov. 14 Lance Kumm
Nov. 14 Aurelle Hall

Federal Income Tax + Provincial Income Tax = *Total Income Tax

_____ _____ _____
_____ _____ _____

_____ _____ _____
_____ _____ _____

Date 2007	Employee	Chq #	Net Claim Code	Total Hrs. Reg.	Total Hrs. O/T	Rate of Pay	Earnings Regular	Earnings Overtime	Gross Earnings	I T**	Deductions CPP	Deductions E I	Net Pay
Nov 21	Lance Kumm												
21	Aurelle Hall												
Nov 28	Lance Kumm												
28	Aurelle Hall												

Income Tax: Employee Name
Nov. 21 Lance Kumm
Nov. 21 Aurelle Hall

Nov. 28 Lance Kumm
Nov. 28 Aurelle Hall

Federal Income Tax + Provincial Income Tax = **Total Income Tax

_____ _____ _____
_____ _____ _____

_____ _____ _____
_____ _____ _____

CHAPTER 7
CHAPTER SUMMARY TEST

Part A

Fill in the blank(s) to complete the statement.

1. The _____ _____ _____ _____ states the maximum hours a worker will work at a regular rate of pay.

2. Form _____ aids the employer in knowing how much to deduct for federal income tax.

3. The rate for CPP will _____ from year to year.

4. _____ _____ _____ has tables available for deductions for CPP and EI.

5. _____ _____ _____ protects employees against losses due to injury or death incurred while on the job.

6. Data from the _____ _____ will provide the needed information to record the payroll entry in the general journal.

7. The _____ _____ _____ _____ in the payroll register identifies how the total gross earnings are to be charged to specific accounts.

8. The credit to Wages and Salaries Payable in recording the payroll entry in the general journal represents _____ _____ .

9. Income Tax Payable is a _____ found on the balance sheet.

10. Each quarter has _____ weeks.

Part B

Answer true or false to the following .

1. The individual earnings record is updated from the general journal.
2. The account distribution columns of the payroll register provide data to say which accounts will be debited to record the total payroll when a journal entry is prepared.
3. CPP Payable is an asset for the employer.
4. Gross pay plus deductions equals net pay.
5. Form TD1 aids in calculating CPP.
6. The employer will match the employee's contribution for CPP.
7. Each quarter has 13 weeks.
8. The normal balance of Income Tax Payable is a credit.
9. The Employment Insurance Premiums Table makes it easy to calculate the amount of deductions for EI.
10. There is a maximum for CPP in a given fiscal year.

Part C

Complete the chart below (use table in text as needed). Use the following information: Before this payroll John Roll had paid CPP of $388.60. This week John earned $600. John is married, and has a net claim code of 4.

Gross Pay	Deductions			Net Pay
	Tax	CPP	EI	

SOLUTIONS TO CHAPTER SUMMARY TEST

Part A

1. Provincial Minimum Wage laws
2. TD1
3. increase
4. Canada Revenue Agency
5. Workers' Compensation Insurance
6. payroll register
7. distribution of expense accounts
8. net pay
9. liability
10. 13

Part B

1. false
2. true
3. false
4. false
5. false
6. true
7. true
8. true
9. true
10. false

Part C

Gross Pay	Deductions			Net Pay
	Tax	CPP	EI	
600.00	76.70 (51.40 + 25.30)	26.32	11.87	485.11

8

The Employer's Tax Responsibilities: Principles and Procedures

SELF-REVIEW QUIZ 8-1

Page 5

Date		Account Title and Description	Post Ref.	Dr.	Cr.

SELF-REVIEW QUIZ 8-2 (1.)

Date		Account Title and Description	Post Ref.	Dr.	Cr.

Date		Account Title and Description	Post Ref.	Dr.	Cr.

SELF-REVIEW QUIZ 8-2 *(2.)*

Income Tax Payable	CPP Payable	EI Payable

(3.) _____ _____

_____ _____

_____ _____

_____ _____

_____ _____

SELF-REVIEW QUIZ 8-3

1. _____ *2.* _____ *3.* _____ *4.* _____

Hold the Lettuce, Withhold the Taxes
SUBWAY Case
Discussion Questions

1. *Federal and provincial income taxes are the amount of income tax that all employees must pay to the government. The amount is based on the level of the employee's earnings. The provincial income tax rate is decided by individual provinces. The federal rate is the same for all taxpayers. Because Stan must pay his employees, he simply collects these taxes from the employees' pay and sends that exact amount to the government by the 15th of the following month. The employer does not pay an employer's share.*

2. *Stan is a small employer. Canada Revenue Agency allows most small business owners to remit every month, while very large employers remit twice or four times a month.*

3. *March's withholdings are due by April 15. If that is a Sunday, Stan should ensure that the amounts are remitted in time to reach the government on the next business day (Monday).*

FORMS FOR MINI EXERCISES

1.

FISHER COMPANY -- GENERAL JOURNAL

Date		Account Title and Description	Post. Ref.	Dr.					Cr.				

2.

Income Tax _____ _____

CPP _____ _____

EI _____ _____

_____

3. _____

_____

_____

_____

4. _____

_____

_____

_____

_____

FORMS FOR EXERCISES

8-1.

Date		Account Title and Description	Post Ref.	Dr.	Cr.

8-2.

Date		Account Title and Description	Post Ref.	Dr.	Cr.

8-3.

Income Tax _____ _____

CPP _____ _____

EI _____ _____

8-4. and 8-5.

Date		Account Title and Description	Post Ref.	Dr.	Cr.

8-6. _____

_____

_____

_____

END OF CHAPTER PROBLEMS

PROBLEM 8A-1. or 8B-1.

(a)

RICE COMPANY
GENERAL JOURNAL   *Page 12*

Date		Account Title and Description	Post Ref.	Dr.	Cr.

(b)

Cheque No. _____   _____

_____   _____

_____   _____

                                                    Total   _____

Cheque No. _____   _____

_____   _____

_____   _____

                                                    Total   _____

Cheque No. _____   _____

_____   _____

_____   _____

                                                    Total   _____

(c)

RICE COMPANY
GENERAL JOURNAL   *Page 13*

Date		Account Title and Description	Post Ref.	Dr.	Cr.

PROBLEM 8A-2. or 8B-2.

(a)

GIBRALTOR CO.
GENERAL JOURNAL

Page 5

Date		Account Title and Description	Post Ref.	Dr.	Cr.

(b)

Cheque Date	Cheque to be issued to:	Cheque Amount
_____	_____	_____
_____	_____	_____
_____	_____	_____
_____	_____	_____

Space below for calculations:

PROBLEM 8A-3. or 8B-3.

(a)

THE CANDY CO.
GENERAL JOURNAL   *Page 7*

Date		Account Title and Description	Post Ref.	Dr.	Cr.

(b)

Cheque Date	Cheque to be issued to	Cheque Amount

Space below for calculations:

PROBLEM 8A-4. or 8B-4.

(a)

RIPCORD PARACHUTE CLUB
GENERAL JOURNAL

Date		Account Title and Description	Post Ref.	Dr.	Cr.

PROBLEM 8A-4. or 8B-4, Cont.

(b)

Income Tax Payable	CPP Payable	EI Payable

LTD Payable	Pension Plan Liability	Medical Plan Payable

Employee Benefits Expense	Wage Expense

(c)

Cheque Date	Cheque to be issued to:	Cheque Amount

Space below for calculations:

PROBLEM 8C-1.

BAWLF HARDWARE CO.
GENERAL JOURNAL

a.

Page 8

Date	Account Title and Description	Post Ref.	Dr.	Cr.

b.

Cheque No. 543 _____ _____

_____

_____

Total _____

Cheque No. 551 _____ _____

_____

_____

Total _____

Cheque No. 567 _____ _____

_____

_____

Total _____

c.

BAWLF HARDWARE CO.
GENERAL JOURNAL

Page 9

Date	Account Title and Description	Post Ref.	Dr.	Cr.

PROBLEM 8C-2.

a.

COUNTERPOINT COUNSELLING CO.
GENERAL JOURNAL   Page 7

Date	Account Title and Description	Post Ref.	Dr.	Cr.

b.

Cheque Date	Cheque to be issued to	Cheque Amount

Space below for calculations:

PROBLEM 8C-3.

WAYLON COMPANY
GENERAL JOURNAL

Page 8

Date		Account Title and Description	Post Ref.	Dr.	Cr.

PROBLEM 8C-4.

WAYLON COMPANY
GENERAL JOURNAL

Page 9

Date		Account Title and Description	Post Ref.	Dr.	Cr.

PROBLEM 8C-5.

a.

MUNCHKIN BAKERY CO.
GENERAL JOURNAL   Page 14

Date	Account Title and Description	Post Ref.	Dr.	Cr.

b.

Cheque Date   Cheque to be issued to: Cheque Amount

_____   _____   _____

_____   _____   _____

_____   _____   _____

_____   _____   _____

Space below for calculations:

PROBLEM 8C-6.

a.

GRIERSON AUTO REPAIR COMPANY
GENERAL JOURNAL

Page 13

Date	Account Title and Description	Post Ref.	Dr.	Cr.

PROBLEM 8C-6, Cont.

b.

Cheque Date	*Cheque to be issued to:*	*Cheque Amount*
_____	_____	_____
_____	_____	_____
_____	_____	_____
_____	_____	_____
_____	_____	_____
_____	_____	_____

Space below for calculations:

REAL WORLD APPLICATIONS

8R-1.

_____
_____
_____
_____
_____
_____
_____
_____
_____
_____

YOU MAKE THE CALL: CRITICAL THINKING/ETHICAL CASE

8R-2.

_____
_____
_____
_____
_____
_____

CONTINUING PROBLEM

1.   **ELDORADO COMPUTER CENTRE - GENERAL JOURNAL**   *Page 6*

Date	Account Title and Description	Post Ref.	Dr.	Cr.

  8-17

CONTINUING PROBLEM

1.   **ELDORADO COMPUTER CENTRE - GENERAL JOURNAL** *Page 7*

Date	Account Title and Description	Post Ref.	Dr.	Cr.

CONTINUING PROBLEM

1.　　　　　　**ELDORADO COMPUTER CENTRE - GENERAL JOURNAL**　　　*Page 8*

Date		Account Title and Description	Post Ref.	Dr.	Cr.

CONTINUING PROBLEM

GENERAL LEDGER OF ELDORADO COMPUTER CENTRE

NAME: CASH   ACCOUNT NO.   1000

Date 2007		Explanation	Post Ref.	Debit	Credit	DR CR	Balance
Dec.	1	Balance Forward	✔			Dr	6 5 1 6 9 1

NAME: PETTY CASH   ACCOUNT NO.   1010

Date 2007		Explanation	Post Ref.	Debit	Credit	DR CR	Balance
Dec.	1	Balance Forward	✔			Dr	1 0 0 0 0

NAME: ACCOUNTS RECEIVABLE   ACCOUNT NO.   1020

Date 2007		Explanation	Post Ref.	Debit	Credit	DR CR	Balance
Dec.	1	Balance Forward	✔			Dr	1 0 2 0 0 0 0

CONTINUING PROBLEM

GENERAL LEDGER OF ELDORADO COMPUTER CENTRE, Cont.

NAME: _PREPAID RENT_   ACCOUNT NO. ___1025___

Date 2007		Explanation	Post Ref.	Debit	Credit	D R C R	Balance
Dec.	1	Balance Forward	✔			Dr	1 6 0 0 0 0

NAME: _SUPPLIES_   ACCOUNT NO. ___1030___

Date 2007		Explanation	Post Ref.	Debit	Credit	D R C R	Balance
Dec.	1	Balance Forward	✔			Dr	1 3 2 0 0

NAME: _MERCHANDISE INVENTORY_   ACCOUNT NO. ___1040___

Date 2007		Explanation	Post Ref.	Debit	Credit	D R C R	Balance

NAME: _COMPUTER SHOP EQUIPMENT_   ACCOUNT NO. ___1080___

Date 2007		Explanation	Post Ref.	Debit	Credit	D R C R	Balance
Dec.	1	Balance Forward	✔			Dr	3 8 0 0 0 0

NAME: _ACCUMULATED AMORTIZATION, COMPUTER SHOP EQUIPMENT_   ACCOUNT NO. ___1081___

Date 2007		Explanation	Post Ref.	Debit	Credit	D R C R	Balance
Dec.	1	Balance Forwatd	✔			Cr	9 9 0 0

NAME: _OFFICE EQUIPMENT_   ACCOUNT NO. ___1090___

Date 2007		Explanation	Post Ref.	Debit	Credit	D R C R	Balance
Dec.	1	Balance Forward	✔			Dr	1 0 5 0 0 0

NAME: _ACCUMULATED AMORTIZATION, OFFICE EQUIPMENT_   ACCOUNT NO. ___1091___

Date 2007		Explanation	Post Ref.	Debit	Credit	D R C R	Balance
Dec.	1	Balance Forward	✔			Cr	2 0 0 0

CONTINUING PROBLEM

GENERAL LEDGER OF ELDORADO COMPUTER CENTRE

NAME: _ACCOUNTS PAYABLE_   ACCOUNT NO. _____ 2000

Date 2007		Explanation	Post Ref.	Debit	Credit	D R C R	Balance
Dec.	1	Balance Forward	✔			Cr	2 0 5 0 00

NAME: _WAGES PAYABLE_   ACCOUNT NO. _____ 2010

Date 2007		Explanation	Post Ref.	Debit	Credit	D R C R	Balance
Dec.	1	Balance Forward	✔				-0-

NAME: _INCOME TAX PAYABLE_   ACCOUNT NO. _____ 2020

Date 2007		Explanation	Post Ref.	Debit	Credit	D R C R	Balance
Dec.	1	Balance Forward	✔			Cr	3 6 1 55

CONTINUING PROBLEM

GENERAL LEDGER OF ELDORADO COMPUTER CENTRE, Cont.

NAME: __CPP PAYABLE__   ACCOUNT NO. ___2030___

Date 2007		Explanation	Post Ref.	Debit	Credit	DR CR	Balance
Dec.	1	Balance Forward	✔			Cr	1 2 2 6 2

NAME: __EI PAYABLE__   ACCOUNT NO. ___2040___

Date 2007		Explanation	Post Ref.	Debit	Credit	DR CR	Balance
Dec.	1	Balance Forward	✔			Cr	5 9 7 4

NAME: __T. FREEDMAN, CAPITAL__   ACCOUNT NO. ___3000___

Date 2007		Explanation	Post Ref.	Debit	Credit	DR CR	Balance
Dec.	1	Balance Forward	✔			Cr	7 4 0 6 0 0

NAME: __T. FREEDMAN, WITHDRAWALS__   ACCOUNT NO. ___3010___

Date 2007		Explanation	Post Ref.	Debit	Credit	DR CR	Balance
Dec.	1	Balance Forward	✔			Dr	2 0 1 5 0 0

CONTINUING PROBLEM

GENERAL LEDGER OF ELDORADO COMPUTER CENTRE, Cont.

NAME: SERVICE REVENUE   4000

Date 2007		Explanation	Post Ref.	Debit	Credit	DR CR	Balance
Dec.	1	Balance Forward	✔			Cr	18 50 0 00

NAME: ADVERTISING EXPENSE   ACCOUNT NO.   5010

Date 2007		Explanation	Post Ref.	Debit	Credit	DR CR	Balance
Dec.	1	Balance Forward	✔				—0—

NAME: RENT EXPENSE   ACCOUNT NO.   5020

Date 2007		Explanation	Post Ref.	Debit	Credit	DR CR	Balance
Dec.	1	Balance Forward	✔				—0—

NAME: UTILITIES EXPENSE   ACCOUNT NO.   5030

Date 2007		Explanation	Post Ref.	Debit	Credit	DR CR	Balance
Dec.	1	Balance Forward	✔				—0—

NAME: PHONE EXPENSE   ACCOUNT NO.   5040

Date 2007		Explanation	Post Ref.	Debit	Credit	DR CR	Balance
Dec.	1	Balance Forward	✔			Dr	1 50 00

NAME: SUPPLIES EXPENSE   ACCOUNT NO.   5050

Date 2007		Explanation	Post Ref.	Debit	Credit	DR CR	Balance
Dec.	1	Balance Forward	✔				—0—

NAME: INSURANCE EXPENSE   ACCOUNT NO.   5060

Date 2007		Explanation	Post Ref.	Debit	Credit	DR CR	Balance
Dec.	1	Balance Forward	✔				—0—

CONTINUING PROBLEM

GENERAL LEDGER OF ELDORADO COMPUTER CENTRE, Cont.

NAME: __POSTAGE EXPENSE__ _____ __5070__

Date 2007		Explanation	Post Ref.	Debit	Credit	D R C R	Balance
Dec.	1	Balance Forward	✔			Dr	2 5 0 0

NAME: __AMORTIZATION, COMPUTER SHOP EQUIPMENT__ _____ ACCOUNT NO. __5080__

Date 2007		Explanation	Post Ref.	Debit	Credit	D R C R	Balance
Dec.	1	Balance Forward	✔				-0-

NAME: __AMORTIZATION, OFFICE EQUIPMENT__ _____ ACCOUNT NO. __5090__

Date 2007		Explanation	Post Ref.	Debit	Credit	D R C R	Balance
Dec.	1	Balance Forward	✔				-0-

NAME: __MISCELLANEOUS EXPENSE__ _____ ACCOUNT NO. __5100__

Date 2007		Explanation	Post Ref.	Debit	Credit	D R C R	Balance
Dec.	1	Balance Forward	✔			Dr	1 0 0 0

NAME: __WAGES EXPENSE__ _____ ACCOUNT NO. __5110__

Date 2007		Explanation	Post Ref.	Debit	Credit	D R C R	Balance
Dec.	1	Balance Forward	✔			Dr	3 0 2 0 0 0

NAME: __PAYROLL BENEFITS EXPENSE__ _____ ACCOUNT NO. __5120__

Date 2007		Explanation	Post Ref	Debit	Credit	D R C R	Balance

ELDORADO COMPUTER CENTRE - PAYROLL REGISTER

Date 2007	Employee	Net Claim Code	Total Hrs. Reg.	Total Hrs. O/T	Rate of Pay	Earnings Regular	Earnings Overtime	Gross Earnings	I T*	Deductions CPP	Deductions EI	Net Pay
Dec 5	Lance Kumm											
5	Aurelle Hall											
Dec 12	Lance Kumm											
12	Aurelle Hall											

Income Tax: Employee Name   Federal Income Tax +   Provincial Income Tax =   *Total Income Tax

Dec. 5 Lance Kumm   _____   _____   _____

Dec. 5 Aurelle Hall   _____   _____   _____

Dec. 12 Lance Kumm   _____   _____   _____

Dec. 12 Aurelle Hall   _____   _____   _____

Date 2007	Employee	Net Claim Code	Total Hrs. Reg.	Total Hrs. O/T	Rate of Pay	Earnings Regular	Earnings Overtime	Gross Earnings	I T**	Deductions CPP	Deductions EI	Net Pay
Dec 19	Lance Kumm											
19	Aurelle Hall											
Dec 24	Lance Kumm											
24	Aurelle Hall											

Income Tax: Employee Name   Federal Income Tax +   Provincial Income Tax =   **Total Income Tax

Dec. 19 Lance Kumm   _____   _____   _____

Dec. 19 Aurelle Hall   _____   _____   _____

Dec. 24 Lance Kumm   _____   _____   _____

Eldorado Computer Centre
Employee Earnings Record
For the Calendar Year 2007

Employee Address:
11224 23B Street
Edmonton, Alberta T6V 2V2

Name of Employee   Lance Kumm
Social Insurance Number 123 456 999
Date of Birth   09/29/74

Week	Net Claim Code	Rate of Pay	Hours Worked	Earnings			Deductions					Net Pay	Chq. No.
				Regular	Overtime	Gross Pay	IT	CPP	EI	Medical	Charitable		
1	1	10/h											
2													
3													
4													
5													
6													
7													
8													

Eldorado Computer Centre
Employee Earnings Record
For the Calendar Year 2007

Employee Address:
22 Fairway Lane
Edmonton, Alberta T6A 1A1

Name of Employee   Aurelle Hall
Social Insurance Number 893 421 777
Date of Birth   01/27/78

Week	Net Claim Code	Rate of Pay	Hours Worked	Earnings			Deductions					Net Pay	Chq. No.
				Regular	Overtime	Gross Pay	IT	CPP	EI	Medical	Charitable		
1	1	10/h											
2													
3													
4													
5													
6													
7													
8													

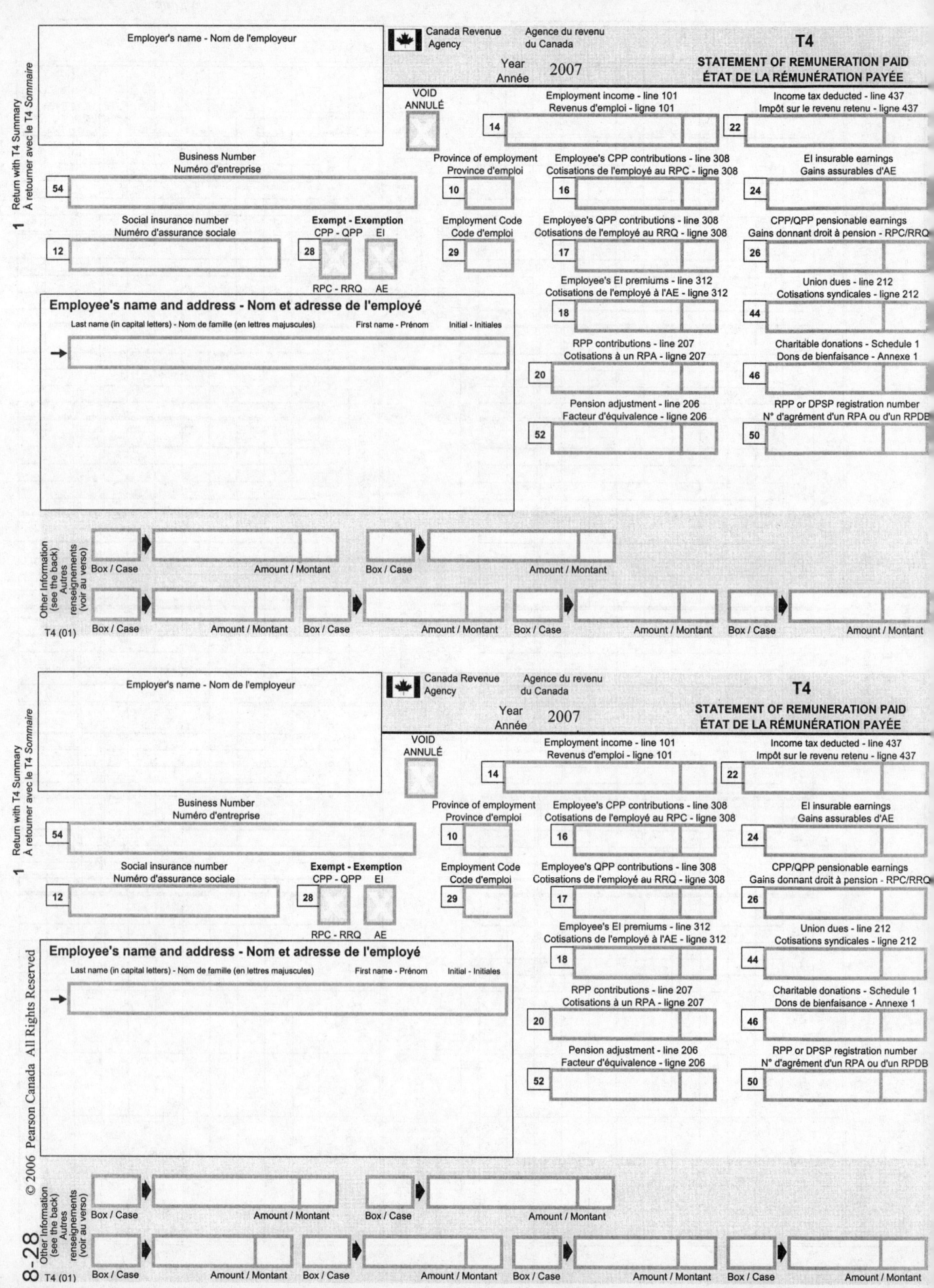

For the year ending December 31, **20**_____

Web Access Code - Code d'accès au Web

0505 **T4** Summary Sommaire

SUMMARY OF REMUNERATION PAID
SOMMAIRE DE LA RÉMUNÉRATION PAYÉE

You have to file your T4 on or before the last day of **February**.
See the information on the back of this form.

Vous devez produire votre déclaration T4 au plus tard le dernier jour de **février**.
Lisez les renseignements au verso de ce formulaire.

Business Number - Numéro d'entreprise

Name and address of employer - Nom et adresse de l'employeur

Total number of T4 slips filed - Nombre total de feuillets T4 produits
88

Employment income - Revenus d'emploi
14

Registered pension plan (RPP) contributions
Cotisations à un régime de pension agréé (RPA)
20

Pension adjustment - Facteur d'équivalence
52

Indicate how many T4 slips are for employees whole addresses are in the U.S.A.

Indiquez le nombre de feuillets T4 émis pour des employés dont l'adresse est aux États-Unis.

Employee's CPP contributions - Cotisations de l'employé au RPC
16

Employer's CPP contributions - Cotisations de l'employeur au RPC
27

Employee's EI premiums - Cotisations de l'employé à l'AE
18

Employer's EI premiums - Cotisations de l'employeur à l'AE
19

Income tax deducted - Impôt sur le revenu retenu
22

Total deductions reports (16 + 27 + 18 + 19 + 22)
Total des retenues déclarées (16 + 27 + 18 + 19 + 22)
80

Minus: remittances - Moins : versements
52

We do not charge or refund a difference of less than $2.

Nous n'exigeons ni ne remboursons une différence inférieure à 2 $.

Difference - Différence

Do not use this area - N'inscrivez rien ici

Last to current
Précédente à courante   Other Autre
90   1**X**   2**X**   3**X**

Pro Forma
91   1**X**   2**X**

Y - A   D - J
93

PD15-1
94   **X**

POF PSF   NLFP APPT
96   **X**   97   **X**

Memo - Note

Prepared by - Établi par

Date

Overpayment - Paiement en trop
84

Balance due - Solde dû
86

Amount enclosed - Somme jointe

Canadian-controlled private corporations or unincorporated employers
Sociétés privées sous contrôle canadien ou employeurs non constitués

SIN of the proprietor(s) or principal owner(s) - NAS du ou des propriétaires
74   75

Person to contact about this return - Personne avec qui communiquer au sujet de cette déclaration
76

Area code
Indicatif régional
78

Telephone number
Numéro de téléphone

Extension
Poste

Certification - Attestation

I certify that the information given in this T4 return (T4 Summary and related T4 slips) is, to the best of my knowledge, correct and complete.
J'atteste que les renseignements fournis dans cette déclaration T4 (le formulaire T4 Sommaire et les feuillets T4 connexes) sont, à ma connaissance, exacts et complets.

Date

Signature of authorized person - Signature d'une personne autorisée

Position or office - Titre ou poste

Canada

8-29

MINI PRACTICE SET

PETE'S MARKET
PAYROLL REGISTER

Date	Employee	Net Claim Code	Weekly Salary	IT*	CPP	EI	Net Pay

Date	Employee	Net Claim Code	Weekly Salary	IT**	CPP	EI	Net Pay

Date	Employee	Net Claim Code	Weekly Salary	IT***	CPP	EI	Net Pay

Date	Employee	Net Claim Code	Weekly Salary	IT****	CPP	EI	Net Pay

For the *, **, ***, **** Notes - please see the next page, 8-31.

MINI PRACTICE SET, Cont.

Information for Pete's Market Payroll Register - Income Tax

Date	Income Tax: Employee Name	Federal Income Tax +	Provincial Income Tax =	*Total Income Tax
_____	_____	_____	_____	_____
	_____	_____	_____	_____
	_____	_____	_____	_____
	Total Income Tax			_____

Date	Income Tax: Employee Name	Federal Income Tax +	Provincial Income Tax =	**Total Income Tax
_____	_____	_____	_____	_____
	_____	_____	_____	_____
	_____	_____	_____	_____
	Total Income Tax			_____

Date	Income Tax: Employee Name	Federal Income Tax +	Provincial Income Tax =	***Total Income Tax
_____	_____	_____	_____	_____
	_____	_____	_____	_____
	_____	_____	_____	_____
	Total Income Tax			_____

Date	Income Tax: Employee Name	Federal Income Tax +	Provincial Income Tax =	****Total Income Tax
_____	_____	_____	_____	_____
	_____	_____	_____	_____
	_____	_____	_____	_____
	Total Income Tax			_____

MINI PRACTICE SET, Cont.

PETE'S MARKET

GENERAL JOURNAL

Page 3

Date	Account Title and Description	Post. Ref.	Dr.	Cr.

MINI PRACTICE SET, Cont.

PETE'S MARKET

GENERAL JOURNAL   Page 4

Date	Account Title and Description	Post. Ref.	Dr.	Cr.

CHAPTER 8
CHAPTER SUMMARY TEST

Part A

Fill in the blank(s) to complete each statement:

1. Only the _____ completes the T4 Summary.
2. The payroll tax expense for the employer is made up of _____ and _____ .
3. The employee is responsible for paying _____ _____ .
4. Deductions are usually paid _____ .
5. CPP Payable is a _____ found on the _____ _____ .
6. Form PD7A summarizes the amounts owed for _____ , _____ and _____ .
7. Employer's expense is computed as _____ X CPP plus _____ X EI .
8. Form _____ is prepared monthly to summarize liabilities for Tax, CPP and EI .
9. A _____ _____ is required to be given to employees by Febuary 28 following the year employed.
10. Monthly remittances are computed as _____ X CPP plus _____ X EI plus _____ X tax .

Part B

Respond true or false to the following:

1. Prepaid Workers' Compensation Insurance is an asset.
2. CPP needs to be estimated at the beginning of the year.
3. Payroll Tax Expense is made up of CPP, EI and Tax.
4. Frequency of remittance relating to Form PD7A is based on current amount of tax liability.
5. Some computer software vendors (for payroll) promise relief from annual manual balancing procedures.
6. The individual earnings record provides the data to prepare T4s.
7. A calendar provides no help to the employer making the payment for tax liabilities.
8. Form PD7A is completed twice a year.
9. A year-end adjusting entry is often needed for workers' compensation.
10. The T4 summary form must be filed not later than 6 months after the employer's fiscal year end.

Part C

Complete the following table:

ACCOUNT	CATEGORY	FOUND ON WHICH REPORT
1. Payroll Tax Expense		
2. CPP Payable		
3. EI Payable		
4. Income Tax Payable		
5. Union Dues Payable		
6. Office Salaries Expense		

SOLUTIONS TO CHAPTER SUMMARY TEST

Part A

1. employer
2. CPP, EI
3. Income Tax
4. monthly
5. liability, Balance Sheet

6. CPP, EI, tax
7. 1, 1.4
8. PD7A
9. T4 Slip
10. 2, 2.4, 1

Part B

1. true
2. false
3. false
4. false
5. true

6. true
7. false
8. false
9. true
10. false

Part C

1. Expense; Income Statement
2. Liability; Balance Sheet
3. Liability; Balance Sheet
4. Liability; Balance Sheet
5. Liability; Balance Sheet
6. Expense; Income Statement

9

Special Journals: Sales and Cash Receipts

SELF-REVIEW QUIZ 9-1

1. _____ 2. _____ 3. _____ 4. _____ 5. _____

SELF-REVIEW QUIZ 9-2

1. _____ 2. _____ 3. _____ 4. _____ 5. _____ 6. _____ 7. _____ 8. _____

SELF-REVIEW QUIZ 9-3

MOSS COMPANY
SALES JOURNAL   *Page 1*

Date		Account Debited	Terms	Invoice No.	Post Ref.	Dr. Acc. Receivable Cr. Sales		

SELF REVIEW QUIZ 9-3, Cont.

MOSS COMPANY
GENERAL JOURNAL   Page 1

Date	Account Title and Description	Post Ref.	Dr.	Cr.

ACCOUNTS RECEIVABLE LEDGER

NAME   JANE COMPANY

ADDRESS   1218 BROADVIEW AVENUE, TORONTO, ON M5X 2A1

Date	Explanation	Post Ref.	Debit	Credit	Dr. Balance

NAME   RALPH COMPANY

ADDRESS   1300 MARINE DRIVE, WEST VANCOUVER, BC V6P 9B6

Date	Explanation	Post Ref.	Debit	Credit	Dr. Balance

SELF-REVIEW QUIZ 9-3, Cont.

PARTIAL GENERAL LEDGER

NAME: ACCOUNTS RECEIVABLE   ACCOUNT NO. ____112____

Date	Explanation	Post Ref.	Debit	Credit	D R C R	Balance

NAME: SALES   ACCOUNT NO. ____411____

Date	Explanation	Post Ref.	Debit	Credit	D R C R	Balance

NAME: SALES RETURNS AND ALLOWANCES   ACCOUNT NO. ____412____

Date	Explanation	Post Ref.	Debit	Credit	D R C R	Balance

SELF-REVIEW QUIZ 9-4

MOSS COMPANY - SALES JOURNAL   Page 1

Date	Accounts Debited	Inv. No.	Post Ref.	Dr. Accts. Rec.	Cr. PST Collected	Cr. GST Collected	Cr. Sales

MOSS COMPANY - GENERAL JOURNAL

Date	Account Title and Description	Post Ref.	Dr.	Cr.

SELF-REVIEW QUIZ 9-4, Cont.

PARTIAL GENERAL LEDGER

NAME: ACCOUNTS RECEIVABLE   ACCOUNT NO. _____ 112 _____

Date	Explanation	Post Ref.	Debit	Credit	D R C R	Balance

NAME: PST COLLECTED   ACCOUNT NO. _____ 210 _____

Date	Explanation	Post Ref.	Debit	Credit	D R C R	Balance

NAME: GST COLLECTED   ACCOUNT NO. _____ 212 _____

Date	Explanation	Post Ref.	Debit	Credit	D R C R	Balance

NAME: SALES   ACCOUNT NO. _____ 411 _____

Date	Explanation	Post Ref.	Debit	Credit	D R C R	Balance

NAME: SALES RETURNS AND ALLOWANCES   ACCOUNT NO. _____ 412 _____

Date	Explanation	Post Ref.	Debit	Credit	D R C R	Balance

PARTIAL ACCOUNTS RECEIVABLE LEDGER

NAME: JANE COMPANY

ADDRESS: 1218 BROADWAY AVENUE, TORONTO, ON M5X 2A1

Date	Explanation	Post Ref.	Debit	Credit	Dr. Balance

NAME: RALPH COMPANY

ADDRESS: 1300 MARINE DRIVE, WEST VANCOUVER, BC V6P 9B6

Date	Explanation	Post Ref.	Debit	Credit	Dr. Balance

SELF-REVIEW QUIZ 9-5

MOORE COMPANY
CASH RECEIPTS JOURNAL

Page 1

Date	Cash Dr.	Accounts Receivable Cr.	Sales Cr.	GST Collected Cr.	Sales Discounts Dr.	Description of Receipt	Post Ref.	Sundry Cr.

SELF-REVIEW QUIZ 9-5, Cont.

PARTIAL GENERAL LEDGER

NAME: CASH   ACCOUNT NO. ____110____

Date 2007		Explanation	Post Ref.	Debit	Credit	DR CR	Balance
May	1	Bal. Fwd.	✔			Dr	6 0 0 00

NAME: ACCOUNTS RECEIVABLE   ACCOUNT NO. ____120____

Date 2007		Explanation	Post Ref.	Debit	Credit	DR CR	Balance
May	1	Bal. Fwd.	✔			Dr	7 4 9 00

NAME: STORE EQUIPMENT   ACCOUNT NO. ____130____

Date 2007		Explanation	Post Ref.	Debit	Credit	DR CR	Balance
May	1	Bal. Fwd.	✔			Dr	6 0 0 0 00

NAME: GST COLLECTED   ACCOUNT NO. ____212____

Date 2007		Explanation	Post Ref.	Debit	Credit	DR CR	Balance
May	1	Bal. Fwd.	✔			Cr	4 9 00

NAME: SALES   ACCOUNT NO. ____410____

Date 2007		Explanation	Post Ref.	Debit	Credit	DR CR	Balance
May	1	Bal. Fwd.	✔			Cr	7 0 0 00

SELF-REVIEW QUIZ 9-5, Cont.

NAME: SALES DISCOUNTS   ACCOUNT NO.   420

Date 2007		Explanation	Post Ref.	Debit	Credit	D R C R	Balance

ACCOUNTS RECEIVABLE LEDGER

NAME   IRENE WELCH

ADDRESS   10 RONG ROAD, TIMMINS, ON P4N 4M3

Date 2007		Explanation	Post Ref.	Debit	Credit	Dr. Balance
May	1	Balance	✔			5 3 5 0 0

NAME   CHANTEL SIMARD

ADDRESS   9017 ROBITAILLE ROAD, MONTREAL, PQ HIK 4R3

Date 2007		Explanation	Post Ref.	Debit	Credit	Dr. Balance
May	1	Balance	✔			2 1 4 0 0

FORMS FOR COMPREHENSIVE DEMONSTRATION PROBLEM

WALTER LANTZ CO.
GENERAL JOURNAL
Page 1

Date	Account Title and Description	Post Ref.	Dr.	Cr.

WALTER LANTZ CO.
SALES JOURNAL
Page 1

Date	Account Debited	Terms	Invoice No.	Post Ref.	Dr. Acc. Receivable Cr. Sales

WALTER LANTZ CO.
CASH RECEIPTS JOURNAL
Page 1

Date	Cash Dr.	Sales Disc. Dr.	Acc. Rec. Cr.	Sales Cr.	Sundry		
					Account Name	Post Ref.	Amount Cr.

FORMS FOR COMPREHENSIVE DEMONSTRATION PROBLEM, Cont.

NAME: __CASH__ ACCOUNT NO. ___111___

Date	Explanation	Post Ref.	Debit	Credit	DR CR	Balance

NAME: __ACCOUNTS RECEIVABLE__ ACCOUNT NO. ___112___

Date	Explanation	Post Ref.	Debit	Credit	DR CR	Balance

NAME: __WALTER LANTZ, CAPITAL__ ACCOUNT NO. ___311___

Date	Explanation	Post Ref.	Debit	Credit	DR CR	Balance

NAME: __SALES__ ACCOUNT NO. ___411___

Date	Explanation	Post Ref.	Debit	Credit	DR CR	Balance

NAME: __SALES RETURNS AND ALLOWANCES__ ACCOUNT NO. ___412___

Date	Explanation	Post Ref.	Debit	Credit	DR CR	Balance

NAME: __SALES DISCOUNTS__ ACCOUNT NO. ___413___

Date	Explanation	Post Ref.	Debit	Credit	DR CR	Balance

FORMS FOR COMPREHENSIVE DEMONSTRATION PROBLEM, Cont.

ACCOUNTS RECEIVABLE LEDGER

NAME   BUZZARD CO.

ADDRESS   1000 SOUTH SHORE HIGHWAY, VANCOUVER, BC V6V 2T2

Date	Explanation	Post Ref.	Debit	Credit	Dr. Balance

NAME   PANDA CO.

ADDRESS   PO BOX 400, YELLOWKNIFE, NWT X1A 1T1

Date	Explanation	Post Ref.	Debit	Credit	Dr. Balance

WALTER LANTZ CO.

SCHEDULE OF ACCOUNTS RECEIVABLE

JULY 31, 2007

NAME: _____   CLASS: _____   DATE: _____

CHAPTER 9
FORMS FOR MINI EXERCISES

1.

2.

3.

   a. _____

   b. _____

   c. _____

4.

FORMS FOR MINI EXERCISES, Concluded

5.   a. _____
      b. _____
      c. _____
      d. _____

6.

BLUE CO.					
SCHEDULE OF ACCOUNTS RECEIVABLE					
MAY 31, 2006					

FORMS FOR EXERCISES

9-1.

Kevin Stone Co.		Accounts Receivable	112

Bill Valley Co.		Sales	412

9-2.

SALES JOURNAL

Page 1

Date	Account Debited	Terms	Invoice No.	Post Ref.	Dr. Acc. Receivable Cr. Sales			

Bass Co.		Accounts Receivable	112	

Ronald Co.		Sales	411	Sales Returns & Allowances	412

GENERAL JOURNAL

Page 1

Date	Account Title and Description	Post Ref.	Dr.	Cr.

Exercises, Cont.

9-3.

CASH RECEIPTS JOURNAL

Page 1

Date	Cash Dr.	Sales Discounts Dr.	Accounts Receivable Cr.	Sales Cr.	Sundry Account Names	Post Ref.	Amount Cr.

9-4.

SALES JOURNAL

Page 1

Date	Account Debited	Terms	Invoice No.	Post Ref.	Dr. Accounts Receivable Cr. Sales

CASH RECEIPTS JOURNAL

Page 1

Date	Cash Dr.	Sales Discounts Dr.	Accounts Receivable Cr.	Sales Cr.	Sundry Account Names	Post Ref.	Amount Cr.

Exercises, Cont.

9-4. Cont.

GENERAL JOURNAL   *Page 1*

Date	Account Title and Description	Post Ref.	Dr.	Cr.

ACCOUNTS RECEIVABLE LEDGER

Boston Co.

Gary Co.

PARTIAL GENERAL LEDGER

Cash   111

Accounts Receivable   113

Edna Cares, Capital   311

Sales   411

Sales Returns & Allowances   412

Sales Discounts   413

EDNA CO.
SCHEDULE OF ACCOUNTS RECEIVABLE
JUNE 30, 2008

_____   _____

_____   _____

_____   _____

9-5.

_____

_____

_____

_____

_____

9-6.

_____

_____

_____

_____

END OF CHAPTER PROBLEMS

PROBLEM 9A-1 or 9B-1.

1.

MAX CO.
SALES JOURNAL

Page 1

Date	Invoice No.	Customer's Name	Post Ref.	Accounts Receivable Dr.	Pizza Sales Cr.	Grocery Sales Cr.

MAX CO.
GENERAL JOURNAL

Page 1

Date	Account Title and Description	Post Ref.	Dr.	Cr.

PROBLEM 9A-1 or 9B-1, Cont.

2.

MAX CO.
ACCOUNTS RECEIVABLE LEDGER

NAME   JOE KASE CO.

ADDRESS   101 VICTORIA ST., LEDUC, AB T9E 4E3

Date	Explanation	Post Ref.	Debit	Credit	Dr. Balance

NAME   LONG CO.

ADDRESS   8 JOSS AVE., EDMONTON, AB   T6A 2R4

Date	Explanation	Post Ref.	Debit	Credit	Dr. Balance

NAME   SUE MOORE CO.

ADDRESS   10 LOST RD., ST. ALBERT, AB   T8N 6E1

Date	Explanation	Post Ref.	Debit	Credit	Dr. Balance

PROBLEM 9A-1 or 9B-1, Concluded

2.

MAX CO.
PARTIAL GENERAL LEDGER

NAME: __ACCOUNTS RECEIVABLE_____ ACCOUNT NO. ___112__

Date		Explanation	Post Ref.	Debit	Credit	D R C R	Balance

NAME: __PIZZA SALES_____ ACCOUNT NO. ___410__

Date		Explanation	Post Ref.	Debit	Credit	D R C R	Balance

NAME: __GROCERY SALES_____ ACCOUNT NO. ___411__

Date		Explanation	Post Ref.	Debit	Credit	D R C R	Balance

NAME: __SALES RETURNS AND ALLOWANCES - GROCERY_____ ACCOUNT NO. ___412__

Date		Explanation	Post Ref.	Debit	Credit	D R C R	Balance

3.

MAX CO.

SCHEDULE OF ACCOUNTS RECEIVABLE

JUNE 30, 2007

PROBLEM 9A-2 or 9B-2.

1.

TED'S AUTO SUPPLY
SALES JOURNAL   *Page 4*

Date	Invoice No.	Customer's Name	Post Ref.	Accounts Receivable Dr.	GST Payable Cr.	Sales Cr.

1.

TED'S AUTO SUPPLY
GENERAL JOURNAL   *Page 2*

Date	Account Title and Description	Post Ref.	Dr.	Cr.

PROBLEM 9A-2 or 9B-2, Cont.

2.

TED'S AUTO SUPPLY
ACCOUNTS RECEIVABLE LEDGER

NAME   LANCE CORNER

ADDRESS   9 ROE ST., OSHAWA, ON L1G 8J3

Date 2008		Explanation	Post Ref.	Debit	Credit	Dr. Balance
Nov	1	Balance	✔			4 0 0 00

NAME   J. SETH

ADDRESS   22 REESE ST., OSHAWA, ON L1J 2X1

Date 2008		Explanation	Post Ref.	Debit	Credit	Dr. Balance
Nov	1	Balance	✔			2 0 0 00

NAME   R. VOLAN

ADDRESS   12 ASTER ROAD, OSHAWA, ON L1H 3B4

Date 2008		Explanation	Post Ref.	Debit	Credit	Dr. Balance
Nov	1	Balance	✔			1 0 0 0 00

PROBLEM 9A-2 or 9B-2, Cont.

2.

TED'S AUTO SUPPLY
PARTIAL GENERAL LEDGER

NAME: ACCOUNTS RECEIVABLE   ACCOUNT NO. _____110_____

Date 2008		Explanation	Post Ref.	Debit	Credit	D R C R	Balance
Nov	1	Bal. Fwd.	✔			Dr	1 6 0 0 0 0

NAME: GST PAYABLE   ACCOUNT NO. _____210_____

Date 2008		Explanation	Post Ref.	Debit	Credit	D R C R	Balance
Nov	1	Bal. Fwd.	✔			Cr	1 6 0 0 0 0

NAME: AUTO PARTS SALES   ACCOUNT NO. _____410_____

Date	Explanation	Post Ref.	Debit	Credit	D R C R	Balance

NAME: SALES RETURNS AND ALLOWANCES   ACCOUNT NO. _____420_____

Date	Explanation	Post Ref.	Debit	Credit	D R C R	Balance

3.

TED'S AUTO SUPPLY
SCHEDULE OF ACCOUNTS RECEIVABLE
NOVEMBER 30, 2008

PROBLEM 9A-3 or 9B-3.

1.

PEAKER'S SNEAKER SHOP
SALES JOURNAL Page 5

Date		Sales Ticket No.	Terms	Account Debited	Post Ref.	Dr. Accounts Receivable Cr. Sales			

1.

PEAKER'S SNEAKER SHOP
GENERAL JOURNAL Page 1

Date		Account Title and Description	Post Ref.	Dr.				Cr.			

PROBLEM 9A-3 or 9B-3, Cont.

1.

PEAKER'S SNEAKER SHOP
CASH RECEIPTS JOURNAL

Page 2

Date	Cash Dr.	Accounts Receivable Cr.	Sales Cr.	Sales Discounts Dr.	Description of Receipt	Post Ref.	Sundry Account Cr.

PROBLEM 9A-3 or 9B-3, Cont.

2.

PEAKER'S SNEAKER SHOP
ACCOUNTS RECEIVABLE LEDGER

NAME   B. DALE

ADDRESS   1822 THE NARROWS ROAD, DARTMOUTH, NS   B2X 7L5

Date 2006		Explanation	Post Ref.	Debit	Credit	Dr. Balance
May	1	Balance	✔			4 0 0 00

NAME   RON LESTER

ADDRESS   18 MASS AVE., KINGSTON, NS   B2A 2G3

Date 2006		Explanation	Post Ref.	Debit	Credit	Dr. Balance
May	1	Balance	✔			8 0 0 00

NAME   PAM PRY

ADDRESS   OLD MILL ROAD, GREENFIELD, QUEENS CO., NS   B0T 3E0

Date 2006		Explanation	Post Ref.	Debit	Credit	Dr. Balance
May	1	Balance	✔			6 0 0 00

NAME   JIM ZON

ADDRESS   2 CHESTNUT ST., HALIFAX, NS   B3K 3D5

Date 2006		Explanation	Post Ref.	Debit	Credit	Dr. Balance
May	1	Balance	✔			4 0 0 00

PROBLEM 9A-3 or 9B-3, Cont.

2.

PEAKER'S SNEAKER SHOP
PARTIAL GENERAL LEDGER

NAME: _CASH_   ACCOUNT NO. ____10____

Date 2006		Explanation	Post Ref.	Debit	Credit	D R C R	Balance
May	1	Bal. Fwd.	✔			Dr	1 5 5 0 0 00

NAME: _ACCOUNTS RECEIVABLE_   ACCOUNT NO. ____12____

Date 2006		Explanation	Post Ref.	Debit	Credit	D R C R	Balance
May	1	Bal. Fwd.	✔			Dr	2 2 0 0 00

NAME: _SNEAKER RACK EQUIPMENT_   ACCOUNT NO. ____14____

Date 2006		Explanation	Post Ref.	Debit	Credit	D R C R	Balance
May	1	Bal. Fwd.	✔			Dr	1 0 0 0 00

NAME: _MARK PEAKER, CAPITAL_   ACCOUNT NO. ____30____

Date 2006		Explanation	Post Ref.	Debit	Credit	D R C R	Balance
May	1	Bal. Fwd.	✔			Cr	4 0 0 0 0 00

NAME: _SALES_   ACCOUNT NO. ____40____

Date 2006		Explanation	Post Ref.	Debit	Credit	D R C R	Balance
May	1	Bal. Fwd.	✔			Cr	2 2 0 0 00

PROBLEM 9A-3 or 9B-3, Cont.

2.

PARTIAL GENERAL LEDGER, Cont.

NAME: _SALES DISCOUNTS_   ACCOUNT NO. ____42____

Date	Explanation	Post Ref.	Debit	Credit	D R C R	Balance

NAME: _SALES RETURNS AND ALLOWANCES_   ACCOUNT NO. ____44____

Date	Explanation	Post Ref.	Debit	Credit	D R C R	Balance

3.

PEAKER'S SNEAKER SHOP

SCHEDULE OF ACCOUNTS RECEIVABLE

MAY 31, 2006

PROBLEM 9A-4 or 9B-4.

1.

BILL'S COSMETIC MARKET
SALES JOURNAL

Page 1

Date	Customer	Sales Invoice	Post Ref.	Accounts Receivable Dr.	PST Payable Cr.	GST Payable Cr.	Lipstick Sales Cr.	Eyeshadow Sales Cr.

PROBLEM 9A-4 or 9B-4, Cont.

1.

BILL'S COSMETIC MARKET
CASH RECEIPTS JOURNAL

Page 1

Date	Cash Dr.	Accounts Receivable Cr.	PST Payable Cr.	GST Payable Cr.	Lipstick Sales Cr.	Eyeshadow Sales Cr.	Description of Receipt	Post Ref.	Sundry Cr.

PROBLEM 9A-4 or 9B-4, Cont.

1.

BILL'S COSMETIC MARKET
GENERAL JOURNAL

Page 1

Date	Account Title and Description	Post Ref.	Dr.	Cr.

2.

BILL'S COSMETIC MARKET
ACCOUNTS RECEIVABLE LEDGER

NAME   ALICE KOY CO.

ADDRESS   2 RYAN ROAD, OTTAWA, ON   K1B 2A5

Date	Explanation	Post Ref.	Debit	Credit	Dr. Balance

NAME   RUSTY NEAL CO.

ADDRESS   4 REEL ROAD, TORONTO, ON   M4G 2Y8

Date	Explanation	Post Ref.	Debit	Credit	Dr. Balance

PROBLEM 9A-4 or 9B-4, Cont.

2.

BILL'S COSMETIC MARKET
ACCOUNTS RECEIVABLE LEDGER, Cont.

NAME   MARIKA SANCHEZ CO.

ADDRESS   14 BONE DRIVE, LONDON, ON N6J 3J6

Date	Explanation	Post Ref.	Debit	Credit	Dr. Balance

NAME   JEFF TONG CO.

ADDRESS   2 MARION RD., SARNIA, ON N7S 8A3

Date	Explanation	Post Ref.	Debit	Credit	Dr. Balance

2.

BILL'S COSMETIC MARKET
PARTIAL GENERAL LEDGER

NAME: CASH   ACCOUNT NO.   10

Date	Explanation	Post Ref.	Debit	Credit	DR CR	Balance

NAME: ACCOUNTS RECEIVABLE   ACCOUNT NO.   12

Date	Explanation	Post Ref.	Debit	Credit	DR CR	Balance

PROBLEM 9A-4 or 9B-4, Cont.

2.
BILL'S COSMETIC MARKET
PARTIAL GENERAL LEDGER, Cont.

NAME: __PST PAYABLE__ ACCOUNT NO. __20__

Date	Explanation	Post Ref.	Debit	Credit	D R C R	Balance

NAME: __GST PAYABLE__ ACCOUNT NO. __22__

Date	Explanation	Post Ref.	Debit	Credit	D R C R	Balance

NAME: __BILL MURRAY, CAPITAL__ ACCOUNT NO. __30__

Date	Explanation	Post Ref.	Debit	Credit	D R C R	Balance

NAME: __LIPSTICK SALES__ ACCOUNT NO. __40__

Date	Explanation	Post Ref.	Debit	Credit	D R C R	Balance

NAME: __SALES RETURNS AND ALLOWANCES, LIPSTICK__ ACCOUNT NO. __42__

Date	Explanation	Post Ref.	Debit	Credit	D R C R	Balance

PROBLEM 9A-4 or 9B-4, Cont.

2.

BILL'S COSMETIC MARKET
PARTIAL GENERAL LEDGER, Cont.

NAME: _EYESHADOW SALES_____ ACCOUNT NO. ____44

Date	Explanation	Post Ref.	Debit	Credit	D R C R	Balance

3.

BILL'S COSMETIC MARKET
SCHEDULE OF ACCOUNTS RECEIVABLE
APRIL 30, 2007

PROBLEM 9A-5 or 9B-5.

1.

PARKER'S SCUBA SHOP
SALES JOURNAL

Page 11

Date	Invoice No.	Customer's Name	Post. Ref.	Accounts Receivable Dr.	HST Payable Cr.	Merchandise Sales Cr.

PROBLEM 9A-5 or 9B-5, Cont.

1.

PARKER'S SCUBA SHOP
CASH RECEIPTS JOURNAL

Page 12

Date	Cash Dr.	Accounts Receivable Cr.	HST Payable Cr.	Merchandise Sales Cr.	Sales Discounts Dr.	Description of Receipt	Post Ref.	Sundry Cr.

PROBLEM 9A-5 or 9B-5, Cont.

1.

PARKER'S SCUBA SHOP
GENERAL JOURNAL

Page 13

Date		Account Title and Description	Post Ref.	Dr.	Cr.

2.

PARKER'S SCUBA SHOP
ACCOUNTS RECEIVABLE LEDGER

NAME   ROLAND DONCASTER

ADDRESS   585 BURKE STREET, BATHURST, NB E2A 2J4

Date 2008		Explanation	Post Ref.	Debit	Credit	Dr. Balance
April	1	Balance	✔			9 0 7 1 5

NAME   J. FELLOWES

ADDRESS   112 CRAFT AVE., CHARLOTTETOWN, PE C1E 3D6

Date 2008		Explanation	Post Ref.	Debit	Credit	Dr. Balance
April	1	Balance	✔			1 4 4 4 5 0

PROBLEM 9A-5 or 9B-5, Cont.   **PARKER'S SCUBA SHOP**
ACCOUNTS RECEIVABLE LEDGER, Cont.

NAME   R. LANGLEY

ADDRESS   67 MAIN STREET, BATHURST, NB E2A 5F5

Date 2008		Explanation	Post Ref.	Debit	Credit	Dr. Balance
April	1	Balance	✔			0

NAME   PHYLLIS LEUNG

ADDRESS   245 CASEMENT CLOSE, EDMUNDSTON, NB E3V 2E4

Date 2008		Explanation	Post Ref.	Debit	Credit	Dr. Balance
April	1	Balance	✔			0

NAME   J. SIMPSON

ADDRESS   65 TALLISMAN CRESC., FREDERICTON, NB E3A 3M1

Date 2008		Explanation	Post Ref.	Debit	Credit	Dr. Balance
April	1	Balance	✔			6 0 6 69

2.   **PARKER'S SCUBA SHOP**
PARTIAL GENERAL LEDGER

NAME: __CASH__   ACCOUNT NO. ___110___

Date 2008		Explanation	Post Ref.	Debit	Credit	DR CR	Balance
April	1	Bal. Fwd.	✔			Dr	1 9 5 3 56

NAME: __ACCOUNTS RECEIVABLE__   ACCOUNT NO. ___120___

Date 2008		Explanation	Post Ref.	Debit	Credit	DR CR	Balance
April	1	Bal. Fwd.	✔			Dr	2 9 5 8 34

PROBLEM 9A-5 or 9B-5, Cont.

2.

PARKER'S SCUBA SHOP
PARTIAL GENERAL LEDGER, Cont.

NAME: __HST PAYABLE__   ACCOUNT NO. ___221___

Date 2008	Explanation	Post Ref.	Debit	Credit	D R C R	Balance

NAME: __MARY PARKER, CAPITAL__   ACCOUNT NO. ___300___

Date 2008	Explanation	Post Ref.	Debit	Credit	D R C R	Balance
April 1	Bal. Fwd.	✔			Cr	28 0 0 0 00

NAME: __MERCHANDISE SALES__   ACCOUNT NO. ___400___

Date 2008	Explanation	Post Ref.	Debit	Credit	D R C R	Balance
April 1	Bal. Fwd.	✔			Cr	74 5 2 3 48

NAME: __SALES RETURNS AND ALLOWANCES__   ACCOUNT NO. ___402___

Date 2008	Explanation	Post Ref.	Debit	Credit	D R C R	Balance
April 1	Bal. Fwd.	✔			Dr	7 5 2 50

NAME: __SALES DISCOUNTS__   ACCOUNT NO. ___404___

Date	Explanation	Post Ref.	Debit	Credit	D R C R	Balance

PROBLEM 9A-5 or 9B-5, Cont.

3.

PARKER'S SCUBA SHOP

SCHEDULE OF ACCOUNTS RECEIVABLE

APRIL 30, 2008

PROBLEM 9C-1.

1.

SALES JOURNAL
Page 3

Date		Invoice No.	Customer's Name	Post Ref.	Accounts Receivable Dr.					Sales Cr.					Sales Cr.				

1.

GENERAL JOURNAL
Page 2

Date		Account Title and Description	Post Ref.	Dr.					Cr.				

PROBLEM 9C-1, Cont.

2. _____

ACCOUNTS RECEIVABLE LEDGER

NAME   CHRIS COWAN CO.

ADDRESS   56 SPADIN AVE.,   EDMONTON, AB T5A 2R7

Date	Explanation	Post Ref.	Debit	Credit	Dr. Balance

NAME   CROSS & CO.

ADDRESS   18 VERLUX STREET, ST. ALBERT, AB T8N 5E3

Date	Explanation	Post Ref.	Debit	Credit	Dr. Balance

NAME   JOAN TIMKINS CO.

ADDRESS   1120 PATRICK ST., MEDICINE HAT, AB T1A 4S6

Date	Explanation	Post Ref.	Debit	Credit	Dr. Balance

PROBLEM 9C-1, Cont. _____

2.

PARTIAL GENERAL LEDGER

NAME: ACCOUNTS RECEIVABLE ACCOUNT NO. _____ 12

Date	Explanation	Post Ref.	Debit	Credit	D R C R	Balance

NAME: CARPET SALES ACCOUNT NO. _____ 40

Date	Explanation	Post Ref.	Debit	Credit	D R C R	Balance

NAME: UPHOLSTERY SALES ACCOUNT NO. _____ 41

Date	Explanation	Post Ref.	Debit	Credit	D R C R	Balance

NAME: SALES RETURNS AND ALLOWANCES ACCOUNT NO. _____ 42

Date	Explanation	Post Ref.	Debit	Credit	D R C R	Balance

3.

SCHEDULE OF ACCOUNTS RECEIVABLE

PROBLEM 9C-2.

1.

SALES JOURNAL

Page 5

Date	Invoice No.	Customer's Name	Post Ref.	Accounts Receivable Dr.	Sales Tax Payable Cr.	Equipment Sales Cr.

1.

GENERAL JOURNAL

Page 3

Date	Account Title and Description	Post Ref.	Dr.	Cr.

PROBLEM 9C-2, Cont.

2.

ACCOUNTS RECEIVABLE LEDGER

NAME   RAY FORTUNA

ADDRESS   82 FIR STREET, REGINA, SK   S4W 3A6

Date 2008		Explanation	Post Ref.	Debit	Credit	Dr. Balance
Sept	1	Balance	✔			2 1 8 0 0 0

NAME   CASSIE HO

ADDRESS   34 SUSSEX RD., SASKATOON, SK   S7H 8J2

Date 2008		Explanation	Post Ref.	Debit	Credit	Dr. Balance
Sept	1	Balance	✔			7 6 3 0 0

NAME   WILMA JORGE

ADDRESS   124 PARTRIDGE WAY, PRINCE ALBERT, SK   S6V 4H2

Date 2008		Explanation	Post Ref.	Debit	Credit	Dr. Balance
Sept	1	Balance	✔			1 3 0 8 0 0

PROBLEM 9C-2, Cont.

2.

PARTIAL GENERAL LEDGER

NAME: _ACCOUNTS RECEIVABLE_ ACCOUNT NO. ___111___

Date 2008		Explanation	Post Ref.	Debit	Credit	D R C R	Balance
Sept	1	Bal. Fwd.	✔			Dr	4 2 5 1 0 0

NAME: _SALES TAX PAYABLE_ ACCOUNT NO. ___212___

Date 2008		Explanation	Post Ref.	Debit	Credit	D R C R	Balance
Sept	1	Bal. Fwd.	✔			Cr	1 7 4 2 5 0

NAME: _EQUIPMENT SALES_ ACCOUNT NO. ___400___

Date	Explanation	Post Ref.	Debit	Credit	D R C R	Balance

NAME: _SALES RETURNS AND ALLOWANCES_ ACCOUNT NO. ___402___

Date	Explanation	Post Ref.	Debit	Credit	D R C R	Balance

3.

SCHEDULE OF ACCOUNTS RECEIVABLE

PROBLEM 9C-3.

1.

SALES JOURNAL   Page 5

Date		Sales Invoice No.	Terms	Account Debited	Post Ref.	Dr. Accounts Receivable Cr. Sales				

1.

GENERAL JOURNAL   Page 7

Date		Account Title and Description	Post Ref.	Dr.				Cr.			

PROBLEM 9C-3, Cont.

2.

CASH RECEIPTS JOURNAL

Page 2

Date	Cash Dr.	Accounts Receivable Cr.	Sales Cr.	Sales Discounts Dr.	Description of Receipt	Post Ref.	Sundry Account Cr.

PROBLEM 9C-3, Cont.

2.

ACCOUNTS RECEIVABLE LEDGER

NAME   CHAPMAN'S DELI

ADDRESS   23 FORTUNE AVE., ST. JOHN, NB   E2M 2J6

Date 2008		Explanation	Post Ref.	Debit	Credit	Dr. Balance
Sept	1	Balance	✔			7 6 4 0 0

NAME   DISCOUNT MEATS

ADDRESS   56 TOWNSHIP BLVD., FREDERICTON, NB   E3A 3S7

Date 2008		Explanation	Post Ref.	Debit	Credit	Dr. Balance
Sept	1	Balance	✔			1 5 6 8 0 0

NAME   PETRA'S MEAT MARKET

ADDRESS   45 MAIN STREET, FREDERICTON, NB   E3B 5H2

Date 2008		Explanation	Post Ref.	Debit	Credit	Dr. Balance
Sept	1	Balance	✔			1 2 3 5 0 0

NAME   VALEMONT VARIETY MEATS

ADDRESS   137 FOREST RD., CHIPMAN, NB   E0E 3H1

Date 2008		Explanation	Post Ref.	Debit	Credit	Dr. Balance
Sept	1	Balance	✔			3 8 7 6 0

PROBLEM 9C-3, Cont.

2.   _____

PARTIAL GENERAL LEDGER

NAME: CASH   ACCOUNT NO. ____110____

Date 2008		Explanation	Post Ref.	Debit	Credit	D R C R	Balance
Sept	1	Bal. Fwd.	✔			Dr	8 7 6 2 3 7

NAME: ACCOUNTS RECEIVABLE   ACCOUNT NO. ____125____

Date 2008		Explanation	Post Ref.	Debit	Credit	D R C R	Balance
Sept	1	Bal. Fwd.	✔			Dr	3 9 5 4 6 0

NAME: MEAT COOLING EQUIPMENT   ACCOUNT NO. ____140____

Date 2008		Explanation	Post Ref.	Debit	Credit	D R C R	Balance
Sept	1	Bal. Fwd.	✔			Dr	9 1 2 5 0 0

NAME: KAREN BLUM, CAPITAL   ACCOUNT NO. ____300____

Date 2008		Explanation	Post Ref.	Debit	Credit	D R C R	Balance
Sept	1	Bal. Fwd.	✔			Cr	5 0 0 0 0 0 0

NAME: SALES   ACCOUNT NO. ____400____

Date 2008		Explanation	Post Ref.	Debit	Credit	D R C R	Balance
Sept	1	Bal. Fwd.	✔			Cr	4 1 7 4 5 8 2

PROBLEM 9C-3, Cont.

2.

_____

PARTIAL GENERAL LEDGER, Cont.

NAME: SALES DISCOUNTS _____ ACCOUNT NO. ____402____

Date		Explanation	Post Ref.	Debit	Credit	D R C R	Balance

NAME: SALES RETURNS AND ALLOWANCES _____ ACCOUNT NO. ____404____

Date		Explanation	Post Ref.	Debit	Credit	D R C R	Balance

3.

_____

SCHEDULE OF ACCOUNTS RECEIVABLE

_____

PROBLEM 9C-4.

1.

SALES JOURNAL
Page 1

Date	Customer	Sales Invoice	Post Ref.	Accounts Receivable Dr.	PST Payable Cr.	GST Payable Cr.	Radio Sales Cr.	Cellular Sales Cr.

PROBLEM 9C-4, Cont.

CASH RECEIPTS JOURNAL

Page 1

Date	Cash Dr.	Accounts Receivable Cr.	PST Payable Cr.	GST Payable Cr.	Radio Sales Cr.	Cellular Sales Cr.	Description of Receipt	Post Ref.	Sundry Cr.

PROBLEM 9C-4, Cont. _____

1.   GENERAL JOURNAL   Page 1

Date		Account Title and Description	Post Ref.	Dr.	Cr.

1.   _____

                              ACCOUNTS RECEIVABLE LEDGER

NAME   KELLY'S REAL ESTATE CO.

ADDRESS   245 CHATTERFORTH RD., NEW WESTMINSTER, BC V3L 2T3

Date		Explanation	Post Ref.	Debit	Credit	Dr. Balance

NAME   MOUNTAIN EXPLORATIONS CO.

ADDRESS   66 ROYAL ROAD, NEW WESTMINSTER, BC V3M 8G4

Date		Explanation	Post Ref.	Debit	Credit	Dr. Balance

PROBLEM 9C-4, Cont.

ACCOUNTS RECEIVABLE LEDGER, Cont.

NAME   WALKINS SAFETY SUPPLY CO.

ADDRESS   11203 FRASER WAY, NEW WESTMINSTER, BC V3L 1A1

Date	Explanation	Post Ref.	Debit	Credit	Dr. Balance

NAME   WELL'S HOTSHOT SERVICE CO.

ADDRESS   23 PITTS AVE., NEW WESTMINSTER, BC V3L 9X2

Date	Explanation	Post Ref.	Debit	Credit	Dr. Balance

3.

PARTIAL GENERAL LEDGER

NAME: __CASH__   ACCOUNT NO. ____105____

Date	Explanation	Post Ref.	Debit	Credit	DR CR	Balance

NAME: __ACCOUNTS RECEIVABLE__   ACCOUNT NO. ____126____

Date	Explanation	Post Ref.	Debit	Credit	DR CR	Balance

PROBLEM 9C-4, Cont.

1.　　　　　　　　_____

PARTIAL GENERAL LEDGER, Cont.

NAME: __PST PAYABLE_____　　ACCOUNT NO. ____210____

Date	Explanation	Post Ref.	Debit	Credit	D R C R	Balance

NAME: __GST PAYABLE_____　　ACCOUNT NO. ____220____

Date	Explanation	Post Ref.	Debit	Credit	D R C R	Balance

NAME: __LOAN PAYABLE_____　　ACCOUNT NO. ____250____

Date	Explanation	Post Ref.	Debit	Credit	D R C R	Balance

NAME: __ROYCE LAMOUREUX, CAPITAL_____　　ACCOUNT NO. ____300____

Date	Explanation	Post Ref.	Debit	Credit	D R C R	Balance

NAME: __RADIO SALES_____　　ACCOUNT NO. ____400____

Date	Explanation	Post Ref.	Debit	Credit	D R C R	Balance

PROBLEM 9C-4, Cont.

1.   ***PARTIAL GENERAL LEDGER, Cont.***

NAME: CELLULAR SALES   ACCOUNT NO.   404

Date	Explanation	Post Ref.	Debit	Credit	D R C R	Balance

NAME: SALES RETURNS AND ALLOWANCES, CELLULAR   ACCOUNT NO.   406

Date	Explanation	Post Ref.	Debit	Credit	D R C R	Balance

2.

SCHEDULE OF ACCOUNTS RECEIVABLE

PROBLEM 9C-5.

1.

			SALES JOURNAL				Page 13

Date	Sales Invoice	Customer's Name	Post Ref.	Accounts Receivable Dr.	HST Payable Cr.	Merchandise Sales Cr.

PROBLEM 9C-5, Cont.

1.

CASH RECEIPTS JOURNAL

Page 17

Date	Cash Dr.	Accounts Receivable Cr.	HST Payable Cr.	Merchandise Sales Cr.	Sales Discounts Dr.	Description of Receipt	Post Ref.	Sundry Cr.

PROBLEM 9C-5, Cont.

1. _____

GENERAL JOURNAL

Page 19

Date	Account Title and Description	Post Ref.	Dr.	Cr.

2. _____

ACCOUNTS RECEIVABLE LEDGER

NAME   BURGESS FANCYS

ADDRESS   177 PORTMOUTH CRESC., ST. JOHN'S, NF   A1C 0S1

Date 2008		Explanation	Post Ref.	Debit	Credit	Dr. Balance
Jan	1	Balance	✔			—0—

NAME   GEORGINA'S COLLECTIONS

ADDRESS   188 FOREST HILL ROAD, ST. JOHN'S, NF   A1C 5H1

Date 2008		Explanation	Post Ref.	Debit	Credit	Dr. Balance
Jan	1	Balance	✔			—0—

PROBLEM 9C-5, Cont.

NAME   HARD-TO-FIND CO.

ADDRESS   47 CLIFF CLOSE, ST. JOHN'S, NF A1C 7E7

Date 2008		Explanation	Post Ref.	Debit	Credit	Dr. Balance
Jan	1	Balance	✔			2 1 4 5 8 4

NAME   PERFECT SALES CO.

ADDRESS   217 ATLANTIC CRESC., ST. JOHN'S, NF A1C 1T1

Date 2008		Explanation	Post Ref.	Debit	Credit	Dr. Balance
Jan	1	Balance	✔			7 6 3 2 0

NAME   STARCRAFT REPRODUCTIONS

ADDRESS   17 HILLHURST CRESC., ST. JOHN'S, NF A1C 0P9

Date 2008		Explanation	Post Ref.	Debit	Credit	Dr. Balance
Jan	1	Balance	✔			1 8 7 6 4 0

2.

PARTIAL GENERAL LEDGER

NAME: CASH   ACCOUNT NO.   111

Date 2008		Explanation	Post Ref.	Debit	Credit	DR CR	Balance
Jan	1	Bal. Fwd.	✔			Dr	2 6 7 5 3 2

NAME: ACCOUNTS RECEIVABLE   ACCOUNT NO.   125

Date 2008		Explanation	Post Ref.	Debit	Credit	DR CR	Balance
Jan	1	Bal. Fwd.	✔			Dr	4 7 8 5 4 4

PROBLEM 9C-5, Cont.

2.
PARTIAL GENERAL LEDGER, Cont.

NAME: _HST PAYABLE_   ACCOUNT NO. ____221____

Date 2008		Explanation	Post Ref.	Debit	Credit	D R C R	Balance
Jan.	1	Bal. Fwd.	✔			Cr	3 1 4 6 9 0

NAME: _MARTHA WORTH, CAPITAL_   ACCOUNT NO. ____300____

Date 2008		Explanation	Post Ref.	Debit	Credit	D R C R	Balance
Jan	1	Bal. Fwd.	✔			Cr	4 8 0 0 0 0 0

NAME: _MERCHANDISE SALES_   ACCOUNT NO. ____400____

Date 2008		Explanation	Post Ref.	Debit	Credit	D R C R	Balance
Jan	1	Bal. Fwd.	✔			Cr	8 2 1 4 5 6 2

NAME: _SALES RETURNS AND ALLOWANCES_   ACCOUNT NO. ____401____

Date 2008		Explanation	Post Ref.	Debit	Credit	D R C R	Balance
Jan	1	Bal. Fwd.	✔			Dr	1 1 4 3 5 6

NAME: _SALES DISCOUNTS_   ACCOUNT NO. ____402____

Date	Explanation	Post Ref.	Debit	Credit	D R C R	Balance

PROBLEM 9C-5, Cont.

3.

SCHEDULE OF ACCOUNTS RECEIVABLE

REAL WORLD APPLICATIONS #9R-1.

SALES JOURNAL   Page 5

Date	Account Debited	Terms	Invoice No.	Post Ref.	Dr. Acc. Receivable Cr. Sales

GENERAL JOURNAL   Page 2

Date	Account Title and Description	Post Ref.	Dr.	Cr.

REAL WORLD APPLICATION #9R-1, Cont.

CASH RECEIPTS JOURNAL

Page 1

Date	Cash Dr.	Accounts Receivable Cr.	Sales Tax Payable Cr.	Sales Cr.	Sales Discounts Dr.	Description of Receipt	Post. Ref.	Sundry Cr.

NAME: _____ CLASS: _____ DATE: _____

REAL WORLD APPLICATION #9R-1, Cont.

_____
_____
_____
_____
_____
_____
_____

REAL WORLD APPLICATION #9R-2.

_____
_____
_____
_____
_____
_____
_____

YOU MAKE THE CALL: CRITICAL THINKING/ETHICAL CASE #9R-3.

_____
_____
_____
_____
_____
_____
_____
_____
_____
_____
_____

CONTINUING PROBLEM

ELDORADO COMPUTER CENTRE
SALES JOURNAL

Page 1

		Account Debited	Terms	Invoice No.	Post. Ref.	Dr. Acc. Receivable Cr. Sales

ELDORADO COMPUTER CENTRE
CASH RECEIPTS JOURNAL

Page 1

Date	Cash Dr.	Sales Disc. Dr.	Acc. Rec. Cr.	Sales Cr.	Sundry		
					Account Name	Post. Ref.	Amount Cr.

ELDORADO COMPUTER CENTRE
GENERAL JOURNAL

Page 9

Date	Account Title and Description	Post. Ref.	Dr.	Cr.

CONTINUING PROBLEM, Cont.

ELDORADO COMPUTER CENTRE
PARTIAL GENERAL LEDGER

NAME: __CASH_____ ACCOUNT NO. ___1000___

Date 2008		Explanation	Post. Ref.	Debit	Credit	D R C R	Balance
Jan.	1	Balance Forward	✔			Dr	1 1 0 8 4 7

NAME: __ACCOUNTS RECEIVABLE_____ ACCOUNT NO. ___1020___

Date 2008		Explanation	Post. Ref.	Debit	Credit	D R C R	Balance
Jan.	1	Balance Forward	✔			Dr	1 1 6 5 0 0 0

NAME: __SALES_____ ACCOUNT NO. ___4010___

Date	Explanation	Post. Ref.	Debit	Credit	D R C R	Balance

NAME: __SALES RETURNS AND ALLOWANCES_____ ACCOUNT NO. ___4020___

Date	Explanation	Post. Ref.	Debit	Credit	D R C R	Balance

NAME: __SALES DISCOUNTS_____ ACCOUNT NO. ___4030___

Date	Explanation	Post. Ref.	Debit	Credit	D R C R	Balance

CONTINUING PROBLEM, Cont.

ACCOUNTS RECEIVABLE SUBSIDIARY LEDGER

NAME   ACCU PAC, INC.   AC101

ADDRESS   11151 - 118 STREET, EDMONTON, AB T5S 2S2

Date 2008		Explanation	Post. Ref.	Debit	Credit	Dr. Balance
Jan.	1	Balance Forward	✔			-0-

NAME   CARSON ENGINEERING CORP.   CA101

ADDRESS   9939 EDMONTON WAY, EDMONTON, AB T5A 9A2

Date 2008		Explanation	Post. Ref.	Debit	Credit	Dr. Balance
Jan.	1	Balance Forward	✔			8 7 5 0 00

NAME   ANTHONY J. PITALE   PI101

ADDRESS   229 DIAMOND RICH AVENUE, EDMONTON, AB T6K 2L7

Date 2008		Explanation	Post. Ref.	Debit	Credit	Dr. Balance
Jan.	1	Balance Forward	✔			-0-

NAME   TAYLOR GOLF   TA101

ADDRESS   232 TAYLOR HEIGHTS, EDMONTON, AB T6E 6R2

Date 2008		Explanation	Post. Ref.	Debit	Credit	Dr. Balance
Jan.	1	Balance Forward	✔			2 9 0 0 00

CONTINUING PROBLEM, Cont.

NAME   VITA NEEDLE COMPANY   VI101

ADDRESS   SUITE 204, 10091 89 STREET, EDMONTON, AB T6F 1S1

Date 2008		Explanation	Post. Ref.	Debit	Credit	Dr. Balance
Jan.	1	Balance Forward	✔			—0—

ELDORADO COMPUTER CENTRE

SCHEDULE OF ACCOUNTS RECEIVABLE

JANUARY 31, 2008

CHAPTER 9
CHAPTER SUMMARY TEST

Part A

Fill in the blank(s) to complete the statement.

1. The credit period is longer than the _____ _____ .
2. The Accounts Receivable Ledger lists in _____ order an account for each customer.
3. Goods purchased for resale to its customers are called _____ _____ .
4. The accounts receivable ledger is updated _____ .
5. The totals of the sales journal are posted to the general ledger account at _____
   _____ .
6. The sale of merchandise on credit is recorded in the _____ _____
7. Sales Discount is a _____ account.
8. Gross profit is net sales less _____ _____ _____ _____
9. In the general ledger, _____ _____ is called the controlling account.
10. A _____ _____ results in the seller reducing its accounts receivable.
11. Sales Returns and Allowances is a _____ account with a _____ balance.
12. Sales Tax Payable is a _____ account with a _____ balance.
13. There is no _____ _____ _____ in a wholesale company.
14. A process that proves the mathematical accuracy of recording transactions in the cash receipts journal is called _____ .
15. The _____ column total in the cash receipts journal is never posted.
16. A listing of the ending balances from the accounts receivable ledger is called a
    _____ _____ _____ _____ .
17. Receipts of cash from any source are recorded in the _____ _____
    _____ .
18. _____ _____ are never taken on sales tax.
19. GST is charged on most sales of _____ and _____ .
20. GST, PST and HST are all _____ to a _____ account at month end.

Part B   (Note that the numbers used are for illustration only and do not necessarily cross-add.)

From the following chart, complete the statements below.

CASH RECEIPTS JOURNAL

Cash Dr.	Accounts Receivable Cr.	GST Payable Cr.	Sales Tax Payable Cr.	Sales Cr.	Sales Discount Dr.	Description of Receipt	Post Ref.	Sundry Cr.
5 5 55		2 2 22	1 1 11	4 4 44		Cash Sale		
6 6 66	8 8 88				7 77			
9 9 9 99						Sold Equipment		9 9 9 99
7 7 7 7 77	2 2 2 2 22	3 3 3 3 33	4 4 4 4 44	5 5 5 5 55	6 6 6 6 66	Totals		1 1 1 1 11

1. EXAMPLE: 1,111.11 is never posted.
2. 2,222.22 is posted to _____ _____ , the controlling account in the general ledger at the end of the month.
3. 3,333.33 is posted to _____ _____ at the end of the month.
4. 4,444.44 is a _____ total, posted to a _____ account.
5. 6,666.66 has a _____ balance that is posted to Sales Discount in the general ledger at the end of the month.
6. 7,777.77 is posted _____ _____ _____ to the cash account in the general ledger.
7. 66.66 should _____ _____ _____ , because the total will be posted to the Cash account in the general ledger at the end of the month.
8. 7.77 is _____ _____ during the month.
9. 88.88 is _____ recorded to the accounts receivable ledger during the month.
10. 44.44 is_____ _____ during the month, because the total of the Sales column is posted at the end of the month to Sales in the general ledger.
11. 999.99 is posted to the _____ _____ during the month, as the total of sundry is never posted.

Part C

Answer true or false to the following statements.

1. Recording a credit memorandum results in Sales Returns and Allowances increasing and Accounts Receivable decreasing.
2. (X) means the accounts receivable ledger has been updated.
3. The total of the sundry column is never posted at the end of the month.
4. A schedule of accounts receivable can be prepared from the general ledger.
5. Cross-footing verifies the accuracy of recording transactions into the general journal.
6. The cash receipts journal records credit sales.

7. The sum of the accounts receivable ledger should be equal to the balance in the controlling account at the end of the month.

8. The sales journal records cash sales and credit sales.

9. A (✔) means the total of sundry is posted monthly.

10. Net sales less Sales Returns and Allowances equals gross profit.

11. Discounts are usually taken on the GST portion of an invoice.

12. Businesses usually have a sales journal to record cash sales.

13. GST is never charged on wholesale sales.

14. Sales Returns and Allowances is a contra-asset account.

15. A discount period is longer than the credit period.

16. Each account in the accounts receivable ledger is debited to record amounts owed by customers.

17. The total of the Provincial Sales Tax Payable is posted at the end of the month to the general ledger.

18. There is a "Dr/Cr" column in accounts receivable ledger accounts.

19. GST is charged for financial services.

20. Gross profit less operating expenses equals net income.

SOLUTIONS TO CHAPTER SUMMARY TEST

Part A

1. discount period
2. alphabetical
3. merchandise inventory
4. daily
5. month end
6. sales journal
7. contra-revenue
8. cost of goods sold
9. Accounts Receivable
10. credit memo
11. contra-revenue, debit
12. liability, credit
13. Provincial Sales Tax
14. cross-footing
15. sundry
16. schedule of accounts receivable
17. Cash Receipts Journal
18. Cash discounts
19. goods, services
20. credited, liability

Part B

1. never posted
2. Accounts Receivable
3. GST Payable
4. credit, liability
5. debit
6. end of month
7. never be posted
8. not posted
9. immediately
10. not posted
11. general ledger

Part C

1. true
2. false
3. true
4. false
5. false
6. false
7. true
8. false
9. false
10. false
11. false
12. false
13. false
14. false
15. false
16. true
17. true
18. false
19. false
20. true

PROBLEM FOR APPENDIX

PETE'S CLOCK SHOPS
GENERAL JOURNAL   *Page 8*

Date	Account Titles and Description	Post Ref.	Dr.	Cr.

PROBLEM FOR APPENDIX, Cont.

PETE'S CLOCK SHOPS
GENERAL JOURNAL

Page 9

Date		Account Titles and Description	Post Ref.	Dr.	Cr.

10

Special Journals: Purchases and Cash Payments

SELF-REVIEW QUIZ 10-1

1. _____	2. _____	3. _____	4. _____	5. _____

SELF-REVIEW QUIZ 10-2

MUNROE CO.
PURCHASES JOURNAL

Page 2

Date	Account Credited	Date of Invoice	Inv. No.	Terms	PR	Accounts Payable Credit	Purchases Debit	Sundry Dr.		
								Account	Post Ref.	Amount

SELF-REVIEW QUIZ 10-2, Cont.

MUNROE CO.
GENERAL JOURNAL

Date	Account Titles and Description	PR	Dr.	Cr.

ACCOUNTS PAYABLE LEDGER

NAME _____ JOHN BUTLER COMPANY _____

ADDRESS _____ 18 REED ROAD, WINNIPEG, MB R2B 8G6 _____

Date	Explanation	Post Ref.	Debit	Credit	Cr. Balance

NAME _____ FLYNN COMPANY _____

ADDRESS _____ 15 FOSS AVE., QUEBEC CITY, PQ G1L 2W4 _____

Date	Explanation	Post Ref.	Debit	Credit	Cr. Balance

PARTIAL GENERAL LEDGER

NAME: _____ EQUIPMENT _____   ACCOUNT NO. _____ 121 _____

Date	Explanation	Post Ref.	Debit	Credit	DR CR	Balance

SELF-REVIEW QUIZ 10-2, Cont.

NAME: ACCOUNTS PAYABLE   ACCOUNT NO. _____212_____

Date		Explanation	Post Ref.	Debit	Credit	D R C R	Balance

NAME: PURCHASES   ACCOUNT NO. _____512_____

Date		Explanation	Post Ref.	Debit	Credit	D R C R	Balance

NAME: PURCHASES RETURNS AND ALLOWANCES   ACCOUNT NO. _____513_____

Date		Explanation	Post Ref.	Debit	Credit	D R C R	Balance

SELF-REVIEW QUIZ 10-3

MELISSA COMPANY
CASH PAYMENTS JOURNAL   Page 2

Date	Chq. No.	Accounts Debited	Post Ref.	Sundry Accounts Dr.	Accounts Payable Dr.	Purchases Discounts Cr.	Cash Cr.

SELF-REVIEW QUIZ 10-3, Cont.

ACCOUNTS PAYABLE LEDGER

NAME: BOB FINKELSTEIN

ADDRESS: 112 FLYING HIGHWAY, MONTREAL, PQ H1K 2H7

Date 2006		Explanation	Post Ref.	Debit	Credit	Cr. Balance
June	1	Balance	✔			3 0 0 0 0

NAME: AL JEEP

ADDRESS: 118 WANG ROAD, LONDON, ON N5X 2Y3

Date 2006		Explanation	Post Ref.	Debit	Credit	Cr. Balance
June	1	Balance	✔			2 0 0 0 0

PARTIAL GENERAL LEDGER

NAME: CASH   ACCOUNT NO. 110

Date 2006		Explanation	Post Ref.	Debit	Credit	DR CR	Balance
June	1	Balance	✔			Dr	7 0 0 0 0

NAME: ACCOUNTS PAYABLE   ACCOUNT NO. 210

Date 2006		Explanation	Post Ref.	Debit	Credit	DR CR	Balance
June	1	Balance	✔			Cr	5 0 0 0 0

NAME: PURCHASES DISCOUNTS   ACCOUNT NO. 511

Date		Explanation	Post Ref.	Debit	Credit	DR CR	Balance

NAME: ADVERTISING EXPENSE   ACCOUNT NO. 610

Date		Explanation	Post Ref.	Debit	Credit	DR CR	Balance

SELF-REVIEW QUIZ 10-4

MUNROE CO.
PURCHASES JOURNAL

Page 2

Date	Description	Date of Invoice	Inv. No.	Terms	PR	Accounts Payable Credit	Purchases Debit	GST Prepaid Debit	Sundry Dr. Account	PR	Amount

MUNROE CO.
GENERAL JOURNAL

Page 1

Date	Account Title and Description	PR	Dr.	Cr.

ACCOUNTS PAYABLE LEDGER

NAME _____ FLYNN CO. _____

ADDRESS _____ 7310 - 34 AVENUE, EDMONTON, AB T6K 2S1 _____

Date		Explanation	Post Ref.	Debit	Credit	Cr. Balance

NAME _____ JOHN BUTLER CO. _____

ADDRESS _____ 20015 NOTTINGHAM BOULEVARD, SHERWOOD PARK, AB T1R 2S2 ____

Date		Explanation	Post Ref.	Debit	Credit	Cr. Balance

PARTIAL GENERAL LEDGER

NAME: ____ EQUIPMENT _____ ACCOUNT NO. ____ 121

Date		Explanation	Post Ref.	Debit	Credit	DR CR	Balance

NAME: ____ GST PREPAID _____ ACCOUNT NO. ____ 125

Date		Explanation	Post Ref.	Debit	Credit	DR CR	Balance

NAME: ____ ACCOUNTS PAYABLE _____ ACCOUNT NO. ____ 212

Date		Explanation	Post Ref.	Debit	Credit	DR CR	Balance

NAME: ____ PURCHASES _____ ACCOUNT NO. ____ 512

Date		Explanation	Post Ref.	Debit	Credit	DR CR	Balance

NAME: ____ PURCHASE RETURNS AND ALLOWANCES _____ ACCOUNT NO. ____ 513

Date		Explanation	Post Ref.	Debit	Credit	DR CR	Balance

FORMS FOR COMPREHENSIVE DEMONSTRATION PROBLEM
J. LING CO.
SALES JOURNAL

Page 1

Date	Invoice No.	Customer's Name	Terms	Post Ref.	Accounts Receivable Dr.	HST Collected Cr.	Sales Cr.

CASH RECEIPTS JOURNAL

Page 1

Date	Cash Dr.	Accounts Receivable Cr.	Sales Cr.	HST Collected Cr.	Sales Discounts Dr.	Description of Receipt	Post Ref.	Sundry Cr.

PURCHASES JOURNAL

Page 1

Date	Account Credited	Date of Inv.	Inv. No.	Terms	Post Ref.	Accounts Payable Cr.	Purchases Dr.	Prepaid HST Dr.	Sundry Account Name	Sundry Post Ref.	Sundry Amount Dr.

CASH PAYMENTS JOURNAL

Page 1

Date	Chq. No.	Account Debited	Post Ref.	Sundry Dr.	Accounts Payable Dr.	Prepaid HST Dr.	Purchases Dr.	Purchases Discounts Cr.	Cash Cr.

FORMS FOR COMPREHENSIVE DEMONSTRATION PROBLEM, Cont.

GENERAL JOURNAL

Page 1

Date	Account Title and Description	PR	Dr.	Cr.

ACCOUNTS RECEIVABLE LEDGER

NAME   BALDER CO.

ADDRESS   1 ROCK RD., QUEBEC CITY, PQ G2J 2W2

Date	Explanation	Post Ref.	Debit	Credit	Dr. Balance

NAME   LEWIS CO.

ADDRESS   15 SMITH AVE., WINNIPEG, MB R4R 8K3

Date	Explanation	Post Ref.	Debit	Credit	Dr. Balance

FORMS FOR COMPREHENSIVE DEMONSTRATION PROBLEM, Concluded

ACCOUNTS PAYABLE LEDGER

NAME — CASE CO.

ADDRESS — 1 LONG RD., BRANDON, MN R7L 2M0

Date	Explanation	Post Ref.	Debit	Credit	Cr. Balance

NAME — NOONE CO.

ADDRESS — 11 MILL RD., WINNIPEG, MN R2P 2T3

Date	Explanation	Post Ref.	Debit	Credit	Cr. Balance

PARTIAL GENERAL LEDGER

Cash   111

Accounts Receivable   112

HST Prepaid   114

Equipment   116

Accounts Payable   210

HST Collected   225

J. Ling, Capital   310

Sales   410

Sales Returns & Allowances 420

Sales Discounts   430

Purchases   510

Purchases Returns & Allowances   520

Purchases Discounts   530

Advertising Expense   601

Salaries Expense   610

CHAPTER 10
FORMS FOR MINI EXERCISES

1. a. _____
    b. _____
    c. _____
    d. _____
    e. _____
    f. _____
    g. _____
    h. _____

2.

3. _____
    _____
    _____
    _____
    _____
    _____
    _____
    _____
    _____

4. a. _____ _____   5. a. _____   d. _____
    b. _____ _____   b. _____   e. _____
    c. _____ _____   c. _____   f. _____

6.

AVE. CO.
SCHEDULE OF ACCOUNTS PAYABLE
MAY 31, 2006

FORMS FOR EXERCISES

10-1.

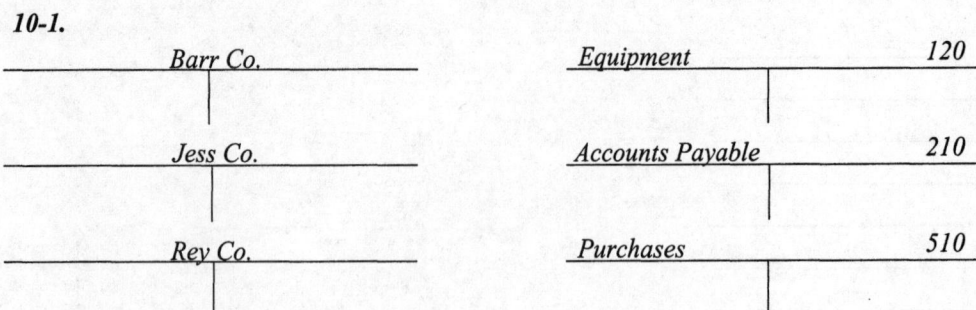

Barr Co.	Equipment 120
Jess Co.	Accounts Payable 210
Rey Co.	Purchases 510

10-2.
                                                                                              Page 1

| Reel Co. | Accounts Payable 211 | Purchase Returns and Allowances 513 |

10-3.

CASH PAYMENTS JOURNAL   Page 2

Date	Chq. No.	Account Debited	Post Ref.				

FORMS FOR EXERCISES, Cont.

10-3, Cont.

| ACCOUNTS PAYABLE LEDGER | PARTIAL GENERAL LEDGER |

ACCOUNTS PAYABLE LEDGER

B. Foss
| | 400

A. James
| | 1,000

J. Ranch
| | 900

B. Swanson
| | 200

PARTIAL GENERAL LEDGER

Cash   110
3,000 |

Accounts Payable   210
| 2,500

Purchases Discounts   511
|

Advertising Expense   610
|

10-4.

MORGAN'S CLOTHING
SCHEDULE OF ACCOUNTS PAYABLE
APRIL 30, 2007

_____
_____
_____
_____

Accounts Payable   210
|

10-5.

Accounts Affected	Category	↑↓	Rules

10-6.

_____
_____
_____
_____
_____
_____

PROBLEM 10A-1 or 10B-1.

JUDY CLARK'S SPORTING GOODS SHOP
PURCHASES JOURNAL

Page 1

Date	Account Credited	Date of Invoice	Inv. No.	Terms	Post Ref.	Accounts Payable Cr.	Purchases Dr.	Sundry Dr.		
								Account	Post Ref.	Amount

PROBLEM 10A-1 or 10B-1, Cont.

JUDY CLARK'S SPORTING GOODS SHOP

ACCOUNTS PAYABLE LEDGER

NAME   ASTER CO.

ADDRESS   12 SMITH ST., BRANTFORD, ON N3R 2T2

Date		Explanation	Post Ref.	Debit	Credit	Cr. Balance

NAME   NORTON CO.

ADDRESS   1071 GRAYSON RD., BRANTFORD, ON N3R 2T2

Date		Explanation	Post Ref.	Debit	Credit	Cr. Balance

NAME   ROLO CO.

ADDRESS   221B BAKER ST., OTTAWA, ON K2A 4N1

Date		Explanation	Post Ref.	Debit	Credit	Cr. Balance

PROBLEM 10A-1 or 10B-1, Cont.

JUDY CLARK'S SPORTING GOODS SHOP

PARTIAL GENERAL LEDGER

NAME: STORE SUPPLIES   ACCOUNT NO. _____ 115

Date	Explanation	Post Ref.	Debit	Credit	D R C R	Balance

NAME: STORE EQUIPMENT   ACCOUNT NO. _____ 121

Date	Explanation	Post Ref.	Debit	Credit	D R C R	Balance

NAME: ACCOUNTS PAYABLE   ACCOUNT NO. _____ 210

Date	Explanation	Post Ref.	Debit	Credit	D R C R	Balance

NAME: PURCHASES   ACCOUNT NO. _____ 510

Date	Explanation	Post Ref.	Debit	Credit	D R C R	Balance

PROBLEM 10A-2 or 10B-2.

MABEL'S NATURAL FOOD STORE
PURCHASES JOURNAL

Page 10

Date	Account Credited	Date of Invoice	Inv. No.	Terms	Post Ref.	Accounts Payable Cr.	Purchases Dr.	Prepaid GST Dr.	Store Supplies Dr.	Sundry Dr.		
										Account	Post Ref.	Amount Dr.

PROBLEM 10A-2 or 10B-2, Cont.

MABEL'S NATURAL FOOD STORE

ACCOUNTS PAYABLE LEDGER

NAME: ATON CO.

ADDRESS: 10174 - 112 ST., YORKTON, SK   S3N 0T1

Date 2006		Explanation	Post Ref.	Debit	Credit	Cr. Balance
May	1	Balance	✔			4 2 8 0 0

NAME: BROWARD CO.

ADDRESS: 415 CHURCHILL ST., REGINA, SK   S4A 8B1

Date 2006		Explanation	Post Ref.	Debit	Credit	Cr. Balance
May	1	Balance	✔			6 4 2 0 0

NAME: MIDDEN CO.

ADDRESS: 5518 VIMY PARK RD., YORKTON, SK   S3N 4V4

Date 2006		Explanation	Post Ref.	Debit	Credit	Cr. Balance
May	1	Balance	✔			1 2 8 4 0 0

NAME: RELAR CO.

ADDRESS: 2415 RED RIVER DR., SASKATOON, SK   S7T 5I2

Date 2006		Explanation	Post Ref.	Debit	Credit	Cr. Balance
May	1	Balance	✔			5 3 5 0 0

GENERAL JOURNAL

Page 2

Date	Account Title and Description	Post Ref.	Dr.	Cr.

PROBLEM 10A-2 or 10B-2, Cont.

MABEL'S NATURAL FOOD STORE
PARTIAL GENERAL LEDGER

NAME: STORE SUPPLIES   ACCOUNT NO. 110

Date	Explanation	Post Ref.	Debit	Credit	DR CR	Balance

NAME: PREPAID GST   ACCOUNT NO. 112

Date 2006		Explanation	Post Ref.	Debit	Credit	DR CR	Balance
May	1	Balance	✔			Dr	4 9 8 00

NAME: OFFICE EQUIPMENT   ACCOUNT NO. 120

Date	Explanation	Post Ref.	Debit	Credit	DR CR	Balance

NAME: ACCOUNTS PAYABLE   ACCOUNT NO. 210

Date 2006		Explanation	Post Ref.	Debit	Credit	DR CR	Balance
May	1	Balance	✔			Cr	2 8 8 9 00

NAME: PURCHASES   ACCOUNT NO. 510

Date 2006		Explanation	Post Ref.	Debit	Credit	DR CR	Balance
May	1	Balance	✔			Dr	1 6 0 0 0 00

NAME: PURCHASES RETURNS AND ALLOWANCES   ACCOUNT NO. 512

Date	Explanation	Post Ref.	Debit	Credit	DR CR	Balance

MABEL'S NATURAL FOOD STORE
SCHEDULE OF ACCOUNTS PAYABLE
MAY 31, 2006

PROBLEM 10A-3 or 10B-3.

JONES' COMPUTER CENTRE

CASH PAYMENTS JOURNAL

Page 5

Date	Chq. No.	Account Debited	Post Ref.	Sundry Dr.	Accounts Payable Dr.	Prepaid GST Dr.	Computer Purchases Dr.	Computer Purchases Discounts Cr.	Cash Cr.

PROBLEM 10A-3 or 10B-3, Cont.

ACCOUNTS PAYABLE LEDGER

NAME: _____ ALVIN CO. _____

ADDRESS: _____ 245 QUEEN ST., LONDON, ON N5X 2T4 _____

Date 2007		Explanation	Post Ref.	Debit	Credit	Cr. Balance
May	1	Balance	✔			1 2 8 4 0 0

NAME: _____ HENRY CO. _____

ADDRESS: _____ 99 VICTORIA ST., LONDON, ON N6H 1B1 _____

Date 2007		Explanation	Post Ref.	Debit	Credit	Cr. Balance
May	1	Balance	✔			6 4 2 0 0

NAME: _____ SOY CO. _____

ADDRESS: _____ P. O. BOX 105, LONDON, ON N5X 8V2 _____

Date 2007		Explanation	Post Ref.	Debit	Credit	Cr. Balance
May	1	Balance	✔			8 5 6 0 0

NAME: _____ XON CO. _____

ADDRESS: _____ 241 RIVER DR., LONDON, ON N6A 2C2 _____

Date 2007		Explanation	Post Ref.	Debit	Credit	Cr. Balance
May	1	Balance	✔			1 4 9 8 0 0

PARTIAL GENERAL LEDGER

NAME: _CASH_____ ACCOUNT NO. _____ 110

Date 2007		Explanation	Post Ref.	Debit	Credit	DR CR	Balance
May	1	Balance	✔			Dr	1 7 0 0 0 0 0

NAME: _PREPAID GST_____ ACCOUNT NO. _____ 132

Date 2007		Explanation	Post Ref.	Debit	Credit	DR CR	Balance
May	1	Balance	✔			Dr	9 6 5 0 0

PROBLEM 10A-3 or 10B-3, Cont. | PARTIAL GENERAL LEDGER, Cont.

NAME: DELIVERY TRUCK   ACCOUNT NO. ___150___

Date	Explanation	Post Ref.	Debit	Credit	DR CR	Balance

NAME: ACCOUNTS PAYABLE   ACCOUNT NO. ___210___

Date 2007	Explanation	Post Ref.	Debit	Credit	DR CR	Balance
May 1	Balance	✔			Cr	4 2 8 0 0 0

NAME: COMPUTER PURCHASES   ACCOUNT NO. ___510___

Date	Explanation	Post Ref.	Debit	Credit	DR CR	Balance

NAME: COMPUTER PURCHASES DISCOUNTS   ACCOUNT NO. ___511___

Date	Explanation	Post Ref.	Debit	Credit	DR CR	Balance

NAME: RENT EXPENSE   ACCOUNT NO. ___610___

Date	Explanation	Post Ref.	Debit	Credit	DR CR	Balance

NAME: UTILITIES EXPENSE   ACCOUNT NO. ___620___

Date	Explanation	Post Ref.	Debit	Credit	DR CR	Balance

JONES' COMPUTER CENTRE
SCHEDULE OF ACCOUNTS PAYABLE
MAY 31, 2007

PROBLEM 10A-4 or 10B-4.

ABBY'S TOY HOUSE
PURCHASES JOURNAL

Page 10

Date	Account Credited	Date of Invoice	Inv. No.	Terms	Post Ref.	Accounts Payable Cr.	Toy Purchases Dr.	Prepaid GST or HST Dr.	Sundry Dr.		
									Account	PR	Amount

PROBLEM 10A-4 or 10B-4, Cont.

ABBY'S TOY HOUSE
CASH PAYMENTS JOURNAL

Page 8

Date	Chq. No.	Account Debited	Post Ref.	Sundry Dr.	Accounts Payable Dr.	Prepaid GST or HST Dr.	Toy Purchases Dr.	Purchases Discounts Cr.	Cash Cr.

PROBLEM 10A-4 or 10B-4, Cont.

ABBY'S TOY HOUSE
CASH RECEIPTS JOURNAL

Page 14

Date	Cash Dr.	Accounts Receivable Cr.	Toy Sales Cr.	GST or HST Payable Cr.	Sales Discounts Dr.	Description of Receipt	Post Ref.	Sundry Cr.

PROBLEM 10A-4 or 10B-4, Cont.

ABBY'S TOY HOUSE
SALES JOURNAL

Page 4

Date	Invoice No.	Customer's Name	Post Ref.	Accounts Receivable Dr.	GST or HST Payable Cr.	Toy Sales Cr.

ABBY'S TOY HOUSE
GENERAL JOURNAL

Page 3

Date	Account Title and Description	Post Ref.	Dr.	Cr.

PROBLEM 10A-4 or 10B-4, Cont.

| ACCOUNTS RECEIVABLE LEDGER |

Please fill in appropriate addresses for your 7% GST or 15% HST answers.

NAME   BILL BURTON
ADDRESS

Date	Explanation	Post Ref.	Debit	Credit	Dr. Balance

NAME   BONNIE FLOW COMPANY
ADDRESS

Date	Explanation	Post Ref.	Debit	Credit	Dr. Balance

NAME   JIM REX
ADDRESS

Date	Explanation	Post Ref.	Debit	Credit	Dr. Balance

NAME   AMY ROSE
ADDRESS

Date	Explanation	Post Ref.	Debit	Credit	Dr. Balance

ABBY'S TOY HOUSE
SCHEDULE OF ACCOUNTS RECEIVABLE
MARCH 31, 2007

NAME: _____ CLASS: _____ DATE: _____

PROBLEM 10A-4 or 10B-4, Cont.

ACCOUNTS PAYABLE LEDGER

Please fill in appropriate addresses for your 7% GST or 15% HST answers.

NAME   MINNIE KATZ

ADDRESS _____

Date	Explanation	Post Ref.	Debit	Credit	Cr. Balance

NAME   SAM KATZ GARAGE

ADDRESS _____

Date	Explanation	Post Ref.	Debit	Credit	Cr. Balance

NAME   EARL MILLER CO.

ADDRESS _____

Date	Explanation	Post Ref.	Debit	Credit	Cr. Balance

NAME   WOODY SMITH

ADDRESS _____

Date	Explanation	Post Ref.	Debit	Credit	Cr. Balance

ABBY'S TOY HOUSE
SCHEDULE OF ACCOUNTS PAYABLE
MARCH 31, 2007

PROBLEM 10A-4 or 10B-4, Cont.

ABBY'S TOY HOUSE - PARTIAL GENERAL LEDGER

NAME: __CASH__   ACCOUNT NO. ___110___

Date	Explanation	Post Ref.	Debit	Credit	D R C R	Balance

NAME: __ACCOUNTS RECEIVABLE__   ACCOUNT NO. ___112___

Date	Explanation	Post Ref.	Debit	Credit	D R C R	Balance

NAME: __PREPAID RENT__   ACCOUNT NO. ___114___

Date	Explanation	Post Ref.	Debit	Credit	D R C R	Balance

NAME: __PREPAID GST or PREPAID HST__   ACCOUNT NO. ___116___

Date	Explanation	Post Ref.	Debit	Credit	D R C R	Balance

NAME: __DELIVERY TRUCK__   ACCOUNT NO. ___121___

Date	Explanation	Post Ref.	Debit	Credit	D R C R	Balance

NAME: __ACCOUNTS PAYABLE__   ACCOUNT NO. ___210___

Date	Explanation	Post Ref.	Debit	Credit	D R C R	Balance

PROBLEM 10A-4 or 10B-4, Cont.

ABBY'S TOY HOUSE - PARTIAL GENERAL LEDGER, Cont.

NAME: GST PAYABLE or HST PAYABLE   ACCOUNT NO. _____ 218

Date	Explanation	Post Ref.	Debit	Credit	D R C R	Balance

NAME: A. ELLEN, CAPITAL   ACCOUNT NO. _____ 310

Date	Explanation	Post Ref.	Debit	Credit	D R C R	Balance

NAME: TOY SALES   ACCOUNT NO. _____ 410

Date	Explanation	Post Ref	Debit	Credit	D R C R	Balance

NAME: SALES RETURNS AND ALLOWANCES   ACCOUNT NO. _____ 412

Date	Explanation	Post Ref.	Debit	Credit	D R C R	Balance

NAME: SALES DISCOUNTS   ACCOUNT NO. _____ 414

Date	Explanation	Post Ref.	Debit	Credit	D R C R	Balance

NAME: TOY PURCHASES   ACCOUNT NO. _____ 510

Date	Explanation	Post Ref.	Debit	Credit	D R C R	Balance

PROBLEM 10A-4 or 10B-4, Cont.

ABBY'S TOY HOUSE - PARTIAL GENERAL LEDGER, Cont.

NAME: __PURCHASES RETURNS AND ALLOWANCES__   ACCOUNT NO. ____512____

Date	Explanation	Post Ref.	Debit	Credit	DR CR	Balance

NAME: __PURCHASES DISCOUNTS__   ACCOUNT NO. ____514____

Date	Explanation	Post Ref.	Debit	Credit	DR CR	Balance

NAME: __SALARIES EXPENSE__   ACCOUNT NO. ____610____

Date	Explanation	Post Ref.	Debit	Credit	DR CR	Balance

NAME: __CLEANING EXPENSE__   ACCOUNT NO. ____612____

Date	Explanation	Post Ref.	Debit	Credit	DR CR	Balance

PROBLEM 10C-1.

Page 1

Date	Account Credited	Date of Invoice	Inv. No.	Terms	Post Ref.	Accounts Payable Cr.	Purchases Dr.	Sundry Dr.		
								Account	Post Ref.	Amount

PROBLEM 10C-1, Cont.

NAME   BRENDAN CO.

ADDRESS   4218 GREYSON ST., RICHMOND, BC V7A 0T1

Date	Explanation	Post Ref.	Debit	Credit	Cr. Balance

NAME   CONVEY CO.

ADDRESS   235 ANTHONY ST., RICHMOND, BC V7D 7V9

Date	Explanation	Post Ref.	Debit	Credit	Cr. Balance

NAME   RELIABLE CO.

ADDRESS   781 PARKER ST., RICHMOND, BC V7C 1T4

Date	Explanation	Post Ref.	Debit	Credit	Cr. Balance

PROBLEM 10C-1, Cont.

NAME: _STORE SUPPLIES_ _____ ACCOUNT NO. ____115____

Date	Explanation	Post Ref.	Debit	Credit	D R C R	Balance

NAME: _STORE EQUIPMENT_ _____ ACCOUNT NO. ____141____

Date	Explanation	Post Ref.	Debit	Credit	D R C R	Balance

NAME: _ACCOUNTS PAYABLE_ _____ ACCOUNT NO. ____210____

Date	Explanation	Post Ref.	Debit	Credit	D R C R	Balance

NAME: _PURCHASES_ _____ ACCOUNT NO. ____510____

Date	Explanation	Post Ref.	Debit	Credit	D R C R	Balance

PROBLEM 10C-2.

Page 21

Date	Account Credited	Date of Invoice	Inv. No.	Terms	Post Ref.	Accounts Payable Cr.	Purchases Dr.	Prepaid GST Dr.	Store Supplies Dr.	Sundry Dr.		
										Account	PR	Amount

PROBLEM 10C-2, Cont.

NAME: EDDYN CO.

ADDRESS: 164 BRONTE STREET, SASKATOON, SK   S7T 5C3

Date 2006		Explanation	Post Ref.	Debit	Credit	Cr. Balance
Aug	1	Balance	✔			8 5 6 0 0

NAME: EUROPEAN IMPORT FABRICS CO.

ADDRESS: 58 JASON STREET, REGINA, SK   S4V 2G4

Date 2006		Explanation	Post Ref.	Debit	Credit	Cr. Balance
Aug	1	Balance	✔			3 2 6 7 0 0

NAME: FORWARD CO.

ADDRESS: 8902 BURKE ROAD, YORKTON, SK   S3N 3J7

Date 2006		Explanation	Post Ref.	Debit	Credit	Cr. Balance
Aug	1	Balance	✔			1 6 7 2 0 0

NAME: LAVOY CO.

ADDRESS: 18 PARK DRIVE, SASKATOON, SK   S7T 5J2

Date 2006		Explanation	Post Ref.	Debit	Credit	Cr. Balance
Aug	1	Balance	✔			5 3 5 0 0

NAME: RELIANT CO.

ADDRESS: 2415 RED RIVER DRIVE, SASKATOON, SK   S7T 0P0

Date 2006		Explanation	Post Ref.	Debit	Credit	Cr. Balance
Aug	1	Balance	✔			2 7 7 3 0 0

PROBLEM 10C-2, Cont.

NAME: STORE SUPPLIES ACCOUNT NO. 130

Date	Explanation	Post Ref.	Debit	Credit	DR CR	Balance

NAME: PREPAID GST ACCOUNT NO. 142

Date 2006	Explanation	Post Ref.	Debit	Credit	DR CR	Balance
Aug 1	Balance	✔			Dr	2 8 7 3 00

NAME: OFFICE EQUIPMENT ACCOUNT NO. 180

Date	Explanation	Post Ref.	Debit	Credit	DR CR	Balance

NAME: ACCOUNTS PAYABLE ACCOUNT NO. 220

Date 2006	Explanation	Post Ref.	Debit	Credit	DR CR	Balance
Aug 1	Balance	✔			Cr	9 1 0 3 00

NAME: PURCHASES ACCOUNT NO. 500

Date 2006	Explanation	Post Ref.	Debit	Credit	DR CR	Balance
Aug 1	Balance	✔			Dr	8 6 3 4 0 00

NAME: PURCHASES RETURNS AND ALLOWANCES ACCOUNT NO. 510

Date 2006	Explanation	Post Ref.	Debit	Credit	DR CR	Balance
Aug 1	Balance	✔			Cr	1 3 7 4 00

PROBLEM 10C-2, Cont.

_____

_____

Page 32

Date		Account Title and Description	Post Ref.	Dr.					Cr.				

_____

_____

PROBLEM 10C-3.

Page ____

Date	Chq. No.	Account Debited	Post Ref.	Sundry Dr.	Accounts Payable Dr.	Prepaid GST Dr.	Welding Purchases Dr.	Purchases Discounts Cr.	Cash Cr.

PROBLEM 10C-3, Cont.

NAME: DOMINION GASES CO.

ADDRESS: 143 - 24 STREET, CAMROSE, AB   T4V 2T2

Date 2008		Explanation	Post Ref.	Debit	Credit	Cr. Balance
May	1	Balance	✔			1 4 8 2 20

NAME: GLOVER GAUGES CO.

ADDRESS: 3223 - 54 AVENUE, EDMONTON, AB   T6B 1C1

Date 2008		Explanation	Post Ref.	Debit	Credit	Cr. Balance
May	1	Balance	✔			8 8 1 71

NAME: MARKER GLOVES CO.

ADDRESS: 477 APEX ROAD, CAMROSE, AB   T4V 9X1

Date 2008		Explanation	Post Ref.	Debit	Credit	Cr. Balance
May	1	Balance	✔			1 8 4 7 48

NAME: PRISM ACCESSORIES CO.

ADDRESS: 5353 CRYSTAL ROAD, CAMROSE, AB   T4V 0L1

Date 2008		Explanation	Post Ref.	Debit	Credit	Cr. Balance
May	1	Balance	✔			3 9 4 2 86

NAME: VERTAL ROD CO.

ADDRESS: 219 FORREST BOULEVARD, EDMONTON, AB   T5K 8E8

Date 2008		Explanation	Post Ref.	Debit	Credit	Cr. Balance
May	1	Balance	✔			2 4 8 0 42

PROBLEM 10C-3, Cont.

STOKES' WHOLESALE WELDING SUPPLIES CO. - PARTIAL GENERAL LEDGER

NAME: __CASH_____ ACCOUNT NO. ____100____

Date 2008		Explanation	Post Ref.	Debit	Credit	DR CR	Balance
May	1	Balance	✔			Dr	2 2 9 4 1 1 8

NAME: __PREPAID GST_____ ACCOUNT NO. ____145____

Date 2008		Explanation	Post Ref.	Debit	Credit	DR CR	Balance
May	1	Balance	✔			Dr	2 4 2 1 1 4

NAME: __DELIVERY TRUCK_____ ACCOUNT NO. ____170____

Date		Explanation	Post Ref.	Debit	Credit	DR CR	Balance

NAME: __ACCOUNTS PAYABLE_____ ACCOUNT NO. ____200____

Date 2008		Explanation	Post Ref.	Debit	Credit	DR CR	Balance
May	1	Balance	✔			Cr	1 0 6 3 4 6 7

NAME: __WELDING PURCHASES_____ ACCOUNT NO. ____500____

Date 2008		Explanation	Post Ref.	Debit	Credit	DR CR	Balance
May	1	Balance	✔			Dr	5 6 4 2 2 2 9

NAME: __WELDING PURCHASES DISCOUNTS_____ ACCOUNT NO. ____510____

Date 2008		Explanation	Post Ref.	Debit	Credit	DR CR	Balance
May	1	Balance	✔			Cr	5 0 6 2 0

PROBLEM 10C-3, Cont.

NAME: _RENT EXPENSE_ _____ ACCOUNT NO. ___670___

Date 2008		Explanation	Post Ref.	Debit	Credit	D R C R	Balance
May	1	Balance	✔			Dr	3 7 3 0 0 0

NAME: _UTILITIES EXPENSE_ _____ ACCOUNT NO. ___690___

Date 2008		Explanation	Post Ref.	Debit	Credit	D R C R	Balance
May	1	Balance	✔			Dr	1 2 0 4 6 6

PROBLEM 10C-4.

1., 2., 3.

Page 17

Date	Account Credited	Date of Invoice	Inv. No.	Terms	Post Ref.	Accounts Payable Cr.	Book Purchases Dr.	Prepaid GST or HST Dr.	Sundry Dr. Account	PR	Amount

PROBLEM 10C-4, Cont.

Page 11

Date	Chq. No.	Account Debited	Post Ref.	Sundry Dr.	Accounts Payable Dr.	Prepaid GST or HST Dr.	Book Purchases Dr.	Purchases Discounts Cr.	Cash Cr.

PROBLEM 10C-4, Cont.

Page 16

Date	Cash Dr.	Accounts Receivable Cr.	Book Sales Cr.	GST or HST Payable Cr.	Sales Discounts Dr.	Description of Receipt	Post Ref.	Sundry Cr.

PROBLEM 10C-4, Cont.

_____

_____   *Page 7*

Date	Invoice No.	Customer's Name	Post Ref.	Accounts Receivable Dr.			GST or HST Payable Cr.			Book Sales Cr.		

_____

_____   *Page 8*

Date	Account Title and Description	Post Ref.	Dr.			Cr.		

PROBLEM 10C-4, Cont.

NAME DISTRICT COLLEGE

ADDRESS

Date		Explanation	Post Ref.	Debit	Credit	Dr. Balance

NAME FIRST CITY LIBRARY

ADDRESS

Date		Explanation	Post Ref.	Debit	Credit	Dr. Balance

NAME FLOWER & COMPANY

ADDRESS

Date		Explanation	Post Ref.	Debit	Credit	Dr. Balance

NAME RURAL BOOKMOBILE CO.

ADDRESS

Date		Explanation	Post Ref.	Debit	Credit	Dr. Balance

PROBLEM 10C-4, Cont.

Please fill in appropriate addresses for your 7% GST or 15% HST answers.

NAME   MILLIGAN BOOK COMPANY

ADDRESS

Date		Explanation	Post Ref.	Debit	Credit	Cr. Balance

NAME   SMITHSONIAN BOOK CO.

ADDRESS

Date		Explanation	Post Ref.	Debit	Credit	Cr. Balance

NAME   SUBURBAN AUTO SALES CO.

ADDRESS

Date		Explanation	Post Ref.	Debit	Credit	Cr. Balance

NAME   WINNIPEG BOOK SUPPLY

ADDRESS

Date		Explanation	Post Ref.	Debit	Credit	Cr. Balance

PROBLEM 10C-4, Cont.

┌──────────────────────────────────────┐
│   │
└──────────────────────────────────────┘

NAME: CASH   ACCOUNT NO. ____110____

Date	Explanation	Post Ref.	Debit	Credit	D R C R	Balance

NAME: ACCOUNTS RECEIVABLE   ACCOUNT NO. ____120____

Date	Explanation	Post Ref.	Debit	Credit	D R C R	Balance

NAME: PREPAID RENT   ACCOUNT NO. ____135____

Date	Explanation	Post Ref.	Debit	Credit	D R C R	Balance

NAME: PREPAID GST or PREPAID HST   ACCOUNT NO. ____138____

Date	Explanation	Post Ref.	Debit	Credit	D R C R	Balance

NAME: DELIVERY TRUCK   ACCOUNT NO. ____180____

Date	Explanation	Post Ref.	Debit	Credit	D R C R	Balance

NAME: ACCOUNTS PAYABLE   ACCOUNT NO. ____210____

Date	Explanation	Post Ref.	Debit	Credit	D R C R	Balance

PROBLEM 10C-4, Cont.

NAME: __GST PAYABLE or HST PAYABLE_____ ACCOUNT NO. ___218__

Date		Explanation	Post Ref.	Debit	Credit	D R C R	Balance

NAME: __B. CARDINAL, CAPITAL_____ ACCOUNT NO. ___310__

Date		Explanation	Post Ref.	Debit	Credit	D R C R	Balance

NAME: __BOOK SALES_____ ACCOUNT NO. ___410__

Date		Explanation	Post Ref.	Debit	Credit	D R C R	Balance

NAME: __SALES RETURNS AND ALLOWANCES_____ ACCOUNT NO. ___412__

Date		Explanation	Post Ref.	Debit	Credit	D R C R	Balance

NAME: __SALES DISCOUNTS_____ ACCOUNT NO. ___414__

Date		Explanation	Post Ref.	Debit	Credit	D R C R	Balance

NAME: __BOOK PURCHASES_____ ACCOUNT NO. ___510__

Date		Explanation	Post Ref.	Debit	Credit	D R C R	Balance

PROBLEM 10C-4, Cont.

NAME: _PURCHASES RETURNS AND ALLOWANCES_____   ACCOUNT NO. _____512_____

Date		Explanation	Post Ref.	Debit	Credit	DR CR	Balance

NAME: _PURCHASES DISCOUNTS_____   ACCOUNT NO. _____514_____

Date		Explanation	Post Ref.	Debit	Credit	DR CR	Balance

NAME: _CLEANING EXPENSE_____   ACCOUNT NO. _____615_____

Date		Explanation	Post Ref.	Debit	Credit	DR CR	Balance

NAME: _SALARIES EXPENSE_____   ACCOUNT NO. _____650_____

Date		Explanation	Post Ref.	Debit	Credit	DR CR	Balance

NAME: _____ CLASS: _____ DATE: _____

REAL WORLD APPLICATIONS, #10R-1.

_____

_____

_____

_____

_____

_____

_____

REAL WORLD APPLICATIONS, #10R-2.

PARTIAL GENERAL LEDGER

Cash	Sales	Purchases Discounts

Accounts Receivable	Sales Discounts	Purchase Returns and Allowances

Notes Payable	Sales Returns and Allowances	Salaries Expense

Accounts Payable	Purchases	

ACCOUNTS RECEIVABLE LEDGER

Blue Co.	Jon Co.	Roff Co.

ACCOUNTS PAYABLE LEDGER

Ralph Co.	Sos Co.	Jingle Co.

_____

_____

_____

_____

_____

YOU MAKE THE CALL: CRITICAL THINKING/ETHICAL CASE, #10R-3.

_____

_____

_____

_____

_____

_____

_____

_____

_____

_____

CONTINUING PROBLEM

ELDORADO COMPUTER CENTRE
PURCHASES JOURNAL

Page 1

Date	Account Credited	Post Ref.	Accounts Payable Cr.	Purchases Dr.	Sundry		
					Account Name	Post Ref.	Amount Dr.

ELDORADO COMPUTER CENTRE
PAYMENTS JOURNAL

Page 1

Date	Chq. No.	Account Debited	Post Ref.	Sundry Dr.	Accounts Payable Dr.	Purchases Discounts Cr.	Cash Cr.

ELDORADO COMPUTER CENTRE
GENERAL JOURNAL

Page 10

Date	Account Title and Description	Post Ref.	Dr.	Cr.

CONTINUING PROBLEM

NOTE: Remember to re-post the entries from Chapter 9.

ELDORADO COMPUTER CENTRE
PARTIAL GENERAL LEDGER

NAME: __CASH__ ACCOUNT NO. ____1000____

Date 2008		Explanation	Post Ref.	Debit	Credit	D R C R	Balance
Jan	1	Balance	✔			Dr	1 1 0 8 4 7

NAME: __PREPAID RENT__ ACCOUNT NO. ____1025____

Date 2008		Explanation	Post Ref.	Debit	Credit	D R C R	Balance
Jan	1	Balance	✔			Dr	1 6 0 0 0 0

NAME: __SUPPLIES__ ACCOUNT NO. ____1030____

Date 2008		Explanation	Post Ref.	Debit	Credit	D R C R	Balance
Jan	1	Balance	✔			Dr	4 5 0 0 0

NAME: __ACCOUNTS PAYABLE__ ACCOUNT NO. ____2000____

Date 2008		Explanation	Post Ref.	Debit	Credit	D R C R	Balance
Jan	1	Balance	✔			Cr	1 0 1 3 0 0

NAME: __INCOME TAX PAYABLE__ ACCOUNT NO. ____2020____

Date 2008		Explanation	Post Ref.	Debit	Credit	D R C R	Balance
Jan	1	Balance	✔			Cr	3 6 0 7 0

CONTINUING PROBLEM

ELDORADO COMPUTER CENTRE
PARTIAL GENERAL LEDGER

NAME: __CPP PAYABLE_____ ACCOUNT NO. ___2030___

Date 2008		Explanation	Post Ref.	Debit	Credit	D R C R	Balance
Jan	1	Balance	✔			Cr	2 4 4 7 4

NAME: __EI PAYABLE_____ ACCOUNT NO. ___2040___

Date 2008		Explanation	Post Ref.	Debit	Credit	D R C R	Balance
Jan	1	Balance	✔			Cr	1 4 3 1 8

NAME: __WAGES EXPENSE_____ ACCOUNT NO. ___5110___

Date 2008		Explanation	Post Ref.	Debit	Credit	D R C R	Balance
Jan	1	Balance	✔			Dr	6 0 3 5 0 0

NAME: __PURCHASES_____ ACCOUNT NO. ___5600___

Date	Explanation	Post Ref.	Debit	Credit	D R C R	Balance

NAME: __PURCHASES RETURNS AND ALLOWANCES_____ ACCOUNT NO. ___5610___

Date	Explanation	Post Ref.	Debit	Credit	D R C R	Balance

NAME: __PURCHASES DISCOUNTS_____ ACCOUNT NO. ___5620___

Date	Explanation	Post Ref.	Debit	Credit	D R C R	Balance

CONTINUING PROBLEM

PARTIAL ACCOUNTS PAYABLE SUBSIDIARY LEDGER

NAME   ALPHA OFFICE CO.   A1

ADDRESS   121 WHITEMUD FREEWAY, EDMONTON, AB T6T 2Z1

Date 2008		Explanation	Post Ref.	Debit	Credit	Cr. Balance
Jan	1	Balance	✔			3 1 8 00

NAME   CITY NEWSPAPER   C2

ADDRESS   10098 EDMONTON WAY, EDMONTON, AB T5A 9S2

Date 2008		Explanation	Post Ref.	Debit	Credit	Cr. Balance
Jan	1	Balance	✔			4 8 0 00

NAME   COMPUTER CONNECTION   C3

ADDRESS   2400, 4421 16 AVENUE, EDMONTON, AB T6R 1A1

Date 2008		Explanation	Post Ref.	Debit	Credit	Cr. Balance
Jan	1	Balance	✔			0

NAME   MULTI SYSTEMS, INC.   M1

ADDRESS   310 N. ESCONDIDO BLVD., EDMONTON, AB T6G 1P1

Date 2008		Explanation	Post Ref.	Debit	Credit	Cr. Balance
Jan.	1	Balance	✔			0

CONTINUING PROBLEM

PARTIAL ACCOUNTS PAYABLE SUBSIDIARY LEDGER

NAME   OFFICE DEPOT   O1

ADDRESS   43 ESCONDIDO AVENUE, EDMONTON, AB T6G 9T9

Date 2008		Explanation	Post Ref.	Debit	Credit	Cr. Balance
Jan	1	Balance	✔			5 0 0 0

NAME   WEST BELL CANADA   W1

ADDRESS   10149 EDMONTON WAY, EDMONTON, AB T5A 9T1

Date 2008		Explanation	Post Ref.	Debit	Credit	Cr. Balance
Jan	1	Balance	✔			1 6 5 0 0

ELDORADO COMPUTER CENTRE

SCHEDULE OF ACCOUNTS PAYABLE

JANUARY 31, 2008

CHAPTER 10
CHAPTER SUMMARY TEST

Part A

Fill in the blank(s) to complete the statement.

1. Accounts Payable represents a potential cash _____ .
2. Individual accounts payable ledger accounts are updated _____.
3. Purchases are added to the cost of _____ _____ .
4. F.O.B. destination means the _____ covers the shipping cost.
5. A journal column total which is never posted is the _____ total.
6. The purchase returns and allowances account has a _____ balance.
7. Purchases represent merchandise for _____ to customers.
8. In the general ledger, the controlling account for the accounts payable ledger is called _____ _____ .
9. A debit memo means the buyer owes _____ money, as merchandise is being returned or an allowance received.
10. The balance in the Accounts Payable controlling account should equal the total of all the accounts payable ledger accounts _____ _____ _____ _____ .
11. The (✔) in the reference column indicates that the _____ _____ _____ has been updated.
12. Purchases Returns and Allowances is increased by a _____ .
13. A debit memorandum issued or a credit memorandum received results in a _____ to Accounts Payable and a _____ to Purchase Returns and Allowances.
14. GST is a _____ _____ tax.
15. List price - trade discount = _____ _____ .
16. The purchases journal minimizes certain repetitive _____ .
17. The total of the purchase discount column is posted at the _____ _____ _____ _____ to the general ledger.
18. After a company inspects received shipments, a _____ _____ is prepared.
19. The cash payments journal records transactions that require a _____ to the cash account.
20. Purchases Discounts is a(n) _____ account.
21. The document which provides the purchasing department with the information to prepare a purchase order is called a _____ _____ .
22. GST paid is _____ from GST collected to arrive at the net amount due.

Part B   *(Note that the numbers used are for illustration only and do not necessarily cross-add.)*

From the following chart, complete the statements below:

CASH PAYMENTS JOURNAL

Description of Payment	Post Ref.	Sundry Dr.	Accounts Payable Dr.	GST Prepaid Dr.	Other Expense Dr.	Purchases Dr.	Purchases Discount Cr.	Cash Cr.
Cash Purchase				2 2 22	1 1 11	4 4 44		5 5 55
Payment on account			8 8 88				7 77	6 6 66
Equipment purchased		8 8 8 88		1 1 1 11				9 9 9 99
Totals		1 1 1 1 11	2 2 2 2 22	3 3 3 3 33	4 4 4 4 44	5 5 5 5 55	6 6 6 6 66	7 7 7 7 77

1. EXAMPLE: 1,111.11 is never posted.
2. 2,222.22 is posted to _____ _____ , the controlling account in the general ledger at the end of the month.
3. 3,333.33 is posted to _____ _____ at the end of the month.
4. 4,444.44 is a _____ total, posted to an _____ account.
5. 6,666.66 has a _____ balance that is posted to Purchases Discount in the general ledger at the end of the month.
6. 7,777.77 is posted _____ _____ _____ to the cash account in the general ledger.
7. 66.66 should _____ _____ _____ , because the total will be posted to the Cash account in the general ledger at the end of the month.
8. 7.77 is _____ _____ during the month.
9. 88.88 is _____ recorded to the accounts payable ledger during the month.
10. 44.44 is _____ _____ during the month, because the total of this column is posted at the end of the month to Purchases in the general ledger.
11. 888.88 is posted to the _____ _____ during the month, as the total of sundry is never posted.

Part C

Answer true or false to the following statements:

1. The purchases journal records only the purchase of merchandise.
2. Purchases Discounts result from paying for purchases within the discount period.
3. The balance in Accounts Payable, the controlling account, should equal the sum of all individual payable ledger accounts at the end of the month.
4. The purchases account is a contra-expense of goods sold account.
5. F.O.B. shipping point means the seller is responsible to cover shipping costs.
6. Freight-In is added to the cost of goods sold.
7. Purchases Discounts are taken on GST amounts.

8. The cash payments journal records outgoing cash.
9. On receiving a purchase order, the seller issues a sales invoice.
10. A purchase requisition is completed before a purchase order.
11. The normal balance of Purchases Discounts is a debit.
12. Returned purchases by a buyer results in a decrease in Purchases Returns and Allowances.
13. On receiving a debit memorandum, the seller will usually issue a credit memorandum.
14. Credit memoranda are always recorded in the general journal.
15. Cash sales are recorded in the cash payments journal.
16. Buyers will occasionally issue a debit memorandum to sellers.
17. A seller's sales discount on sales is the buyer's purchases discount.
18. Freight-In records the amount of shipping costs incurred in bringing merchandise into the store.
19. Trade discounts occur because of timely payments of one's bills.
20. Buying of equipment on account is usually recorded in the general journal.

SOLUTIONS TO CHAPTER SUMMARY TEST

Part A

1. outflow
2. daily
3. goods sold
4. vendor (shipper)
5. sundry
6. credit
7. resale
8. Accounts Payable
9. less
10. at end of month
11. Accounts Payable Ledger
12. credit
13. debit, credit
14. value added
15. selling price
16. postings
17. end of the month
18. receiving report
19. credit
20. contra-expense
21. purchase requisition
22. subtracted

Part B

1. never posted
2. Accounts Payable
3. GST Prepaid
4. debit, expense
5. credit
6. end of month
7. never be posted
8. not posted
9. immediately
10. not posted
11. Equipment account

Part C

1. false
2. true
3. true
4. false
5. false
6. true
7. false
8. true
9. true
10. true
11. false
12. false
13. true
14. false
15. false
16. true
17. true
18. true
19. false
20. false

11

The Synoptic (Combined) Journal

SELF-REVIEW QUIZ 11-1

1. _____ 2. _____ 3. _____ 4. _____ 5. _____

SELF-REVIEW QUIZ 11-2

1. _____ 2. _____ 3. _____ 4. _____ 5. _____

6. _____ 7. _____ 8. _____ 9. _____ 10. _____

FORMS FOR MINI EXERCISES

1. _____

_____

_____

2.

Date	Account Title and Description	Post. Ref.	Dr.	Cr.

3. a. _____ b. _____ c. _____ d. _____ e. _____

4. _____ _____ _____ _____

FORMS FOR EXERCISES

11-1.
_____

11-2.

    a. _____

    _____

    b. _____

    _____

    c. _____

    _____

    d. _____

    _____

11-3.
_____

_____

_____

_____

11-4.
_____

_____

_____

_____

_____

_____

11-5.
_____

_____

_____

_____

_____

_____

PROBLEM 11A-1 or 11B-1.

ANN KUHL, M.D.
SYNOPTIC JOURNAL

Page 1

Date	Explanation	Post Ref.	Sundry		Medical Supplies Dr.	A. Kuhl, Withdrawals Dr.	Cleaning Expense Dr.	Professional Fees Cr.	Chq. No.	Alberta Bank	
			Dr.	Cr.						Dr.	Cr.

PROBLEM 11A-2 or 11B-2.

NATHAN FOX, M.D.
SYNOPTIC JOURNAL

Date		Explanation	Post Ref.	Bank of Regina			Chq. No.	Professional Fees Cr.
				Dr.		Cr.		
May	1	Balance	✔	8 0 0 0 0 0				8 9 0 0 0 0

PROBLEM 11A-2 or 11B-2, Cont.

NATHAN FOX, M.D.
SYNOPTIC JOURNAL

Page 14

| Salaries Expense Dr. | Payroll Deductions | | | Medical Supplies Dr. | Sundry | |
	Income Tax Payable Cr.	CPP Payable Cr.	EI Payable Cr.		Dr.	Cr.
1 5 0 0 0 0				6 0 0 0 0	5 0 0 0 0	1 7 0 0 0 0

PROBLEM 11A-3 or 11B-3.

DEBRA CLARK, M.D.
SYNOPTIC JOURNAL

Date	Explanation	Chq. No.	Post Ref.	Sundry Dr.	Sundry Cr.	Cash Dr.	Cash Cr.

PROBLEM 11A-4 OR 11B-4.

Please use the form in the fold-out section at the end of this study guide

PROBLEM 11A-3 or 11B-3, Cont.

DEBRA CLARK, M.D.
SYNOPTIC JOURNAL

Page 1

Accounts Receivable		Accounts Payable		Office Equipment Dr.	Medical Fees Cr.
Dr.	Cr.	Dr.	Cr.		

PROBLEM 11A-4 or 11B-4, Cont.

ACCOUNTS RECEIVABLE LEDGER

NAME   PETE DALEY

ADDRESS   155 MAIN STREET, DAUPHIN, MB R7N 3T4

Date	Explanation	Post Ref.	Debit	Credit	Dr. Balance

NAME   ALICE SMALL

ADDRESS   67 MAPLE STREET, DAUPHIN, MB R7N 7T9

Date	Explanation	Post Ref.	Debit	Credit	Dr. Balance

ACCOUNTS PAYABLE LEDGER

NAME   FRESH AIR COMPANY

ADDRESS   159 PORTSMOUTH CRESC., BRANDON, MB R7B 4P1

Date	Explanation	Post Ref.	Debit	Credit	Cr. Balance

NAME   RAL COMPANY

ADDRESS   416 KINGSWAY AVE., DAUPHIN, MB R7N 1C1

Date	Explanation	Post Ref.	Debit	Credit	Cr. Balance

NAME   ROLE COMPANY

ADDRESS   188 FRANKLIN AVE., BRANDON, MB R7A 2A1

Date	Explanation	Post Ref.	Debit	Credit	Cr. Balance

PROBLEM 11A-4 or 11B-4, Cont.

PARTIAL GENERAL LEDGER

NAME: __CASH__ ACCOUNT NO. ____111____

Date		Explanation	Post Ref	Debit	Credit	D R C R	Balance

NAME: __ACCOUNTS RECEIVABLE__ ACCOUNT NO. ____112____

Date		Explanation	Post Ref	Debit	Credit	D R C R	Balance

NAME: __PREPAID INSURANCE__ ACCOUNT NO. ____113____

Date		Explanation	Post Ref	Debit	Credit	D R C R	Balance

NAME: __PREPAID GST__ ACCOUNT NO. ____115____

Date		Explanation	Post Ref	Debit	Credit	D R C R	Balance

NAME: __CLEANING EQUIPMENT__ ACCOUNT NO. ____121____

Date		Explanation	Post Ref	Debit	Credit	D R C R	Balance

NAME: __ACCOUNTS PAYABLE__ ACCOUNT NO. ____211____

Date		Explanation	Post Ref	Debit	Credit	D R C R	Balance

NAME: __BANK LOAN PAYABLE__ ACCOUNT NO. ____212____

Date		Explanation	Post Ref	Debit	Credit	D R C R	Balance

PROBLEM 11A-4 or 11B-4, Cont.

PARTIAL GENERAL LEDGER, Cont.

NAME: **GST PAYABLE**   **ACCOUNT NO.** _____ **215**

Date	Explanation	Post Ref	Debit	Credit	D R C R	Balance

NAME: **PST PAYABLE**   **ACCOUNT NO.** _____ **217**

Date	Explanation	Post Ref	Debit	Credit	D R C R	Balance

NAME: **B. SULLIVAN, CAPITAL**   **ACCOUNT NO.** _____ **311**

Date	Explanation	Post Ref	Debit	Credit	D R C R	Balance

NAME: **CLEANING SALES**   **ACCOUNT NO.** _____ **411**

Date	Explanation	Post Ref	Debit	Credit	D R C R	Balance

NAME: **SALES DISCOUNTS**   **ACCOUNT NO.** _____ **412**

Date	Explanation	Post Ref	Debit	Credit	D R C R	Balance

NAME: **PURCHASES**   **ACCOUNT NO.** _____ **511**

Date	Explanation	Post Ref	Debit	Credit	D R C R	Balance

NAME: **PURCHASES RETURNS AND ALLOWANCES**   **ACCOUNT NO.** _____ **512**

Date	Explanation	Post Ref	Debit	Credit	D R C R	Balance

NAME: **PURCHASES DISCOUNTS**   **ACCOUNT NO.** _____ **513**

Date	Explanation	Post Ref	Debit	Credit	D R C R	Balance
					Cr	

PROBLEM 11A-4 or 11B-4, Concluded

Accounts Receivable Ledger Listing:

_____ _____
_____ _____
_____ _____
_____ _____
_____ _____

Accounts Payable Ledger Listing:

_____ _____
_____ _____
_____ _____
_____ _____
_____ _____

Proof of Synoptic Journal:

	Debit	Credit
_____	_____	_____
_____	_____	_____
_____	_____	_____
_____	_____	_____
_____	_____	_____
_____	_____	_____
_____	_____	_____
_____	_____	_____
_____	_____	_____
_____	_____	_____
_____	_____	_____
_____	_____	_____
_____	_____	_____
_____	_____	_____
_____	_____	_____
_____	_____	_____
_____	_____	_____

PROBLEM 11C-1.

SYNOPTIC JOURNAL

Page 1

Date	Explanation	Post Ref.	Sundry Dr.	Sundry Cr.	Medical Supplies Dr.	J. Reid, Withdrawals Dr.	Cleaning Expense Dr.	Professional Fees Cr.	Chq. No.	Bank of New Brunswick Dr.	Bank of New Brunswick Cr.

PROBLEM 11C-2.

SYNOPTIC JOURNAL

Date		Explanation	Post Ref.	Bank of Vancouver Dr.		Bank of Vancouver Cr.		Chq. No.	Professional Fees Cr.	
June	1	Balance	✔	9 0 0 0 00					1 3 2 0 0 00	

PROBLEM 11C-2, Cont.

SYNOPTIC JOURNAL

Salaries Expense Dr.	Payroll Deductions			Dental Supplies Dr.	Sundry	
	Income Tax Payable Cr.	CPP Cr.	EI Cr.		Dr.	Cr.
5 5 0 0 00				9 0 0 00	6 5 0 00	2 8 5 0 00

PROBLEM 11C-3.

SYNOPTIC JOURNAL

Date	Explanation	Chq. No.	Post Ref.	Sundry		Cash	
				Dr.	Cr.	Dr.	Cr.

PROBLEM 11C-4.

Please use the form in the fold-out section at the end of this study guide

11-16

PROBLEM 11C-3, Cont.

Accounts Receivable		Accounts Payable		Office Equipment	Optometric Fees
Dr.	Cr.	Dr.	Cr.	Dr.	Cr.

PROBLEM 11C-4, Cont.

ACCOUNTS RECEIVABLE LEDGER

NAME   J. FRESNEL

ADDRESS   2314 ISLAND HIGHWAY, DUNCAN BC V8L 8R2

Date	Explanation	Post Ref.	Debit	Credit	Dr. Balance

NAME   VINCE LOMBARDI

ADDRESS   1124 CEDAR AVE., DUNCAN BC V9L 0K0

Date	Explanation	Post Ref.	Debit	Credit	Dr. Balance

ACCOUNTS PAYABLE LEDGER

NAME   APEX COMPANY

ADDRESS   46 FIR ST., VANCOUVER, BC V6N 2L7

Date	Explanation	Post Ref.	Debit	Credit	Cr. Balance

NAME   COLTER & CO.

ADDRESS   12420 - 50 ST., EDMONTON AB T5M 4R1

Date	Explanation	Post Ref.	Debit	Credit	Cr. Balance

NAME   SATTRAP CO.

ADDRESS   711 KINGSWAY AVE., VANCOUVER BC V7A 2L0

Date	Explanation	Post Ref.	Debit	Credit	Cr. Balance

PROBLEM 11C-4, Cont.

PARTIAL GENERAL LEDGER

NAME: __CASH__   ACCOUNT NO. ___111___

Date	Explanation	Post Ref	Debit	Credit	D R C R	Balance

NAME: __ACCOUNTS RECEIVABLE__   ACCOUNT NO. ___112___

Date	Explanation	Post Ref	Debit	Credit	D R C R	Balance

NAME: __PREPAID INSURANCE__   ACCOUNT NO. ___113___

Date	Explanation	Post Ref	Debit	Credit	D R C R	Balance

NAME: __PREPAID GST__   ACCOUNT NO. ___115___

Date	Explanation	Post Ref	Debit	Credit	D R C R	Balance

NAME: __REPAIR EQUIPMENT__   ACCOUNT NO. ___121___

Date	Explanation	Post Ref	Debit	Credit	D R C R	Balance

NAME: __ACCOUNTS PAYABLE__   ACCOUNT NO. ___211___

Date	Explanation	Post Ref	Debit	Credit	D R C R	Balance

NAME: __BANK LOAN PAYABLE__   ACCOUNT NO. ___212___

Date	Explanation	Post Ref	Debit	Credit	D R C R	Balance

PROBLEM 11C-4, Cont. | PARTIAL GENERAL LEDGER, Cont. |

NAME: GST PAYABLE   ACCOUNT NO. ___215___

Date	Explanation	Post Ref	Debit	Credit	DR CR	Balance

NAME: PST PAYABLE   ACCOUNT NO. ___217___

Date	Explanation	Post Ref	Debit	Credit	DR CR	Balance

NAME: F. SCHRAGGE, CAPITAL   ACCOUNT NO. ___311___

Date	Explanation	Post Ref	Debit	Credit	DR CR	Balance

NAME: F. SCHRAGGE, WITHDRAWALS   ACCOUNT NO. ___312___

Date	Explanation	Post Ref	Debit	Credit	DR CR	Balance

NAME: APPLIANCE SALES   ACCOUNT NO. ___411___

Date	Explanation	Post Ref	Debit	Credit	DR CR	Balance

NAME: SALES DISCOUNTS   ACCOUNT NO. ___412___

Date	Explanation	Post Ref	Debit	Credit	DR CR	Balance

NAME: REPAIRS REVENUE   ACCOUNT NO. ___413___

Date	Explanation	Post Ref	Debit	Credit	DR CR	Balance

NAME: PURCHASES   ACCOUNT NO. ___511___

Date	Explanation	Post Ref	Debit	Credit	DR CR	Balance

PROBLEM 11C-4, Concluded

NAME: __PURCHASES DISCOUNTS__   ACCOUNT NO. ___513___

Date	Explanation	Post. Ref.	Debit	Credit	D R C R	Balance

Accounts Receivable Ledger Listing:

_____   _____
_____   _____
_____   _____
_____   _____
_____   _____

Accounts Payable Ledger Listing:

_____   _____
_____   _____
_____   _____
_____   _____
_____   _____

Proof of Synoptic Journal:

                                          Debit   Credit

_____   _____   _____
_____   _____   _____
_____   _____   _____
_____   _____   _____
_____   _____   _____
_____   _____   _____
_____   _____   _____
_____   _____   _____
_____   _____   _____
_____   _____   _____
_____   _____   _____
_____   _____   _____
_____   _____   _____
_____   _____   _____
_____   _____   _____
_____   _____   _____
_____   _____   _____
_____   _____   _____
_____   _____   _____

REAL WORLD APPLICATIONS, #11R-1.

REAL WORLD APPLICATIONS, #11R-2 and 11R-3.

_____
_____
_____
_____
_____
_____
_____
_____
_____
_____
_____
_____
_____
_____
_____
_____
_____
_____
_____
_____
_____
_____
_____
_____
_____
_____
_____
_____
_____
_____
_____
_____
_____
_____
_____
_____
_____
_____
_____
_____
_____
_____
_____
_____

CONTINUING PROBLEM

ELDORADO COMPUTER CENTRE
SYNOPTIC JOURNAL

Date	Explanation	Chq. No.	Post Ref.	Sundry		Cash	
				Dr.	Cr.	Dr.	Cr.

CONTINUING PROBLEM, Cont'd.

Page 1

Accounts Receivable				Accounts Payable				Service Revenue Cr.	Sales Cr.
Dr.		Cr.		Dr.		Cr.			

CONTINUING PROBLEM, Cont.

ELDORADO COMPUTER CENTRE
GENERAL LEDGER

NAME: __CASH__ ACCOUNT NO. ___1000___

Date 2008		Explanation	Post Ref	Debit	Credit	DR CR	Balance
Jan	31	Balance Forward	✔			Dr	1 0 6 5 4 8

NAME: __PETTY CASH__ ACCOUNT NO. ___1010___

Date 2008		Explanation	Post Ref	Debit	Credit	DR CR	Balance
Jan	31	Balance Forward	✔			Dr	1 0 0 0 0

NAME: __ACCOUNTS RECEIVABLE__ ACCOUNT NO. ___1020___

Date 2008		Explanation	Post Ref	Debit	Credit	DR CR	Balance
Jan	31	Balance Forward	✔			Dr	1 1 9 5 0 0 0

NAME: __PREPAID INSURANCE__ ACCOUNT NO. ___1023___

Date 2008		Explanation	Post Ref	Debit	Credit	DR CR	Balance

NAME: __PREPAID RENT__ ACCOUNT NO. ___1025___

Date 2008		Explanation	Post Ref	Debit	Credit	DR CR	Balance
Jan	31	Balance Forward	✔			Dr	2 8 0 0 0 0

NAME: __SUPPLIES__ ACCOUNT NO. ___1030___

Date 2008		Explanation	Post Ref	Debit	Credit	DR CR	Balance
Jan	31	Balance Forward	✔			Dr	7 5 0 0 0

CONTINUING PROBLEM, Cont.

ELDORADO COMPUTER CENTRE
GENERAL LEDGER

NAME: **MERCHANDISE INVENTORY**　　　　　ACCOUNT NO. _____ 1040

Date 2008		Explanation	Post Ref	Debit	Credit	DR CR	Balance
Jan	31	Balance Forward	✔			Dr	7 0 0 0 0

NAME: **COMPUTER SHOP EQUIPMENT**　　　　　ACCOUNT NO. _____ 1080

Date 2008		Explanation	Post Ref	Debit	Credit	DR CR	Balance
Jan	31	Balance Forward	✔			Dr	3 8 0 0 0 0

NAME: **ACCUMULATED AMORTIZATION, COMPUTER SHOP EQUIPMENT**　ACCOUNT NO. _____ 1081

Date 2008		Explanation	Post Ref	Debit	Credit	DR CR	Balance
Jan	31	Balance Forward	✔			Cr	9 9 0 0

NAME: **OFFICE EQUIPMENT**　　　　　ACCOUNT NO. _____ 1090

Date 2008		Explanation	Post Ref	Debit	Credit	DR CR	Balance
Jan	31	Balance Forward	✔			Dr	1 0 5 0 0 0

NAME: **ACCUMULATED AMORTIZATION, OFFICE EQUIPMENT**　　ACCOUNT NO. _____ 1091

Date 2008		Explanation	Post Ref	Debit	Credit	DR CR	Balance
Jan	31	Balance Forward	✔			Cr	2 0 0 0

NAME: **ACCOUNTS PAYABLE**　　　　　ACCOUNT NO. _____ 2000

Date 2008		Explanation	Post Ref	Debit	Credit	DR CR	Balance
Jan	31	Balance Forward	✔			Cr	8 9 5 0 0

CONTINUING PROBLEM, Cont.

ELDORADO COMPUTER CENTRE
GENERAL LEDGER

NAME: WAGES PAYABLE ACCOUNT NO. 2010

Date 2008		Explanation	Post Ref	Debit	Credit	D R C R	Balance
Jan	31	Balance Forward	✔				─0─

NAME: INCOME TAX PAYABLE ACCOUNT NO. 2020

Date 2008		Explanation	Post Ref	Debit	Credit	D R C R	Balance
Jan	31	Balance Forward	✔				─0─

NAME: CPP PAYABLE ACCOUNT NO. 2030

Date 2008		Explanation	Post Ref	Debit	Credit	D R C R	Balance
Jan	31	Balance Forward	✔				─0─

NAME: EI PAYABLE ACCOUNT NO. 2040

Date 2008		Explanation	Post Ref	Debit	Credit	D R C R	Balance
Jan	31	Balance Forward	✔				─0─

NAME: T. FREEDMAN, CAPITAL ACCOUNT NO. 3000

Date 2008		Explanation	Post Ref	Debit	Credit	D R C R	Balance
Jan	31	Balance Forward	✔			Cr	7 4 0 6 0 0

NAME: T. FREEDMAN, WITHDRAWALS ACCOUNT NO. 3010

Date 2008		Explanation	Post Ref	Debit	Credit	D R C R	Balance
Jan	31	Balance Forward	✔			Dr	2 0 1 5 0 0

CONTINUING PROBLEM, Cont.

ELDORADO COMPUTER CENTRE
GENERAL LEDGER

NAME: __INCOME SUMMARY__   ACCOUNT NO. ____3020__

Date 2008	Explanation	Post Ref	Debit	Credit	D R C R	Balance

NAME: __SERVICE REVENUE__   ACCOUNT NO. ____4000__

Date 2008		Explanation	Post Ref	Debit	Credit	D R C R	Balance
Jan	31	Balance Forward	✔			Cr	2 7 2 5 0 00

NAME: __SALES__   ACCOUNT NO. ____4010__

Date 2008		Explanation	Post Ref	Debit	Credit	D R C R	Balance
Jan	31	Balance Forward	✔			Cr	9 7 0 0 00

NAME: __SALES RETURNS AND ALLOWANCES__   ACCOUNT NO. ____4020__

Date 2008		Explanation	Post Ref	Debit	Credit	D R C R	Balance
Jan	31	Balance Forward	✔			Dr	4 0 0 00

NAME: __SALES DISCOUNTS__   ACCOUNT NO. ____4030__

Date 2008		Explanation	Post Ref	Debit	Credit	D R C R	Balance
Jan	31	Balance Forward	✔			Dr	2 2 0 00

NAME: __ADVERTISING EXPENSE__   ACCOUNT NO. ____5010__

Date 2008		Explanation	Post Ref	Debit	Credit	D R C R	Balance
Jan	31	Balance Forward	✔			Dr	4 8 0 00

CONTINUING PROBLEM, Cont.

ELDORADO COMPUTER CENTRE
GENERAL LEDGER

NAME: __RENT EXPENSE_____ ACCOUNT NO. ____5020__

Date 2008		Explanation	Post Ref	Debit	Credit	DR CR	Balance
Jan	31	Balance Forward	✔				0

NAME: __UTILITIES EXPENSE_____ ACCOUNT NO. ____5030__

Date 2008		Explanation	Post Ref	Debit	Credit	DR CR	Balance
Jan	31	Balance Forward	✔			Dr	4 8 6 0 0

NAME: __PHONE EXPENSE_____ ACCOUNT NO. ____5040__

Date 2008		Explanation	Post Ref	Debit	Credit	DR CR	Balance
Jan	31	Balance Forward	✔			Dr	3 1 5 0 0

NAME: __SUPPLIES EXPENSE_____ ACCOUNT NO. ____5050__

Date 2008		Explanation	Post Ref	Debit	Credit	DR CR	Balance
Jan	31	Balance Forward	✔				0

NAME: __INSURANCE EXPENSE_____ ACCOUNT NO. ____5060__

Date 2008		Explanation	Post Ref	Debit	Credit	DR CR	Balance
Jan	31	Balance Forward	✔				0

NAME: __POSTAGE EXPENSE_____ ACCOUNT NO. ____5070__

Date 2008		Explanation	Post Ref	Debit	Credit	DR CR	Balance
Jan	31	Balance Forward	✔			Dr	2 5 0 0

11-30   © 2006 Pearson Canada All Rights Reserved

CONTINUING PROBLEM, Cont.

ELDORADO COMPUTER CENTRE
GENERAL LEDGER

NAME: __AMORTIZATION EXPENSE, COMPUTER SHOP EQUIPMENT__   ACCOUNT NO. ___5080___

Date 2008		Explanation	Post Ref	Debit	Credit	D R C R	Balance
Jan.	31	Balance Forward	✔				−0−

NAME: __AMORTIZATION EXPENSE, OFFICE EQUIPMENT__   ACCOUNT NO. ___5090___

Date 2008		Explanation	Post Ref	Debit	Credit	D R C R	Balance
Jan	31	Balance Forward	✔				−0−

NAME: __MISCELLANEOUS EXPENSE__   ACCOUNT NO. ___5100___

Date 2008		Explanation	Post Ref	Debit	Credit	D R C R	Balance
Jan	31	Balance Forward	✔			Dr	1 0 0 0

NAME: __WAGES EXPENSE__   ACCOUNT NO. ___5110___

Date 2008		Explanation	Post Ref	Debit	Credit	D R C R	Balance
Jan	31	Balance Forward	✔			Dr	1 1 6 5 8 7

NAME: __PAYROLL BENEFITS EXPENSE__   ACCOUNT NO. ___5120___

Date 2008		Explanation	Post Ref	Debit	Credit	D R C R	Balance
Jan	31	Balance Forward	✔			Dr	4 1 2 1 5

NAME: __INTEREST EXPENSE__   ACCOUNT NO. ___5130___

Date 2008		Explanation	Post Ref	Debit	Credit	D R C R	Balance

CONTINUING PROBLEM, Cont.

ELDORADO COMPUTER CENTRE
GENERAL LEDGER

NAME: _BAD DEBTS EXPENSE_   ACCOUNT NO. ___5140___

Date 2008		Explanation	Post Ref	Debit	Credit	DR CR	Balance

NAME: _PURCHASES_   ACCOUNT NO. ___5600___

Date 2008		Explanation	Post Ref	Debit	Credit	DR CR	Balance
Jan	31	Balance Forward	✔			Dr	9 5 0 00

NAME: _PURCHASES RETURNS AND ALLOWANCES_   ACCOUNT NO. ___5610___

Date 2008		Explanation	Post Ref	Debit	Credit	DR CR	Balance
Jan	31	Balance Forward	✔			Cr	1 0 0 00

NAME: _PURCHASES DISCOUNTS_   ACCOUNT NO. ___5620___

Date 2008		Explanation	Post Ref	Debit	Credit	DR CR	Balance
Jan	31	Balance Forward	✔			Cr	1 7 50

NAME: _FREIGHT IN_   ACCOUNT NO. ___5630___

Date 2008		Explanation	Post Ref	Debit	Credit	DR CR	Balance

CONTINUING PROBLEM, Cont.

ELDORADO COMPUTER CENTRE

TRIAL BALANCE

FEBRUARY 29, 2008

CHAPTER 11
CHAPTER SUMMARY TEST

Part A

Fill in the blank(s) to complete the statements.

1. Under the modified cash basis, long-lived assets as well as items like insurance premiums and supplies will be_____ .

2. In a Synoptic Journal that uses accrual accounting, _____ and _____ _____ are recorded in the sales column.

3. In the cash basis accounting the owner's share of CPP as well as EI is recorded when they are _____ .

4. A service company with no inventories might use the _____ _____ of accounting.

5. When using the modified cash basis , there are no titles in the chart of accounts for Accounts _____ or Accounts _____ .

6. A strictly cash basis approach may result in the _____ _____ being distorted.

7. A combination of cash and accrual methods is known as the _____ _____ of accounting.

8. A synoptic journal that uses accrual accounting will have columns for Accounts _____ and Accounts _____ .

9. _____ and _____ entries could be recorded in the sundry columns of a synoptic journal.

10. In the modified cash system, _____ records can be employed to keep track of information about receivables or payables.

Part B

From the information below, indicate what account and posting effect will result from the following transactions. Be sure to do both the debit and the credit portions. This company uses the accrual basis of accounting.

CHART OF ACCOUNTS

ASSETS
Cash
Accounts Receivable
Prepaid Rent
Cleaning Equipment

LIABILITIES
Accounts Payable

OWNER'S EQUITY
M. Owens, Capital
REVENUE
Cleaning Fees Earned
EXPENSES
Salary Expense
Advertising Expense
Repairs Expense

Date	Explanation	Chq.	Post Ref.	Sundry Dr.	Sundry Cr.	Cash Dr.	Cash Cr.	Accounts Receivable Dr.	Accounts Receivable Cr.	Accounts Payable Dr.	Accounts Payable Cr.	Cleaning Equipment Dr.	Cleaning Fees Cr.

a. Posted immediately to general ledger. The total of the sundry column is not posted.
b. Recorded immediately to accounts receivable ledger. The sum of the column will be posted at the end of month to controlling account.
c. Recorded immediately to account payable ledger. The sum of the column will be posted at end of month to controlling account.
d. Not posted at this time; the total of column will be posted at end of month.

		Dr.	Account	Transactions	Cr.	Account
EXAMPLE:	1	a	Prepaid Rent	Paid three months rent in advance	d	Cash
	2			Earned cleaning fees on account		
	3			Bought cleaning equipment on account		
	4			Paid salaries		
	5			Paid advertising bill		
	6			Cleaning fees received		
	7			Received half of cleaning fees previously earned from past sales		
	8			Purchase cleaning equipment for cash		
	9			Received bill for repairs to cleaning equipment		

Part C

Answer true or false to the following statements.

1. In a modified cash system, there are no subsidiary ledgers for accounts receivable or accounts payable.
2. In the cash basis system, the owner's share of CPP as well as EI is recorded when they are paid.
3. A synoptic journal is used mainly by large businesses.
4. The totals of the sundry column of the synoptic journal are never posted.
5. The hybrid method is another name for accrual accounting.
6. The prepaid GST/HST account cannot be used in the hybrid method.
7. Payroll tax expense is a liability.
8. The hybrid method requires no adjusting entries.
9. Closing entries are always prepared in the general journal no matter whether a synoptic journal is used or not.
10. Synoptic journals cannot be used in an accrual accounting approach.
11. Notes payable in a hybrid method result from buying inexpensive supplies.
12. A doctor would not use a synoptic journal.
13. Headings of synoptic journals are dictated by Income Tax Act regulations.
14. Insurance premiums are never adjusted in a modified cash system.
15. A (✔ in a synoptic journal using accrual accounting means a subsidiary ledger has been updated.
16. Synoptic journals are usually used with additional special journals.
17. Trial balances are obtained directly from the synoptic journal.
18. In a cash basis approach, there are account titles for CPP and EI.
19. Long-lived assets are not depreciated in a modified cash system.
20. A strict cash basis of accounting would distort financial reports.

CHAPTER 11
SOLUTIONS TO CHAPTER SUMMARY TEST

Part A

1. adjusted
2. credit, cash sales
3. paid
4. cash method
5. Receivable, Payable

6. financial reports (statements)
7. hybrid method
8. Payable, Receivable
9. adjusting, closing
10. memorandum (informal)

Part B

	DR. ACCOUNT		CR. ACCOUNT
1.	a	Prepaid rent	d	Cash
2.	b	Accounts Receivable	d	Cleaning Fees
3.	d	Cleaning Equipment	c	Accounts Payable
4.	a	Salaries Expense	d	Cash
5.	a	Advertising Expense	d	Cash
6.	d	Cash	d	Cleaning Fees
7.	d	Cash	b	Accounts Receivable
8.	d	Cleaning Equipment	d	Cash
9.	a	Repairs Expense	c	Accounts Payable

Part C

1. true
2. true
3. false
4. true
5. false
6. false
7. false
8. false
9. false
10. false
11. false
12. false
13. false
14. false
15. true
16. false
17. false
18. false
19. false
20. true

12

Preparing a Worksheet
for a Merchandising Company

SELF-REVIEW QUIZ 12-1

GENERAL JOURNAL

Date	Account Title and Description	Post. Ref.	Dr.	Cr.

SELF-REVIEW QUIZ 12-2

Use a blank, fold-out worksheet which is found at the end of this study guide.

FORMS FOR MINI EXERCISES

1.   **GENERAL JOURNAL**   *Page 1*

Date		Account Title and Description	Post Ref.	Dr.	Cr.
2a.					

2b. _____

3.   *a.* _____   *d.* _____
        b. _____   *e.* _____
        c. _____   *f.* _____

4. _____
_____
_____
_____
_____
_____
_____

5.
A _____ *B* _____ *C* _____ *D* _____ *E* _____ *F* _____

FORMS FOR EXERCISES

12-1.

a. _____

b. _____

c. _____

d. _____

e. _____

f. _____

g. _____

h. _____

12-2.

a. _____
_____
_____

b. _____
_____
_____

c. _____
_____
_____

d. _____
_____
_____

12-3.

Accounts Affected	Category	↑↓	Rules

12-4.

a. _____

b. _____

c. _____

12-5.

Use a blank, fold-out worksheet which is found at the end of this study guide.

END OF CHAPTER PROBLEMS

PROBLEM 12A-1 or 12B-1.

a. Net Sales:

b. Cost of Goods Sold:

c. Gross Profit:

d. Net Income:

PROBLEM 12A-2 OR 12B-2; PROBLEM 12A-3 OR 12B-3; PROBLEM 12A-4 OR 12B-4:

Use a blank, fold-out worksheet which is found at the end of this study guide

PROBLEM 12C-1.

a. Net Sales:

b. Cost of Goods Sold:

c. Gross Profit:

d. Net Income:

PROBLEM 12C-2; PROBLEM 12C-3; PROBLEM 12C-4, and the CONTINUING PROBLEM

Use a blank, fold-out worksheet which is found at the end of this study guide.

REAL WORLD APPLICATIONS, #12R-1, 12R-2, AND 12R-3.

_____
_____
_____
_____
_____
_____
_____
_____
_____
_____
_____
_____
_____
_____
_____
_____
_____
_____
_____
_____
_____
_____
_____
_____
_____
_____
_____
_____
_____
_____
_____
_____
_____
_____
_____
_____
_____
_____
_____
_____

CHAPTER 12
CHAPTER SUMMARY TEST

Part A

Fill in the blank(s) to complete the statement.

1. A continuous record of inventory is not kept in a _____ _____ system.
2. Net sales less cost of goods sold equals _____ _____ .
3. The _____ _____ system keeps a continual track of the quantity and cost of the inventory on hand.
4. In the periodic inventory system, all purchases of merchandise during the period are recorded in the _____ account.
5. Net purchases equals purchases less both _____ _____ _____ _____ as well as_____ _____ .
6. Gross profit minus _____ equals net income.
7. When the periodic system is used, _____ _____ remains unchanged.
8. A liability on the balance sheet which records money received for sale or service not yet performed is called_____ _____ .
9. Purchase discounts _____ the total cost of merchandise sold.
10. The ending inventory of period one becomes the _____ _____ of period two.
11. At the end of a period, the inventory account is _____ .
12. Ending inventory is _____ from the cost of goods available for sale.
13. Freight-In _____ the cost of goods sold.
14. Gross sales less sales discounts and sales returns and allowances equals _____ _____ .
15. Beginning inventory plus net purchases equals _____ _____ _____ _____ _____ _____ .
16. Beginning inventory at the end of the period is assumed to be _____ , and thus a _____ .
17. Sales returns and allowances are used in calculating _____ _____ .
18. Ending inventory represents goods not yet _____ .
19. Net purchases are _____ in the cost of goods available for sale.
20. Purchases are increased by a _____ .

Part B

Answer true or false to the following statements.

1. Unearned Revenue is shown on the income statement.
2. A trial balance can be placed directly on a worksheet.
3. Ending inventory of one period is the beginning inventory of the following period.
4. Beginning and ending inventory figures are combined on a worksheet.
5. Cost of goods sold is decreased by purchases.
6. Unearned Revenue is a liability.
7. Sales Discounts is a temporary account.
8. Ending merchandise inventory can only be found on the balance sheet.
9. Perpetual inventory keeps a continuous record of inventory.
10. Net income always means cash is received.
11. Freight-In is subtracted from cost of goods sold.
12. The adjustment process updates the inventory account.
13. Net purchases is the same as total purchases.
14. Ending merchandise inventory of the current period is found only on the balance sheet.
15. Income Summary is used in the adjustment of merchandise inventory.
16. A merchandise company does not need a cost of goods sold section on the income statement.
17. A perpetual system is often used by companies with low volume and high unit prices.
18. Merchandise inventory that is sold is assumed to be a liability.
19. Merchandise Inventory is an asset.
20. All companies give sale discounts.
21. Purchases reduce the cost of goods sold.
22. The ending inventory is ususally calculated by using an inventory sheet.
23. Merchandise Inventory (beginning) found on the balance sheet from the prior period will also be placed in the cost of goods sold section of the balance sheet.
24. Inventory is taken 12 times per year.
25. Ending inventory increases cost of goods sold.
26. Sales means cash is received right away.
27. Gross profit and net income mean the same.
28. Purchases discounts reduce the cost of goods sold.
29. Ending inventory is only placed in the credit column in the balance sheet section of the worksheet.
30. Purchases replace ending inventory in a periodic system.
31. There are no temporary accounts in a post-closing trial balance.
32. Unearned Storage Fees is a liability.
33. Purchases Discounts are shown in the credit column in the income statement on the worksheet.
34. Beginning inventory is always assumed sold by end of a period if the periodic inventory system is used.
35. Gross sales are shown on the balance sheet.
36. Accumulated Amortization is increased by a debit.
37. Purchases Returns and Allowances is found on a balance sheet.
38. The Sales Returns and Allowances account has a normal balance of a debit.
39. Gross profit plus expenses equals net income.
40. Merchandise Inventory is never listed on a trial balance.

SOLUTIONS TO CHAPTER SUMMARY TEST

Part A

1. periodic inventory
2. Gross Profit
3. perpetual inventory
4. Purchases
5. Purchase Returns and Allowances, Purchases Discounts
6. Expenses
7. Beginning inventory
8. Unearned Revenue
9. reduce
10. beginning inventory
11. adjusted
12. deducted (subtracted)
13. increases
14. Net Sales
15. cost of goods available for sale
16. sold, cost
17. net sales
18. sold
19. included
20. debit

Part B

1. false	11. false	21. false	31. true
2. true	12. true	22. true	32. true
3. true	13. false	23. false	33. true
4. false	14. false	24. false	34. true
5. false	15. true	25. false	35. false
6. true	16. false	26. false	36. false
7. true	17. true	27. false	37. false
8. false	18. false	28. true	38. true
9. true	19. true	29. false	39. false
10. false	20. false	30. false	40. false

13

Completion of the Accounting Cycle for a Merchandising Company

SELF-REVIEW QUIZ 13-1

1. _____
   _____
   _____

SELF-REVIEW QUIZ 13-1, Cont.

2.

_____
_____
_____

3.

_____
_____
_____

SELF-REVIEW QUIZ 13-2

GENERAL JOURNAL

Page 2

Date		Account Title and Description	Post Ref.	Dr.	Cr.

SELF-REVIEW QUIZ 13-3

Situation 1
Situation 2
Situation 3

SELF-REVIEW QUIZ 13-2

FORMS FOR MINI EXERCISES

1. _____
_____
_____
_____

2. _____
_____
_____
_____
_____

3. _____
_____
_____
_____
_____

4. a. _____   f. _____
    b. _____   g. _____
    c. _____   h. _____
    d. _____   i. _____
    e. _____   j. _____

5. a.

GENERAL JOURNAL

Date		Account Title and Description	Post. Ref.	Dr.	Cr.

b. _____

FORMS FOR EXERCISES
COST OF GOODS SOLD

13-1.

_____
_____
_____
_____
_____
_____
_____
_____
_____
_____
_____

13-2.

a. _____
b. _____
c. _____
d. _____
e. _____
f. _____
g. _____

13-3.

A. SLOW CO.
GENERAL JOURNAL   Page 8

Exercises (continued)

13-4.

A. SLOW CO.
BALANCE SHEET
DECEMBER 31, 2007

13-5.

a.

Salaries Expense   Salaries Payable

b.

Salaries Expense   Salaries Payable

c.

Salaries Expense   Cash

PROBLEM 13A-1 or 13B-1.

PORTER'S PANTS CO.

INCOME STATEMENT

FOR THE YEAR ENDED DECEMBER 31, 2006

PROBLEM 13A-2 or 13B-2.

JAMES COMPANY

STATEMENT OF OWNER'S EQUITY

FOR THE YEAR ENDED DECEMBER 31, 2008

PROBLEM 13A-2 or 13B-2, Concluded

JAMES COMPANY

BALANCE SHEET

DECEMBER 31, 2008

PROBLEM 13A-3 or 13B-3.

Use a blank, fold-out worksheet which is located at the end of this study guide.

JAY'S SUPPLIES

INCOME STATEMENT

FOR THE YEAR ENDED DECEMBER 31, 2007

PROBLEM 13A-3 or 13B-3.

JAY'S SUPPLIES

STATEMENT OF OWNER'S EQUITY

FOR THE YEAR ENDED DECEMBER 31, 2007

13-12

PROBLEM 13A-3 or 13B-3, Cont.

JAY'S SUPPLIES

BALANCE SHEET

DECEMBER 31, 2007

PROBLEM 13A-3 or 13B-3, Cont.

JAY'S SUPPLIES
GENERAL JOURNAL   *Page 2*

Date	Account Title and Description	Post Ref.	Dr.	Cr.

PROBLEM 13A-3 or 13B-3, Cont.

JAY'S SUPPLIES
GENERAL JOURNAL   *Page 3*

Date	Account Title and Description	Post Ref.	Dr.	Cr.

PROBLEM 13A-4 or 13B-4.

Use a blank, fold-out worksheet which is located at the end of this study guide.

CALLAHAN LUMBER

INCOME STATEMENT

FOR THE YEAR ENDED DECEMBER 31, 2007

PROBLEM 13A-4 or 13B-4, Cont.

CALLAHAN LUMBER

STATEMENT OF OWNER'S EQUITY

FOR THE YEAR ENDED DECEMBER 31, 2007

PROBLEM 13A-4 or 13B-4, Cont.

CALLAHAN LUMBER

BALANCE SHEET

DECEMBER 31, 2007

PROBLEM 13A-4 or 13B-4, Cont.

CALLAHAN LUMBER
GENERAL JOURNAL

Page 2

Date	Account Title and Description	Post Ref.	Dr.	Cr.

PROBLEM 13A-4 or 13B-4, Cont.

13-19

PROBLEM 13A-4 or 13B-4, Cont.

CALLAHAN LUMBER
GENERAL JOURNAL

Page 3

Date	Account Title and Description	Post Ref.	Dr.	Cr.

PROBLEM 13A-4 or 13B-4, Cont.

CALLAHAN LUMBER - GENERAL LEDGER

NAME: __CASH__   ACCOUNT NO. ____110__

Date	Explanation	Post Ref	Debit	Credit	D R C R	Balance

NAME: __ACCOUNTS RECEIVABLE__   ACCOUNT NO. ____111__

Date	Explanation	Post Ref	Debit	Credit	D R C R	Balance

NAME: __MERCHANDISE INVENTORY__   ACCOUNT NO. ____112__

Date	Explanation	Post Ref	Debit	Credit	D R C R	Balance

NAME: __LUMBER SUPPLIES__   ACCOUNT NO. ____113__

Date	Explanation	Post Ref	Debit	Credit	D R C R	Balance

NAME: __PREPAID INSURANCE__   ACCOUNT NO. ____114__

Date	Explanation	Post Ref	Debit	Credit	D R C R	Balance

NAME: __LUMBER EQUIPMENT__   ACCOUNT NO. ____121__

Date	Explanation	Post Ref	Debit	Credit	D R C R	Balance

PROBLEM 13A-4 or 13B-4, Cont.

NAME: ACCUMULATED AMORTIZATION, LUMBER EQUIPMENT   ACCOUNT NO. 122

Date	Explanation	Post Ref	Debit	Credit	D R C R	Balance

NAME: ACCOUNTS PAYABLE   ACCOUNT NO. 220

Date	Explanation	Post Ref	Debit	Credit	D R C R	Balance

NAME: WAGES PAYABLE   ACCOUNT NO. 221

Date	Explanation	Post Ref	Debit	Credit	D R C R	Balance

NAME: J. CALLAHAN, CAPITAL   ACCOUNT NO. 330

Date	Explanation	Post Ref	Debit	Credit	D R C R	Balance

NAME: J. CALLAHAN, WITHDRAWALS   ACCOUNT NO. 331

Date	Explanation	Post Ref	Debit	Credit	D R C R	Balance

NAME: INCOME SUMMARY   ACCOUNT NO. 332

Date	Explanation	Post Ref	Debit	Credit	D R C R	Balance

PROBLEM 13A-4 or 13B-4, Cont.

NAME: __SALES_____ ACCOUNT NO. ____440__

Date	Explanation	Post Ref	Debit	Credit	D R C R	Balance

NAME: __SALES RETURNS AND ALLOWANCES_____ ACCOUNT NO. ____441__

Date	Explanation	Post Ref	Debit	Credit	D R C R	Balance

NAME: __PURCHASES_____ ACCOUNT NO. ____550__

Date	Explanation	Post Ref	Debit	Credit	D R C R	Balance

NAME: __PURCHASES DISCOUNTS_____ ACCOUNT NO. ____551__

Date	Explanation	Post Ref	Debit	Credit	D R C R	Balance

NAME: __PURCHASES RETURNS AND ALLOWANCES_____ ACCOUNT NO. ____552__

Date	Explanation	Post Ref	Debit	Credit	D R C R	Balance

NAME: __WAGES EXPENSE_____ ACCOUNT NO. ____660__

Date	Explanation	Post Ref	Debit	Credit	D R C R	Balance

PROBLEM 13A-4 or 13B-4, Cont.

NAME: __ADVERTISING EXPENSE_____   ACCOUNT NO. ____661__

Date	Explanation	Post Ref	Debit	Credit	D R C R	Balance

NAME: __RENT EXPENSE_____   ACCOUNT NO. ____662__

Date	Explanation	Post Ref	Debit	Credit	D R C R	Balance

NAME: __AMORTIZATION EXPENSE, LUMBER EQUIPMENT_____   ACCOUNT NO. ____663__

Date	Explanation	Post Ref	Debit	Credit	D R C R	Balance

NAME: __LUMBER SUPPLIES EXPENSE_____   ACCOUNT NO. ____664__

Date	Explanation	Post Ref	Debit	Credit	D R C R	Balance

NAME: __INSURANCE EXPENSE_____   ACCOUNT NO. ____665__

Date	Explanation	Post Ref	Debit	Credit	D R C R	Balance

PROBLEM 13A-4 or 13B-4, Concluded

CALLAHAN LUMBER							
POST-CLOSING TRIAL BALANCE							
DECEMBER 31, 2007							

NAME: _____ CLASS: _____ DATE: _____

PROBLEM 13C-1.

_____

_____

_____

PROBLEM 13C-2.

_____

_____

PROBLEM 13C-2, Concluded

BALANCE SHEET

PROBLEM 13C-3.

Use a blank, fold-out worksheet which is located at the end of this study guide.

INCOME STATEMENT

PROBLEM 13C-3, Cont.

_____

STATEMENT OF OWNER'S EQUITY

_____

PROBLEM 13C-3, Cont.

BALANCE SHEET

PROBLEM 13C-3, Cont. _____

_____ *Page 4*

Date		Account Title and Description	Post Ref.	Dr.	Cr.

PROBLEM 13C-3, Cont.

PROBLEM 13C-3, Cont.

_____

_____ *Page 5*

Date		Account Title and Description	Post Ref.	Dr.	Cr.

PROBLEM 13C-4.

Use a blank, fold-out worksheet which is located at the end of this study guide.

_____

INCOME STATEMENT

_____

PROBLEM 13C-4, Cont.

_____

STATEMENT OF OWNER'S EQUITY

_____

PROBLEM 13C-4, Cont.

_____

BALANCE SHEET _____

_____

PROBLEM 13C-4, Cont.

_____

_____ *Page 5*

Date		Account Title and Description	Post Ref.	Dr.	Cr.

13-37

PROBLEM 13C-4, Cont.

_____

_____   *Page 6*

Date		Account Title and Description	Post Ref.	Dr.		Cr.	

PROBLEM 13C-4, Cont.

NAME: CASH   ACCOUNT NO. 1100

Date		Explanation	Post Ref	Debit	Credit	DR CR	Balance

NAME: ACCOUNTS RECEIVABLE   ACCOUNT NO. 1110

Date		Explanation	Post Ref	Debit	Credit	DR CR	Balance

NAME: MERCHANDISE INVENTORY   ACCOUNT NO. 1120

Date		Explanation	Post Ref	Debit	Credit	DR CR	Balance

NAME: SUPPLIES   ACCOUNT NO. 1130

Date		Explanation	Post Ref	Debit	Credit	DR CR	Balance

NAME: PREPAID INSURANCE   ACCOUNT NO. 1140

Date		Explanation	Post Ref	Debit	Credit	DR CR	Balance

NAME: PREPAID GST   ACCOUNT NO. 1150

Date		Explanation	Post Ref	Debit	Credit	DR CR	Balance

NAME: EQUIPMENT   ACCOUNT NO. 1210

Date		Explanation	Post Ref	Debit	Credit	DR CR	Balance

PROBLEM 13C-4, Cont.

NAME: _ACCUMULATED AMORTIZATION, EQUIPMENT_ _____ ACCOUNT NO. ____1220__

Date		Explanation	Post Ref	Debit	Credit	D R C R	Balance

NAME: _ACCOUNTS PAYABLE_ _____ ACCOUNT NO. ____2200__

Date		Explanation	Post Ref	Debit	Credit	D R C R	Balance

NAME: _WAGES PAYABLE_ _____ ACCOUNT NO. ____2210__

Date		Explanation	Post Ref	Debit	Credit	D R C R	Balance

NAME: _GST COLLECTED_ _____ ACCOUNT NO. ____2220__

Date		Explanation	Post Ref	Debit	Credit	D R C R	Balance

NAME: _W. BRENNAN, CAPITAL_ _____ ACCOUNT NO. ____3300__

Date		Explanation	Post Ref	Debit	Credit	D R C R	Balance

NAME: _W. BRENNAN, WITHDRAWALS_ _____ ACCOUNT NO. ____3310__

Date		Explanation	Post Ref	Debit	Credit	D R C R	Balance

NAME: _INCOME SUMMARY_ _____ ACCOUNT NO. ____3320__

Date		Explanation	Post Ref	Debit	Credit	D R C R	Balance

PROBLEM 13C-4, Cont.

NAME: _SALES_ ACCOUNT NO. ___4400

Date		Explanation	Post Ref	Debit	Credit	D R C R	Balance

NAME: _SALES RETURNS AND ALLOWANCES_ ACCOUNT NO. ___4410

Date		Explanation	Post Ref	Debit	Credit	D R C R	Balance

NAME: _PURCHASES_ ACCOUNT NO. ___5500

Date		Explanation	Post Ref	Debit	Credit	D R C R	Balance

NAME: _PURCHASES DISCOUNTS_ ACCOUNT NO. ___5510

Date		Explanation	Post Ref	Debit	Credit	D R C R	Balance

NAME: _PURCHASES RETURNS AND ALLOWANCES_ ACCOUNT NO. ___5520

Date		Explanation	Post Ref	Debit	Credit	D R C R	Balance

NAME: _WAGES EXPENSE_ ACCOUNT NO. ___6600

Date		Explanation	Post Ref	Debit	Credit	D R C R	Balance

PROBLEM 13C-4, Cont.

NAME: __ADVERTISING EXPENSE_____ ACCOUNT NO. ___6610___

Date		Explanation	Post Ref	Debit	Credit	D R C R	Balance

NAME: __RENT EXPENSE_____ ACCOUNT NO. ___6620___

Date		Explanation	Post Ref	Debit	Credit	D R C R	Balance

NAME: __AMORTIZATION EXPENSE, EQUIPMENT_____ ACCOUNT NO. ___6630___

Date		Explanation	Post Ref	Debit	Credit	D R C R	Balance

NAME: __SUPPLIES EXPENSE_____ ACCOUNT NO. ___6640___

Date		Explanation	Post Ref	Debit	Credit	D R C R	Balance

NAME: __INSURANCE EXPENSE_____ ACCOUNT NO. ___6650___

Date		Explanation	Post Ref	Debit	Credit	D R C R	Balance

PROBLEM 13C-4, Concluded

_____

POST-CLOSING TRIAL BALANCE

_____

REAL WORLD APPLICATIONS, #13R-1.

CHAN COMPANY

INCOME STATEMENT

FOR THE YEAR ENDED DECEMBER 31, 2008

REAL WORLD APPLICATIONS, #13R-2.

GREGOT COMPANY
BALANCE SHEET
DECEMBER 31, 2006

REAL WORLD APPLICATIONS, #13R-3.

_____

_____

_____

_____

_____

ELDORADO COMPUTER CENTRE
GENERAL JOURNAL

Page 9

Date	Account Title and Description	Post Ref.	Dr.	Cr.

CONTINUING PROBLEM, Cont.

ELDORADO COMPUTER CENTRE
GENERAL LEDGER

NAME: CASH   ACCOUNT NO. ____1000____

Date 2008		Explanation	Post Ref	Debit	Credit	DR CR	Balance
Sept	30	Balance	✔			Dr	2 8 3 2 3 1

NAME: PETTY CASH   ACCOUNT NO. ____1010____

Date 2008		Explanation	Post Ref	Debit	Credit	DR CR	Balance
Sept	30	Balance	✔			Dr	1 0 0 0 0

NAME: ACCOUNTS RECEIVABLE   ACCOUNT NO. ____1020____

Date 2008		Explanation	Post Ref	Debit	Credit	DR CR	Balance
Sept	30	Balance	✔			Dr	2 1 6 2 0 0 0

NAME: PREPAID RENT   ACCOUNT NO. ____1025____

Date 2008		Explanation	Post Ref	Debit	Credit	DR CR	Balance
Sept	30	Balance	✔			Dr	5 2 0 0 0 0

NAME: SUPPLIES   ACCOUNT NO. ____1030____

Date 2008		Explanation	Post Ref	Debit	Credit	DR CR	Balance
Sept	30	Balance	✔			Dr	1 8 6 0 5 2

NAME: PREPAID INSURANCE   ACCOUNT NO. ____1035____

Date 2008		Explanation	Post Ref	Debit	Credit	DR CR	Balance
Sept	30	Balance	✔			Dr	1 8 4 6 0 0

CONTINUING PROBLEM, Cont.

ELDORADO COMPUTER CENTRE
GENERAL LEDGER

NAME: __MERCHANDISE INVENTORY__   ACCOUNT NO. ___1040___

Date 2008		Explanation	Post Ref	Debit	Credit	DR CR	Balance
Sept	30	Balance	✔			Dr	7 0 0 0 0 0

NAME: __COMPUTER SHOP EQUIPMENT__   ACCOUNT NO. ___1080___

Date 2008		Explanation	Post Ref	Debit	Credit	DR CR	Balance
Sept	30	Balance	✔			Dr	3 8 0 0 0 0

NAME: __ACCUM. AMORTIZATION, COMPUTER SHOP EQUIPMENT__   ACCOUNT NO. ___1081___

Date 2008		Explanation	Post Ref	Debit	Credit	DR CR	Balance
Sept	30	Balance	✔			Cr	9 9 0 0

NAME: __OFFICE EQUIPMENT__   ACCOUNT NO. ___1090___

Date 2008		Explanation	Post Ref	Debit	Credit	DR CR	Balance
Sept	30	Balance	✔			Dr	1 0 5 0 0 0

NAME: __ACCUM. AMORTIZATION, OFFICE EQUIPMENT__   ACCOUNT NO. ___1091___

Date 2008		Explanation	Post Ref	Debit	Credit	DR CR	Balance
Sept	30	Balance	✔			Cr	2 0 0 0

NAME: __ACCOUNTS PAYABLE__   ACCOUNT NO. ___2000___

Date 2008		Explanation	Post Ref	Debit	Credit	DR CR	Balance
Sept	30	Balance	✔			Cr	4 3 6 2 0 0

CONTINUING PROBLEM, Cont.

ELDORADO COMPUTER CENTRE
GENERAL LEDGER

NAME: WAGES PAYABLE   ACCOUNT NO. 2010

Date 2008		Explanation	Post Ref	Debit	Credit	D R C R	Balance
Sept	30	Balance	✔				0

NAME: DUE TO CRA   ACCOUNT NO. 2020

Date 2008		Explanation	Post Ref	Debit	Credit	D R C R	Balance
Sept	30	Balance	✔				0

NAME: UNEARNED SERVICE REVENUE   ACCOUNT NO. 2050

Date 2008		Explanation	Post Ref	Debit	Credit	D R C R	Balance
Sept	30	Balance	✔			Cr	4 8 0 0 0 0

NAME: GST PAYABLE   ACCOUNT NO. 2060

Date 2008		Explanation	Post Ref	Debit	Credit	D R C R	Balance
Sept	30	Balance	✔			Cr	1 1 4 9 8 3

NAME: GST RECOVERABLE   ACCOUNT NO. 2066

Date 2008		Explanation	Post Ref	Debit	Credit	D R C R	Balance
Sept	30	Balance	✔			Dr	8 1 8 6 4

NAME: T. FREEDMAN, CAPITAL   ACCOUNT NO. 3000

Date 2008		Explanation	Post Ref	Debit	Credit	D R C R	Balance
Sept	30	Balance	✔			Cr	7 4 0 6 0 0

CONTINUING PROBLEM, Cont.

ELDORADO COMPUTER CENTRE
GENERAL LEDGER

NAME: __T. FREEDMAN, WITHDRAWALS_____ ACCOUNT NO. ____3010____

Date 2008		Explanation	Post Ref	Debit	Credit	D R C R	Balance
Sept	30	Balance	✔			Dr	1 8 7 3 5 0 0

NAME: __INCOME SUMMARY_____ ACCOUNT NO. ____3020____

Date 2008		Explanation	Post Ref	Debit	Credit	D R C R	Balance

NAME: __SERVICE REVENUE_____ ACCOUNT NO. ____4000____

Date 2008		Explanation	Post Ref	Debit	Credit	D R C R	Balance
Sept	30	Balance	✔			Cr	7 6 8 0 6 0 0

NAME: __SALES_____ ACCOUNT NO. ____4010____

Date 2008		Explanation	Post Ref	Debit	Credit	D R C R	Balance
Sept	30	Balance	✔			Cr	9 6 4 4 8 0 0

NAME: __SALES RETURNS AND ALLOWANCES_____ ACCOUNT NO. ____4020____

Date 2008		Explanation	Post Ref	Debit	Credit	D R C R	Balance
Sept	30	Balance	✔			Dr	4 0 0 0 0

NAME: __SALES DISCOUNTS_____ ACCOUNT NO. ____4030____

Date 2008		Explanation	Post Ref	Debit	Credit	D R C R	Balance
Sept	30	Balance	✔			Dr	2 2 0 0 0

CONTINUING PROBLEM, Cont.

ELDORADO COMPUTER CENTRE
GENERAL LEDGER

NAME: SERVICE CONTRACTS SOLD   ACCOUNT NO.   4050

Date 2008		Explanation	Post Ref	Debit	Credit	D R C R	Balance
Sept	30	Balance	✔				0

NAME: ADVERTISING EXPENSE   ACCOUNT NO.   5010

Date 2008		Explanation	Post Ref	Debit	Credit	D R C R	Balance
Sept	30	Balance	✔			Dr	2 7 1 6 3 7

NAME: RENT EXPENSE   ACCOUNT NO.   5020

Date 2008		Explanation	Post Ref	Debit	Credit	D R C R	Balance
Sept	30	Balance	✔				0

NAME: UTILITIES EXPENSE   ACCOUNT NO.   5030

Date 2008		Explanation	Post Ref	Debit	Credit	D R C R	Balance
Sept	30	Balance	✔			Dr	2 4 8 2 1 5

NAME: PHONE EXPENSE   ACCOUNT NO.   5040

Date 2008		Explanation	Post Ref	Debit	Credit	D R C R	Balance
Sept	30	Balance	✔			Dr	1 9 8 0 0 4

NAME: SUPPLIES EXPENSE   ACCOUNT NO.   5050

Date 2008		Explanation	Post Ref	Debit	Credit	D R C R	Balance
Sept	30	Balance	✔			Dr	2 8 6 0 0

CONTINUING PROBLEM, Cont.

ELDORADO COMPUTER CENTRE
GENERAL LEDGER

NAME: INSURANCE EXPENSE   ACCOUNT NO. 5060

Date 2008		Explanation	Post Ref	Debit	Credit	DR CR	Balance
Sept	30	Balance	✔				-0-

NAME: POSTAGE EXPENSE   ACCOUNT NO. 5070

Date 2008		Explanation	Post Ref	Debit	Credit	DR CR	Balance
Sept	30	Balance	✔			Dr	1 7 6 1 1

NAME: AMORTIZATION EXPENSE, COMPUTER SHOP EQUIPMENT   ACCOUNT NO. 5080

Date 2008		Explanation	Post Ref	Debit	Credit	DR CR	Balance
Sept	30	Balance	✔				-0-

NAME: AMORTIZATION EXPENSE, OFFICE EQUIPMENT   ACCOUNT NO. 5090

Date 2008		Explanation	Post Ref	Debit	Credit	DR CR	Balance
Sept	30	Balance	✔				-0-

NAME: MISCELLANEOUS EXPENSE   ACCOUNT NO. 5100

Date 2008		Explanation	Post Ref	Debit	Credit	DR CR	Balance
Sept	30	Balance	✔			Dr	1 4 3 1 2

NAME: WAGES EXPENSE   ACCOUNT NO. 5110

Date 2008		Explanation	Post Ref	Debit	Credit	DR CR	Balance
Sept	30	Balance	✔			Dr	4 8 3 9 9 2

CONTINUING PROBLEM, Cont.

ELDORADO COMPUTER CENTRE
GENERAL LEDGER

NAME: __PAYROLL BENEFITS EXPENSE__ ACCOUNT NO. __5120__

Date 2008		Explanation	Post Ref	Debit	Credit	D R C R	Balance
Sept	30	Balance	✔			Dr	4 1 2 1 5

NAME: __BAD DEBTS EXPENSE__ ACCOUNT NO. __5140__

Date 2008		Explanation	Post Ref	Debit	Credit	D R C R	Balance

NAME: __PURCHASES__ ACCOUNT NO. __5600__

Date 2008		Explanation	Post Ref	Debit	Credit	D R C R	Balance
Sept	30	Balance	✔			Dr	6 8 4 1 4 0 6

NAME: __PURCHASES RETURNS AND ALLOWANCES__ ACCOUNT NO. __5610__

Date 2008		Explanation	Post Ref	Debit	Credit	D R C R	Balance
Sept	30	Balance	✔			Cr	4 2 2 1 8

NAME: __PURCHASES DISCOUNTS__ ACCOUNT NO. __5620__

Date 2008		Explanation	Post Ref	Debit	Credit	D R C R	Balance
Sept	30	Balance	✔			Cr	1 4 5 2 0

NAME: __FREIGHT IN__ ACCOUNT NO. __5630__

Date 2008		Explanation	Post Ref	Debit	Credit	D R C R	Balance
Sept	30	Balance	✔			Dr	1 1 6 5 8 2

CONTINUING PROBLEM, *Cont.*

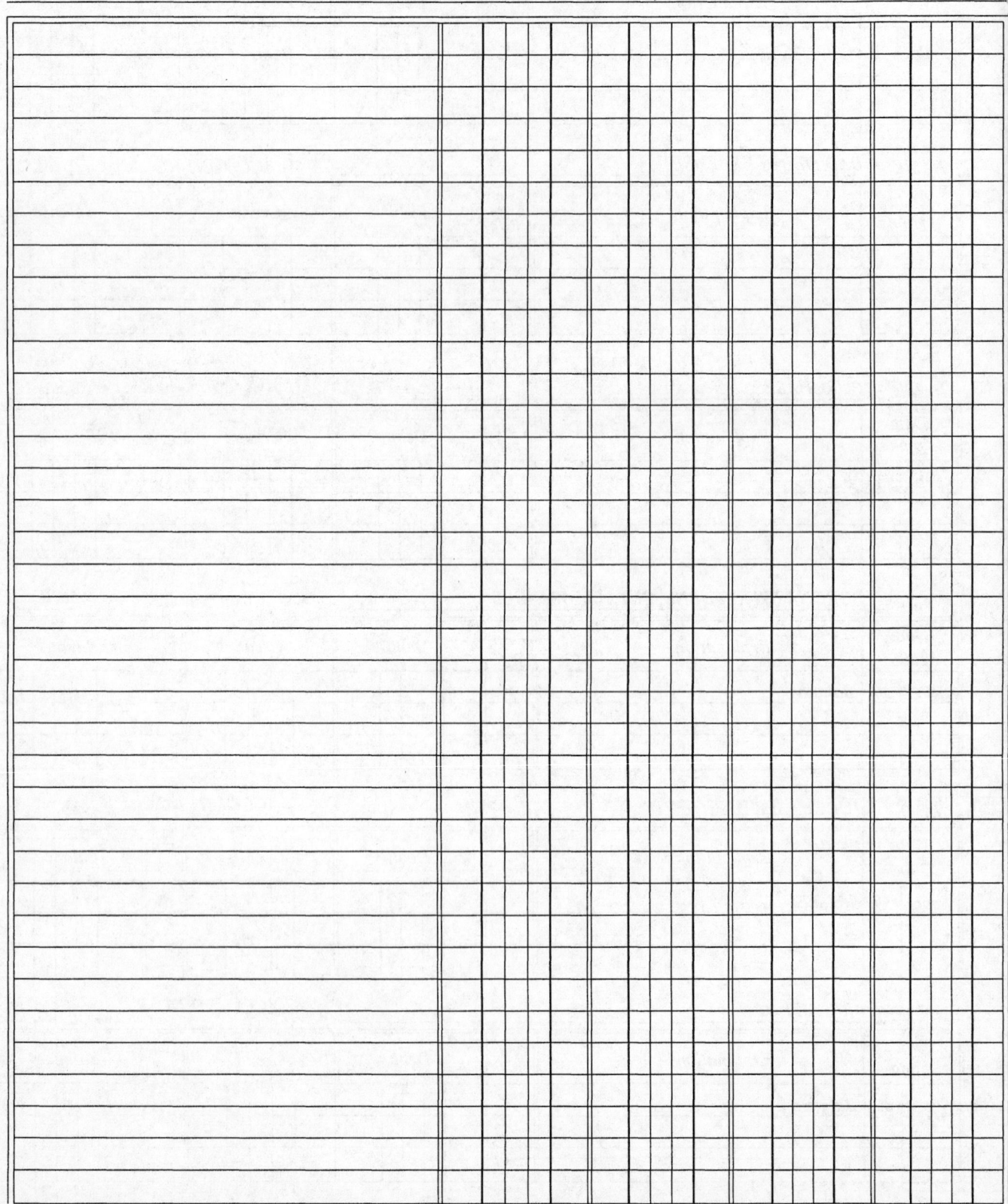

ELDORADO COMPUTER CENTRE

INCOME STATEMENT

FOR THE YEAR ENDED SEPTEMBER 30, 2008

CONTINUING PROBLEM, Cont.

ELDORADO COMPUTER CENTRE

STATEMENT OF OWNER'S EQUITY

FOR THE YEAR ENDED SEPTEMBER 30, 2008

ELDORADO COMPUTER CENTRE

BALANCE SHEET

SEPTEMBER 30, 2008

CHAPTER 13
CHAPTER SUMMARY TEST

Part A

Fill in the blank(s) to complete each statement:

1. _____ expenses are related to sales activity.
2. Cash or other assets that will be converted into cash during the normal operating cycle of the company or one year, whichever is longer, are called _____ _____ .
3. Mortgage Payable is an example of a _____ _____ .
4. The income statement uses _____ _____ figures for inventory.
5. On the worksheet, the _____ figure for capital is never found.
6. _____ expenses are related to the administrative function.
7. The left-most columns of financial reports are used for_____ .
8. The post-closing trial balance contains no _____ accounts.
9. Selling and administrative expenses can be combined as _____ _____ .
10. Long-lived assets used for the production or sale of other assets or services are referred to as _____ _____ .
11. Reversing entries are used only if assets are _____ and have no previous balance and liabilities are _____ and have no previous balance.
12. Debts or obligations that are to be paid using current assets are called _____ _____ .
13. A reversing entry follows certain _____ entries.
14. In the adjusting process, the beginning inventory of the period is transferred to the _____ _____ account.
15. Prepaid insurance is a _____ _____ .
16. The gross profit figure is found on the _____ _____ .

Part B

Answer true or false to the following statements.

1. Accumulated Amortization is an expense.
2. The normal balance of the merchandise inventory account is a debit.
3. Formal reports contain no debit or credit columns.
4. Unearned Rent is a liability.
5. Reversing entries are not applied to all adjustments.
6. Cost of goods sold contains only ending inventory.
7. The post-closing trial balance would not contain any unearned revenue accounts.
8. Net sales less cost of goods sold equals gross profit.
9. Operating expenses include administative expenses.
10. Long-term liabilities are due within one year.
11. Ending inventory is closed directly to cost of goods sold.
12. An adjusting entry for accrued wages is never reversed.
13. Closing entries will update the merchandise inventory account.
14. Supplies is considered part of plant and equipment.
15. An adjusting entry with an asset decreasing and with no previous balance cannot be reversed.
16. Beginning merchandise inventory of a period is assumed sold by end of the period.
17. Reversing entries switch closing entries the first day of the new period.
18. An operating cycle of a business must be one year.
19. Reversing entries are optional at the end of each month before the close of the year.
20. Merchandise Inventory is a temporary account.

CHAPTER 13
SOLUTIONS TO CHAPTER SUMMARY TEST

Part A

1. Selling
2. current assets
3. long-term liability
4. two separate
5. ending
6. Administrative
7. subtotalling
8. temporary
9. operating expenses
10. Capital Assets
11. increasing, increasing
12. current liabilities
13. adjusting
14. Income Summary
15. permanent account or Current Asset
16. income statement

Part B

1. false
2. true
3. true
4. true
5. true
6. false
7. false
8. true
9. true
10. false
11. false
12. false
13. false
14. false
15. true
16. true
17. false
18. false
19. false
20. false

MINI PRACTICE SET *Use a blank, fold-out worksheet which is located at the end of this study guide.*

THE CORNER DRESS SHOP
GENERAL JOURNAL
Page 4

Date	Account Title and Description	Post Ref.	Dr.	Cr.

13-58

MINI PRACTICE SET, Cont.

THE CORNER DRESS SHOP
GENERAL JOURNAL

Date	Account Title and Description	Post Ref.	Dr.	Cr.

MINI PRACTICE SET, Cont.

THE CORNER DRESS SHOP - PAYROLL REGISTER

Employee	Net Claim Code	Salary	Cumulative CPP	Tax*
Mel Case				
Jane Holl				
Jackie Moore				

*Federal and Provincial Income Taxes combined

MINI PRACTICE SET, Cont.

PAYROLL REGISTER, Cont.

	Deductions				Net Pay	Chq. No.
	C P P	E I	Health	Charitable		

THE CORNER DRESS SHOP
SALES JOURNAL

Page 3

Date	Invoice No.	Customer's Name	Post Ref.	Accounts Receivable Dr.	GST Collected Cr.	Dress Sales Cr.

MINI PRACTICE SET, Cont.

THE CORNER DRESS SHOP
CASH RECEIPTS JOURNAL

Page 6

Date	Invoice No.	Description of Receipt	Post Ref.	Sundry Cr.	Accounts Receivable Cr.	GST Collected Cr.	Sales Cr.	Sales Discounts Dr.	Cash Dr.

MINI PRACTICE SET, Cont.

THE CORNER DRESS SHOP
PURCHASES JOURNAL

Page 4

Date	Account Credited	Date of Invoice	Invoice No.	Post Ref.	Accounts Payable Cr.	Purchases Dr.	GST Prepaid Dr.	Sundry Dr.		
								Account	Post Ref.	Amount

MINI PRACTICE SET, Cont.

THE CORNER DRESS SHOP
CASH PAYMENTS JOURNAL

Page 7

Date	Chq. No.	Account Debited	Post Ref.	Sundry Dr.	Accounts Payable Dr.	GST Prepaid Dr.	Purchases Dr.	Purchases Discount Cr.	Cash Cr.

MINI PRACTICE SET, Cont.

THE CORNER DRESS SHOP
AUXILIARY PETTY CASH RECORD

Date	Voucher No.	Description	Receipts	Payment	Category of Payment				
					Postage Expense	Delivery Expense	Account	Sundry Amount	

13-65

MINI PRACTICE SET, Cont.

ACCOUNTS RECEIVABLE LEDGER

NAME: BING COMPANY

ADDRESS:

Date		Explanation	Post Ref.	Debit	Credit	Dr. Balance

NAME: MORRIS COMPANY

ADDRESS:

Date		Explanation	Post Ref.	Debit	Credit	Dr. Balance

NAME: RONALD COMPANY

ADDRESS:

Date 2007		Explanation	Post Ref.	Debit	Credit	Dr. Balance
Mar.	1	Balance				5 5 9 0 7 5

NAME: SALLY'S STORE

ADDRESS:

Date 2007		Explanation	Post Ref.	Debit	Credit	Dr. Balance
Mar.	1	Balance				2 7 8 0 1 8

THE CORNER DRESS SHOP
SCHEDULE OF ACCOUNTS RECEIVABLE
MARCH 31, 2007

MINI PRACTICE SET, Cont.

ACCOUNTS PAYABLE LEDGER

NAME: BLEW COMPANY

ADDRESS: _____

Date 2007		Explanation	Post Ref.	Debit	Credit	Cr. Balance
Mar.	1	Balance				2 5 6 8 0 0

NAME: DRESSES BY SHELLEY

ADDRESS: _____

Date 2007		Explanation	Post Ref.	Debit	Credit	Cr. Balance
Mar.	1	Balance				1 5 2 4 7 5

NAME: JONES COMPANY

ADDRESS: _____

Date		Explanation	Post Ref.	Debit	Credit	Cr. Balance

NAME: SILK MAGIC

ADDRESS: _____

Date 2007		Explanation	Post Ref.	Debit	Credit	Cr. Balance
Mar.	1	Balance				7 4 9 0 0

THE CORNER DRESS SHOP
SCHEDULE OF ACCOUNTS PAYABLE
MARCH 31, 2007

MINI PRACTICE SET, Cont.

THE CORNER DRESS SHOP - GENERAL LEDGER

NAME: CASH   ACCOUNT NO. 1110

Date	Explanation	Post Ref	Debit	Credit	D R C R	Balance

NAME: PETTY CASH   ACCOUNT NO. 1115

Date	Explanation	Post Ref	Debit	Credit	D R C R	Balance

NAME: ACCOUNTS RECEIVABLE   ACCOUNT NO. 1120

Date	Explanation	Post Ref	Debit	Credit	D R C R	Balance

NAME: OFFICE SUPPLIES   ACCOUNT NO. 1135

Date	Explanation	Post Ref	Debit	Credit	D R C R	Balance

NAME: PREPAID RENT   ACCOUNT NO. 1140

Date	Explanation	Post Ref	Debit	Credit	D R C R	Balance

NAME: PREPAID INSURANCE   ACCOUNT NO. 1145

Date	Explanation	Post Ref	Debit	Credit	D R C R	Balance

MINI PRACTICE SET, Cont.

NAME: GST PREPAID _____ ACCOUNT NO. _____ 1150

Date		Explanation	Post Ref	Debit	Credit	D R C R	Balance

NAME: INVENTORY _____ ACCOUNT NO. _____ 1210

Date		Explanation	Post Ref	Debit	Credit	D R C R	Balance

NAME: COMPUTER AND OFFICE EQUIPMENT _____ ACCOUNT NO. _____ 1330

Date		Explanation	Post Ref	Debit	Credit	D R C R	Balance

NAME: ACC. AMORT. - COMPUTER & OFFICE EQUIPMENT _____ ACCOUNT NO. _____ 1335

Date		Explanation	Post Ref	Debit	Credit	D R C R	Balance

NAME: COMPUTER SOFTWARE _____ ACCOUNT NO. _____ 1340

Date		Explanation	Post Ref	Debit	Credit	D R C R	Balance

NAME: ACC. AMORT. - COMPUTER SOFTWARE _____ ACCOUNT NO. _____ 1345

Date		Explanation	Post Ref	Debit	Credit	D R C R	Balance

MINI PRACTICE SET, Cont.

NAME: DELIVERY TRUCK   ACCOUNT NO.   _____ 1350

Date		Explanation	Post Ref	Debit	Credit	D R C R	Balance

NAME: ACC. AMORT.-DELIVERY TRUCK   ACCOUNT NO.   _____ 1355

Date		Explanation	Post Ref	Debit	Credit	D R C R	Balance

NAME: ACCOUNTS PAYABLE   ACCOUNT NO.   _____ 2100

Date		Explanation	Post Ref	Debit	Credit	D R C R	Balance

NAME: WAGES PAYABLE   ACCOUNT NO.   _____ 2200

Date		Explanation	Post Ref	Debit	Credit	D R C R	Balance

NAME: INCOME TAXES PAYABLE   ACCOUNT NO.   _____ 2330

Date		Explanation	Post Ref	Debit	Credit	D R C R	Balance

NAME: EI PAYABLE   ACCOUNT NO.   _____ 2335

Date		Explanation	Post Ref	Debit	Credit	D R C R	Balance

MINI PRACTICE SET, Cont.

NAME: __CPP PAYABLE__ ACCOUNT NO. ___2340___

Date		Explanation	Post Ref	Debit	Credit	D R C R	Balance

NAME: __MEDICAL PLAN PAYABLE__ ACCOUNT NO. ___2350___

Date		Explanation	Post Ref	Debit	Credit	D R C R	Balance

NAME: __CHARITABLE DONATIONS PAYABLE__ ACCOUNT NO. ___2360___

Date		Explanation	Post Ref	Debit	Credit	D R C R	Balance

NAME: __GST COLLECTED__ ACCOUNT NO. ___2400___

Date		Explanation	Post Ref	Debit	Credit	D R C R	Balance

NAME: __RENT RECEIVED IN ADVANCE__ ACCOUNT NO. ___2500___

Date		Explanation	Post Ref	Debit	Credit	D R C R	Balance

NAME: __B. LOEB, CAPITAL__ ACCOUNT NO. ___3110___

Date		Explanation	Post Ref	Debit	Credit	D R C R	Balance

MINI PRACTICE SET, Cont.

NAME: B. LOEB, WITHDRAWALS _____ ACCOUNT NO. ____ 3120

Date	Explanation	Post Ref	Debit	Credit	D R C R	Balance

NAME: INCOME SUMMARY _____ ACCOUNT NO. ____ 3380

Date	Explanation	Post Ref	Debit	Credit	D R C R	Balance

NAME: SALES _____ ACCOUNT NO. ____ 4110

Date	Explanation	Post Ref	Debit	Credit	D R C R	Balance

NAME: SALES DISCOUNTS _____ ACCOUNT NO. ____ 4140

Date	Explanation	Post Ref	Debit	Credit	D R C R	Balance

NAME: SALES RETURNS & ALLOWANCES _____ ACCOUNT NO. ____ 4150

Date	Explanation	Post Ref	Debit	Credit	D R C R	Balance

NAME: RENTAL INCOME _____ ACCOUNT NO. ____ 4200

Date	Explanation	Post Ref	Debit	Credit	D R C R	Balance

MINI PRACTICE SET, Cont.

NAME: __PURCHASES_____ ACCOUNT NO. ___5040___

Date	Explanation	Post Ref	Debit	Credit	D R C R	Balance

NAME: __PURCHASES DISCOUNTS_____ ACCOUNT NO. ___5140___

Date	Explanation	Post Ref	Debit	Credit	D R C R	Balance

NAME: __PURCHASES RETURNS & ALLOWANCES_____ ACCOUNT NO. ___5150___

Date	Explanation	Post Ref	Debit	Credit	D R C R	Balance

NAME: __WAGES EXPENSE_____ ACCOUNT NO. ___5400___

Date	Explanation	Post Ref	Debit	Credit	D R C R	Balance

NAME: __EI EXPENSE_____ ACCOUNT NO. ___5430___

Date	Explanation	Post Ref	Debit	Credit	D R C R	Balance

NAME: __CPP EXPENSE_____ ACCOUNT NO. ___5440___

Date	Explanation	Post Ref	Debit	Credit	D R C R	Balance

NAME: __POSTAL EXPENSE_____ ACCOUNT NO. ___5500___

Date	Explanation	Post Ref	Debit	Credit	D R C R	Balance

MINI PRACTICE SET, Cont.

NAME: __INSURANCE EXPENSE_____ ACCOUNT NO. ___5510__

Date		Explanation	Post Ref	Debit	Credit	D R C R	Balance

NAME: __CLEANING EXPENSE_____ ACCOUNT NO. ___5520__

Date		Explanation	Post Ref	Debit	Credit	D R C R	Balance

NAME: __RENT EXPENSE_____ ACCOUNT NO. ___5530__

Date		Explanation	Post Ref	Debit	Credit	D R C R	Balance

NAME: __DELIVERY EXPENSE_____ ACCOUNT NO. ___5540__

Date		Explanation	Post Ref	Debit	Credit	D R C R	Balance

NAME: __AMORT. EXP-COMP & OFFICE EQUIP._____ ACCOUNT NO. ___5550__

Date		Explanation	Post Ref	Debit	Credit	D R C R	Balance

NAME: __AMORT. EXP - SOFTWARE_____ ACCOUNT NO. ___5560__

Date		Explanation	Post Ref	Debit	Credit	D R C R	Balance

MINI PRACTICE SET, Cont.

NAME: _AMORT. EXPENSE - DELIVERY TRUCK_____   ACCOUNT NO. ___5570___

Date	Explanation	Post Ref	Debit	Credit	D R / C R	Balance

NAME: __ACCOUNTING EXPENSE_____   ACCOUNT NO. ___5590___

Date	Explanation	Post Ref	Debit	Credit	D R / C R	Balance

NAME: __MISCELLANEOUS EXPENSE_____   ACCOUNT NO. ___5595___

Date	Explanation	Post Ref	Debit	Credit	D R / C R	Balance

MINI PRACTICE SET, Cont.

THE CORNER DRESS SHOP

INCOME STATEMENT

FOR THE MONTH ENDED MARCH 31, 2007

MINI PRACTICE SET, Cont.

THE CORNER DRESS SHOP

STATEMENT OF OWNER'S EQUITY

FOR THE MONTH ENDED MARCH 31, 2007

MINI PRACTICE SET, Cont.

THE CORNER DRESS SHOP
BALANCE SHEET
MARCH 31, 2007

MINI PRACTICE SET, Concluded

THE CORNER DRESS SHOP
POST-CLOSING TRIAL BALANCE
MARCH 31, 2007

14

Accounting for Bad Debts

SELF-REVIEW QUIZ 14-1

1. _____ 2. _____ 3. _____ 4. _____ 5. _____

SELF-REVIEW QUIZ 14-2

SELF-REVIEW QUIZ 14-3

1. _____ 2. _____ 3. _____ 4. _____ 5. _____

FORMS FOR MINI EXERCISES

1. *a.*

b. _____ *b.*

_____

c. _____

_____

2. *A.* _____

B. _____

C. _____

D. _____

FORMS FOR MINI EXERCISES, Cont.

Date		Account Title and Description	Post Ref.		Dr.				Cr.			
3.												
4.												
5.												

14-3

FORMS FOR EXERCISES

14-1.

JETSON CO.
PARTIAL BALANCE SHEET
DECEMBER 31, 2006

14-2.

Date	Account Title and Description	Post Ref.	Dr.	Cr.

14-3.

Date	Account Title and Description	Post Ref.	Dr.	Cr.

Exercises, Cont.

14-4. a.

Date		Account Title and Description	Post Ref.	Dr.					Cr.				

b.

Date		Account Title and Description	Post Ref.	Dr.					Cr.				

14-5.

Date		Account Title and Description	Post Ref.	Dr.					Cr.				

PROBLEM 14A-1 or 14B-1.

PALTER CO.
GENERAL JOURNAL

Page 14

Date		Account Title and Description	Post Ref.	Dr.	Cr.

PROBLEM 14A-2 or 14B-2.

ALVIE CO.
GENERAL JOURNAL   *Page 5*

	Date		Account Title and Description	Post Ref.	Dr.	Cr.
a.						
c.						

ALVIE CO.

PARTIAL BALANCE SHEET

DECEMBER 31, 2007

b.			

PROBLEM 14A-3 or 14B-3.

T. J. RACK
GENERAL JOURNAL

Page 4

Date	Account Title and Description	Post Ref.	Dr.	Cr.

PROBLEM 14A-4 or 14B-4.   **SIMON COMPANY**
                                     GENERAL JOURNAL   *Page 2*

Date		Account Title and Description	Post Ref.	Dr.	Cr.

PROBLEM 14A-4 or 14B-4, Cont.   **SIMON COMPANY**
PARTIAL GENERAL LEDGER

NAME: __ALLOWANCE FOR DOUBTFUL ACCOUNTS_____   ACCOUNT NO. ____114____

Date		Explanation	Post Ref	Debit	Credit	D R C R	Balance

NAME: __INCOME SUMMARY_____   ACCOUNT NO. ____312____

Date		Explanation	Post Ref	Debit	Credit	D R C R	Balance

NAME: __BAD DEBTS EXPENSE_____   ACCOUNT NO. ____612____

Date		Explanation	Post Ref	Debit	Credit	D R C R	Balance

SIMON COMPANY

PARTIAL BALANCE SHEET

DECEMBER 31, 2007

PROBLEM 14C-1.

_____

_____

Page 5

Date	Account Title and Description	Post Ref.	Dr.	Cr.

PROBLEM 14C-2.

a., c.

_____

_____

Page 8

Date		Account Title and Description	Post Ref.	Dr.	Cr.

b.

_____

_____

_____

PROBLEM 14C-3.

_____

_____

Page 9

Date		Account Title and Description	Post Ref.	Dr.	Cr.

14-13

NAME: _____ CLASS: _____ DATE: _____

PROBLEM 14C-4.

_____

_____

Page 2

Date	Account Title and Description	Post Ref.	Dr.	Cr.

PROBLEM 15A-2 or 15B-2, Cont.

Inventory Item _____

Date	Received			Sold			Balance		
	Units	Cost per Unit	Total	Units	Cost per Unit	Total	Units	Cost per Unit	Total

Inventory Item _____

Date	Received			Sold			Balance		
	Units	Cost per Unit	Total	Units	Cost per Unit	Total	Units	Cost per Unit	Total

Inventory Item _____

Date	Received			Sold			Balance		
	Units	Cost per Unit	Total	Units	Cost per Unit	Total	Units	Cost per Unit	Total

PROBLEM 14C-4, Cont.

NAME: ALLOWANCE FOR DOUBTFUL ACCOUNTS   ACCOUNT NO.   1124

Date		Explanation	Post Ref	Debit	Credit	D R C R	Balance

NAME: INCOME SUMMARY   ACCOUNT NO.   3100

Date		Explanation	Post Ref	Debit	Credit	D R C R	Balance

NAME: BAD DEBTS EXPENSE   ACCOUNT NO.   6125

Date		Explanation	Post Ref	Debit	Credit	D R C R	Balance

_____

_____

NAME: _____ CLASS: _____ DATE: _____

REAL WORLD APPLICATIONS, #14R-1 and 14R-2.

AND YOU MAKE THE CALL: CRITICAL THINKING/ETHICAL CASE, #14R-3.

14-17

CONTINUING PROBLEM

ELDORADO COMPUTER CENTRE

GENERAL JOURNAL

Date	Account Title and Description	Post Ref.	Dr.	Cr.

GENERAL JOURNAL

Date	Account Title and Description	Post Ref.	Dr.	Cr.

CHAPTER 14
CHAPTER SUMMARY TEST

Part A
Fill in the blank(s) to complete the statement.

1. Under the allowance method, in estimating bad debts, you may use either the _____ _____ or the _____ _____ approach.
2. Bad Debts Expense is a(n)_____ account.
3. In writing off an account in the allowance method, the account _____ _____ _____ is not involved.
4. The Income Tax Act supports the _____ _____ _____ method of estimating bad debts.
5. A debit balance in the _____ _____ _____ _____ indicates that the estimate for bad debts was too low.
6. Allowance for Doubtful Accounts is categorized as a _____ account.
7. Accounts Receivable less Allowance for Doubtful Accounts equals _____ _____ _____ .
8. A revenue account found in the other income section of an income statement is the _____ _____ _____ .
9. Customers' accounts, according to days past due, are listed in the _____ _____ _____ _____ .
10. In the income statement approach, any existing balance in the allowance for doubtful accounts may be _____ .

Part B

Answer true or false to the following.

1. Bad debts expense is classified as an operating expense.
2. Using the direct method, the account Bad Debts Recovered is used when an account is reinstated only in the same year the sale is made.
3. The direct method fulfills the requirements of the Income Tax Act.
4. The direct method follows the matching principle.
5. When an account is written off in the allowance method, bad debts expense is debited.
6. The normal balance of allowance for doubtful accounts is a credit.
7. In the direct method, accounts receivable is reported at net.
8. The balance sheet approach to estimating bad debts expense using the allowance method will adjust the balance in the allowance account.
9. Using the direct write-off method, a debit to bad debts expense and a credit to accounts receivable means a customer's account is thought to be uncollectible.
10. Net realizable value is a ledger account with a debit balance.
11. Net realizable value equals accounts receivable less the allowance for doubtful accounts.
12. An aging of the accounts receivable is used for the direct write-off method.
13. The direct write-off method shows net realized value.
14. The direct write-off method needs an allowance account.
15. Bad debts expense is reported on the income statement.
16. A debit to accounts receivable and a credit to bad debts recovered means that a bad debt has been recovered in the same year as the sale took place.
17. A debit to bad debts expense and a credit to the allowance for doubtful accounts means that a customer's account has been declared uncollectible.

18. Using the allowance method, a debit to allowance for doubtful accounts and a credit to accounts receivable means that an account receivable is thought to be uncollectible.

19. The income statement approach usually estimates bad debts expense on a percent of net credit sales.

CHAPTER 14
SOLUTIONS TO CHAPTER SUMMARY TEST

Part A

1. income statement; balance sheet
2. temporary
3. Bad Debts Expense
4. Bad Debts Reserve
5. Allowance for Doubtful Accounts
6. contra-asset
7. Net Realizable Value
8. Bad Debts Recovered
9. Aging of accounts receivable
10. ignored

Part B

1. true
2. false
3. true
4. false
5. false
6. true
7. false
8. true
9. true
10. false
11. true
12. false
13. false
14. false
15. true
16. false
17. false
18. true
19. true

15

Accounting for Merchandise Inventory

SELF-REVIEW QUIZ 15-1

GENERAL JOURNAL

Page 2

Date	Account Title and Description	Post Ref.	Dr.	Cr.

NAME: _____ CLASS: _____ DATE: _____

SELF--REVIEW QUIZ 15-2

GENERAL JOURNAL Page 4

Date		Account Title and Description	Post Ref.	Dr.	Cr.

15-2

SELF-REVIEW QUIZ 15-2, Cont.

Merchandise Inventory

Product #1: X Product   **INVENTORY REPORT FORM**   Item _____

Date		Purchased	Sold		Balance	

Product #2: Z Product   **INVENTORY REPORT FORM**   Item _____

Date		Purchased	Sold		Balance	

SELF-REVIEW QUIZ 15-3

1.

a. Specific Invoice								
b. Weighted-Average								
c. FIFO								
d. LIFO								

2.

a. _____   b. _____   c. _____

SELF REVIEW QUIZ 15-4

1.

	COST		RETAIL	

2.

a. _____   b. _____   c. _____   d. _____   e. _____

How Not to Say "Oops, We're Out of That!"
Subway CASE
Discussion Questions

1. Stan insists on a physical count because he is worried about spoilage, and the unexpected success of the sweet onion chicken teriyaki has made it hard to predict sales (and inventory) accurately.

2. Stan might choose a weighted average method of accounting for inventory costs because it takes into account the number of units purchased at each amount, not a simple average cost. This method assigns an equal unit cost to each unit of inventory; so when the income statement is prepared, net income will not fluctuate as much as with other methods.

3. A Subway restaurant owner might choose the LIFO method because tomato, lettuce, pepper and onion prices are so volatile. This method allows the restaurant owner to monitor costs and profits better when prices change rapidly.

FORMS FOR MINI EXERCISES

1.

1 Accounts Affected	2 Category	↑ 3 ↓	4 Rules
Merchandise Inventory		↓	
Cost of Goods Sold		↑	

2.

GENERAL JOURNAL

Date	Account Title and Description	Post. Ref.	Dr.	Cr.
3.				
4.				

FORMS FOR MINI EXERCISES, Cont.

5.

	Units	Cost per Unit

FIFO

LIFO

Weighted-Average

6.

A

B

C

D

E

7.

A

B

C

D

FORMS FOR EXERCISES

15-1.

GENERAL JOURNAL

Date		Account Title and Description	Post Ref.	Dr.	Cr.

15-2.

INVENTORY REPORT FORM

Item ___U47___

Date		Purchased	Sold	Balance

FORMS FOR EXERCISES, Cont.

15-3.

GENERAL JOURNAL

Date	Account Title and Description	Post Ref.	Dr.	Cr.

| Cash | 111 | Merchandise Inventory 114 | Accounts Payable | 201 |

| Sales | 401 |

| Cost of Goods Sold | 501 |

FORMS FOR EXERCISES, Cont.

15-4.

Inventory Item _____

Date	Received				Sold				Balance			
	Units	Cost per Unit		Total	Units	Cost per Unit		Total	Units	Cost per Unit		Total

15-5.

	Units	Cost per Unit

FIFO

LIFO

Weighted-Average

FORMS FOR EXERCISES, Cont.

15-6.

_____

_____

_____

_____

_____

_____

15-7.

	COST	RETAIL

15-8.

PROBLEM 15A-1 or 15B-1.   **WREN COMPANY**
                                GENERAL JOURNAL   Page 2

Date		Account Title and Description	Post Ref.	Dr.	Cr.

PROBLEM 15A-2 or 15B-2.

BEST ELECTRONICS
GENERAL JOURNAL   Page 2

Date		Account Title and Description	Post Ref.	Dr.	Cr.

15-14

PROBLEM 15A-2 or 15B-2, Cont.

Inventory Item _____

Date	Received			Sold			Balance		
	Units	Cost per Unit	Total	Units	Cost per Unit	Total	Units	Cost per Unit	Total

Inventory Item _____

Date	Received			Sold			Balance		
	Units	Cost per Unit	Total	Units	Cost per Unit	Total	Units	Cost per Unit	Total

Inventory Item _____

Date	Received			Sold			Balance		
	Units	Cost per Unit	Total	Units	Cost per Unit	Total	Units	Cost per Unit	Total

PROBLEM 15A-2 or 15B-2, Cont.

NAME: __CASH_____ ACCOUNT NO. ___101___

Date		Explanation	Post Ref	Debit	Credit	D R C R	Balance

NAME: __MERCHANDISE INVENTORY_____ ACCOUNT NO. ___114___

Date		Explanation	Post Ref	Debit	Credit	D R C R	Balance

NAME: __ACCOUNTS PAYABLE_____ ACCOUNT NO. ___201___

Date		Explanation	Post Ref	Debit	Credit	D R C R	Balance

NAME: __SALES_____ ACCOUNT NO. ___401___

Date		Explanation	Post Ref	Debit	Credit	D R C R	Balance

NAME: __SALES RETURNS AND ALLOWANCES_____ ACCOUNT NO. ___402___

Date		Explanation	Post Ref	Debit	Credit	D R C R	Balance

NAME: __COST OF GOODS SOLD_____ ACCOUNT NO. ___501___

Date		Explanation	Post Ref	Debit	Credit	D R C R	Balance

PROBLEM 15A-3 or 15B-3.

Date	Received			Sold			Balance		
	Units	Cost per Unit	Total	Units	Cost per Unit	Total	Units	Cost per Unit	Total

PROBLEM 15A-4 *or* 16B-4.

PROBLEM 15A-5 or 15B-5.

	Cost	Retail

PROBLEM 15A-6 or 15B-6.

PROBLEM 15C-1.

_____

_____

Date	Account Title and Description	Post Ref.	Dr.	Cr.

PROBLEM 15C-2.

_____

Date		Account Title and Description	Post Ref.		Dr.					Cr.				
												\		

PROBLEM 15C-2, Cont.

Inventory Item _____

Date	Received			Sold			Balance		
	Units	Cost per Unit	Total	Units	Cost per Unit	Total	Units	Cost per Unit	Total

Inventory Item _____

Date	Received			Sold			Balance		
	Units	Cost per Unit	Total	Units	Cost per Unit	Total	Units	Cost per Unit	Total

Inventory Item _____

Date	Received			Sold			Balance		
	Units	Cost per Unit	Total	Units	Cost per Unit	Total	Units	Cost per Unit	Total

PROBLEM 15C-2, Cont.

NAME: __CASH__ ACCOUNT NO. ___101___

Date	Explanation	Post Ref.	Debit	Credit	DR CR	Balance

NAME: __MERCHANDISE INVENTORY__ ACCOUNT NO. ___114___

Date	Explanation	Post Ref.	Debit	Credit	DR CR	Balance

NAME: __ACCOUNTS PAYABLE__ ACCOUNT NO. ___201___

Date	Explanation	Post Ref	Debit	Credit	DR CR	Balance

NAME: __SALES__ ACCOUNT NO. ___401___

Date	Explanation	Post Ref.	Debit	Credit	DR CR	Balance

NAME: __SALES RETURNS AND ALLOWANCES__ ACCOUNT NO. ___402___

Date	Explanation	Post Ref.	Debit	Credit	DR CR	Balance

NAME: __COST OF GOODS SOLD__ ACCOUNT NO. ___501___

Date	Explanation	Post Ref.	Debit	Credit	DR CR	Balance

PROBLEM 15C-3.

PROBLEM 15C-4.

PROBLEM 15C-5.

PROBLEM 15C-6.

Date	Received			Sold			Balance		
	Units	Cost per Unit	Total	Units	Cost per Unit	Total	Units	Cost per Unit	Total

REAL WORLD APPLICATIONS, #16R-1.

a. _____

b. _____

c. _____

d. _____

YOU MAKE THE CALL: CRITICAL THINKING/ETHICAL CASE, #16R-2.

CONTINUING PROBLEM

ELDORADO COMPUTER CENTRE

	Units	Cost per Unit

FIFO

LIFO

Weighted-Average

CHAPTER 15
CHAPTER SUMMARY TEST

Part A

Fill in the blank(s) to complete the statement.

1. The net income will not fluctuate as much as other methods when the _____ method is used.
2. The most recent costs are assigned to ending inventory when the _____ method is used.
3. If ending inventory is understated, net income will be _____ .
4. In the _____ _____ system, purchases and sales of inventory are recorded in the inventory account.
5. _____ _____ plus cost of goods purchased equals cost of goods available for sale.
6. What costs are assigned by various possible inventory methods determines _____
    _____ _____ .
7. Consigned goods are the property of the _____ and will be added to its inventory.
8. The _____ method assumes that the ending inventory is made up of the old inventory.
9. In the _____ _____ system, the inventory account is not updated by each sale or purchase of inventory made during the period.
10. The flow of goods and costs are the same in the _____ _____ _____ .
11. The principle of _____ makes financial statements more reliable.
12. During inflation, FIFO produces the _____ net income.
13. The _____ principle tells why a company makes a change in the preparation of its financial reports.
14. If beginning inventory is overstated, net income will be _____ .

Part B

Match the term in the column on the left to the definition, example, or phrase in the column on the right. Be sure to use a letter only once.

__c__ 1. LIFO	a. Cost ratio
_____ 2. Specific invoice	b. Compromise between LIFO and FIFO
_____ 3. Perpetual inventory system	c. Newest goods sold first
_____ 4. Not used in a perpetual system	d. Merchandise inventory
_____ 5. Matches current costs with current selling prices	e. Net income overstated
	f. Accountant will determine it
_____ 6. Gross Profit	g. Consignee
_____ 7. Ending inventory overstated	h. Auto dealer
_____ 8. FIFO	i. Actual physical movement
_____ 9. Current asset	j. LIFO
_____ 10. Retail method	k. Affects gross profit
_____ 11. Flow of goods	l. Old goods sold first
_____ 12. Sells consigned goods	m. Continual running balance of the inventory account
_____ 13. Weighted-average	n. Cost percentage
_____ 14. Selling price	o. Purchases account
_____ 15. Flow of costs	

Part C

Answer true or false to the following:

1. A cost percentage is essential in order to calculate estimated cost of goods sold in the gross profit method.
2. A mistake in calculating ending inventory takes three accounting periods to self-correct.
3. Weighted average costs are usually between LIFO and FIFO.
4. Goods in transit "F.O.B. destination" are added to the buyer's cost of inventory.
5. LIFO cannot be used in a periodic system.
6. If ending inventory is understated, net income is understated.
7. The specific invoice method is easy to use for goods with a large unit volume and small unit prices.
8. A perpetual inventory system is necessary to prepare interim financial statements.
9. The retail inventory method calculates ending inventory at cost by multiplying the gross margin ratio times ending inventory at retail.
10. FIFO assumes that old inventory is sold evenly throughout the year.
11. Damaged goods are never added to the cost of inventory.
12. LIFO always matches the physical flow of goods.
13. Recent costs are matched with sales in FIFO.
14. No freight-in account is used in a perpetual inventory system.
15. If beginning inventory is overstated, net income is understated.
16. The perpetual inventory system records the sale of goods directly into cost of goods sold.
17. Purchases returns and allowances cannot be used in a periodic inventory system.
18. Goods are added to the inventory of consignees.

SOLUTIONS TO CHAPTER SUMMARY TEST

Part A

1. weighted-average	6. flow of costs	11. consistency
2. FIFO	7. consignor	12. highest
3. understated	8. LIFO	13. disclosure
4. perpetual inventory	9. periodic inventory	14. understated
5. Beginning inventory	10. specific invoice method	

Part B

1. c	6. n	11. i
2. h	7. e	12. g
3. m	8. l	13. b
4. o	9. d	14. k
5. j	10. a	15. f

Part C

1. true	6. true	11. false	16. true
2. false	7. false	12. false	17. false
3. true	8. false	13. false	18. false
4. false	9. false	14. true	
5. false	10. false	15. true	

16

Partnerships and Corporations

SELF-REVIEW QUIZ 16-1

1.	2.	3.	4.	5.

SELF-REVIEW QUIZ 16-2

	FRENCH	SMALL	TOTAL
Salary Allowance			
Interest on Capital Investments:			
Total Interest Allowance			
Total Salary and Interest Allowance			
Net Income			
Less: Salary and Interest			
Income to be distributed equally			
Share of Net Income to Partners			

SELF-REVIEW QUIZ 16-3

1.	2.	3.	4.	5.

SELF-REVIEW QUIZ 16-4

1.	2.	3.	4.	5.	6.

SELF-REVIEW QUIZ 16-5

1.

Date		Account Title and Description	Post Ref.	Dr.	Cr.

2.

	Preferred	Common
Dividends for Preferred		
Dividends for Common		
Amount remaining to be divided		
Total Number of Shares		
Preferred		
Common		
Total		
Preferred		
Common		
Total		

SELF-REVIEW QUIZ 16-6

1.

Page 14

Date		Account Title and Description	Post Ref.	Dr.					Cr.				

2.

Page 6

Date		Account Title and Description	Post Ref.	Dr.					Cr.				

3.

Page 14

Date		Account Title and Description	Post Ref.	Dr.				Cr.			

FORMS FOR MINI EXERCISES

1.

Page 4

Date		Account Title and Description	Post Ref.	Dr.	Cr.

2.

Page 2

Date		Account Title and Description	Post Ref.	Dr.	Cr.

3.

Page 2

Date		Account Title and Description	Post Ref.	Dr.	Cr.

16-4

MINI EXERCISES, Cont.

4.

5.

6.

7.

MINI EXERCISES, Cont.

8.   Page 1

Date		Account Title and Description	Post Ref.		Dr.					Cr.				

9.

EXERCISES

16-1.

Page 1

Date	Account Title and Description	Post Ref.	Dr.	Cr.

16-2.

GENERAL JOURNAL

Date	Account Title and Description	Post Ref.	Dr.	Cr.

16-3.

Page 4

	Date	Account Title and Description	Post Ref.	Dr.	Cr.
a.					
b.					

EXERCISES, Cont.

16-4.

GENERAL JOURNAL

Date	Account Title and Description	Post Ref.	Dr.	Cr.

16-5.

Year	Dividend to Preferred Shares	Dividend to Common Shares

16-6.

SCUPPER CORPORATION
SHAREHOLDERS' EQUITY
DECEMBER 31, 2006

Working Area:

EXERCISES, Cont.

16-7.

Page 2

Date		Account Title and Description	Post Ref.	Dr.				Cr.			

16-8.

Page 3

Date		Account Title and Description	Post Ref.	Dr.				Cr.			

16-9.

GENERAL JOURNAL

Date		Account Title and Description	Post Ref.	Dr.				Cr.			

PROBLEM 16A-1.

	BELL	SHELL	TOTAL
16-10			

PROBLEM 16A-2.

Page 3

Date	Account Title and Description	Post Ref.	Dr.	Cr.

PROBLEM 16A-2, Cont.

1.

NAME: _PREFERRED SHARES_   ACCOUNT NO. ____310____

Date 2007	Explanation	Post Ref	Debit	Credit	D R C R	Balance

NAME: _COMMON SHARES_   ACCOUNT NO. ____312____

Date	Explanation	Post Ref	Debit	Credit	D R C R	Balance

2.

PROBLEM 16A-3.

Situation	Dividends paid	2004 0	2005 $46,000	2006 $78,000	2007 0	2008 $82,000
a.	PREFERRED					
	COMMON					
b.	PREFERRED					
	COMMON					
c.	PREFERRED					
	COMMON					

PROBLEM 16A-3, Cont.

WORK AREA

PROBLEM 16A-4.

XENON CORPORATION
SHAREHOLDERS' EQUITY
JULY 31, 2008

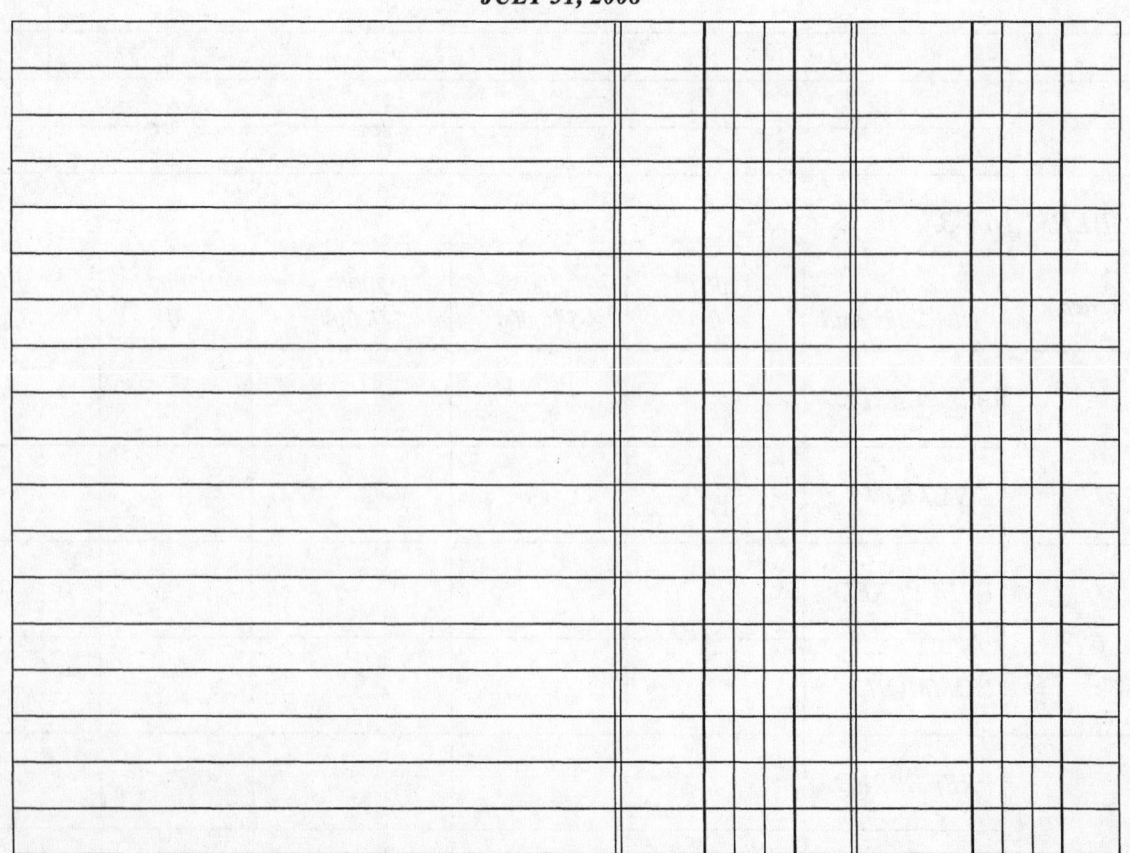

PROBLEM 16B-1.

	BELL	SHELL	TOTAL

PROBLEM 16B-2.

Page 3

Date	Account Title and Description	Post Ref.	Dr.	Cr.

PROBLEM 16B-2, Cont.

1.

NAME: __PREFERRED SHARES__   ACCOUNT NO. ____310____

Date 2007		Explanation	Post Ref	Debit	Credit	D R C R	Balance

NAME: __COMMON SHARES__   ACCOUNT NO. ____312____

Date		Explanation	Post Ref	Debit	Credit	D R C R	Balance

2.

PROBLEM 16B-3.

Situation	Dividends paid	2004 0	2005 $16,000	2006 $80,000	2007 $84,000	2008 $120,000
a.	PREFERRED					
	COMMON					
b.	PREFERRED					
	COMMON					
c.	PREFERRED					
	COMMON					

PROBLEM 16B-3, Cont.

WORK AREA

PROBLEM 16B-4.

XENON CORPORATION
SHAREHOLDER'S EQUITY
JULY 31, 2008

PROBLEM 16C-1.

	CONKLIN	DUNLEVY	FRANKLIN	TOTAL

PROBLEM 16C-2.

Date		Account Title and Description	Post Ref.	Dr.	Cr.

PROBLEM 16C-2, Cont.

1.

NAME: __PREFERRED SHARES__ ACCOUNT NO. __310__

Date		Explanation	Post Ref	Debit	Credit	D R C R	Balance

NAME: __COMMON SHARES__ ACCOUNT NO. __312__

Date		Explanation	Post Ref	Debit	Credit	D R C R	Balance

2.

KINCAID CORPORATION LTD.
SHAREHOLDERS' EQUITY - PAID-IN CAPITAL SECTION
JULY 31, 2006

PROBLEM 16C-3.

Situation	Dividends paid	2004	2005	2006	2007	2008
a.	PREFERRED					
	COMMON					
b.	PREFERRED					
	COMMON					
c.	PREFERRED					
	COMMON					

PROBLEM 16C-3, Cont.

WORK AREA

PROBLEM 16C-4.

BITWHERE CORPORATION LTD.
SHAREHOLDERS' EQUITY
JULY 31, 2008

SOLUTIONS TO REAL WORLD APPLICATIONS, #16R-1.

SOLUTIONS TO REAL WORLD APPLICATION, #16R-3.

SOLUTIONS TO YOU MAKE THE CALL:
CRITICAL THINKING/ETHICAL CASE, #16R-3.

SOLUTIONS TO YOU MAKE THE CALL:
CRITICAL THINKING/ETHICAL CASE, #16R-4.

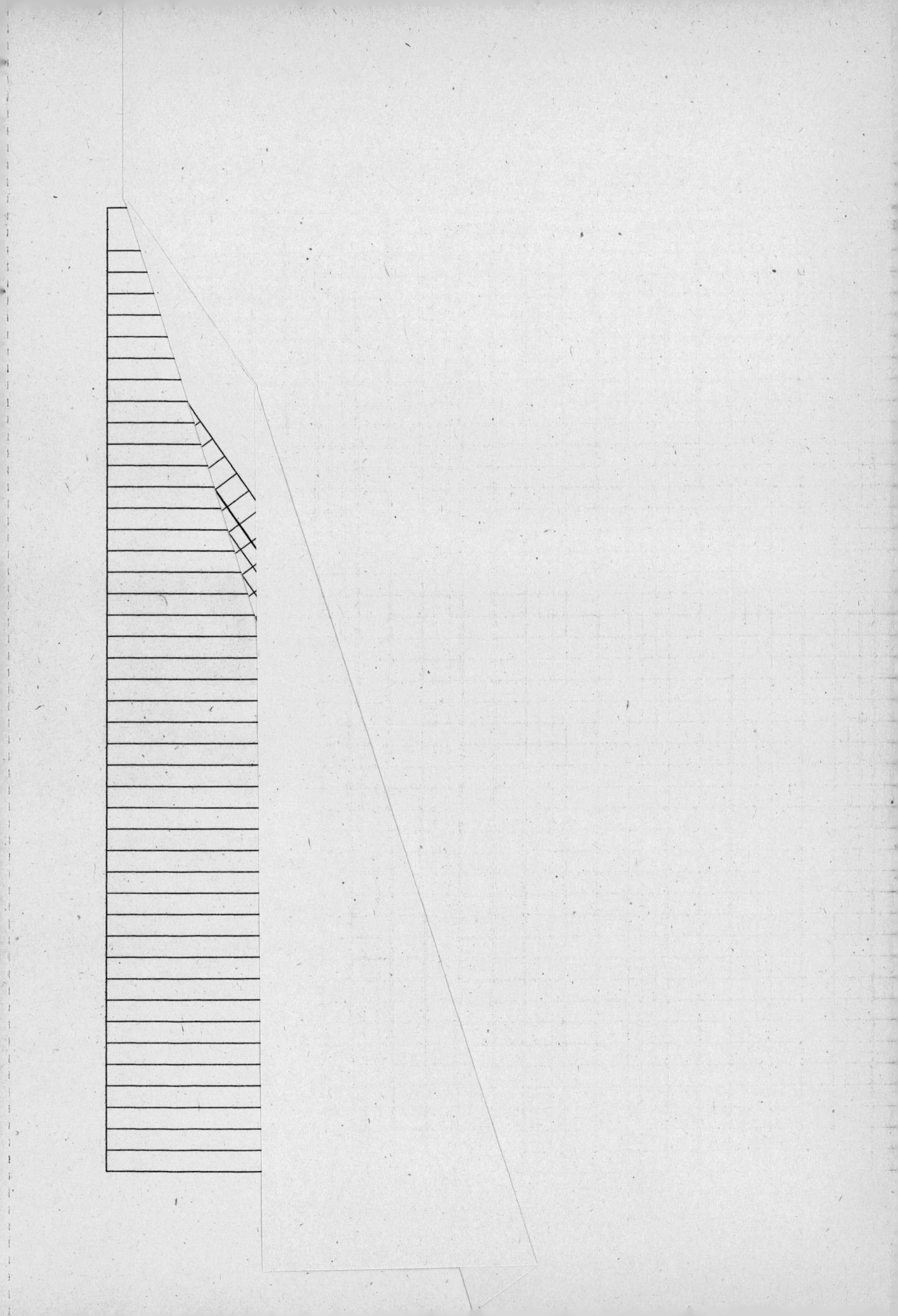